The Evolution of Soviet Security Strategy

1965-1975

The Evolution of Soviet Security Strategy

1965-1975

AVIGDOR HASELKORN

PUBLISHED BY

Crane, Russak &
Company, Inc.

NEW YORK

National Strategy
Information Center, Inc.

The Evolution of Soviet Security Strategy, 1965-1975

Published in the United States by
Crane, Russak & Company, Inc.
347 Madison Avenue
New York, N.Y. 10017

© 1978 by National Strategy Information Center, Inc.
111 East 58th Street
New York, N.Y. 10022

Library Edition: ISBN: 0-8448-1273-0
Paperbound Edition: ISBN: 0-8448-1272-2
LC 77-85316

Strategy Paper No. 31

Printed in the United States of America

Table of Contents

Preface

In *The Evolution of Soviet Security Strategy, 1965-1975,* Avigdor Haselkorn outlines the development since 1965 of a long-range, unified, and coherent strategic design aimed at the establishment of a Soviet-sponsored collective security system all along the periphery of the Soviet Union. This strategy, which could result in a gradual expansion of the Soviet sphere of domination without ever directly challenging the United States, is in large part an outgrowth of the USSR's powerful "two-front complex" stimulated by the emergence in the 1960s of a new eastern front against Communist China.

In their efforts to acquire more mobile, powerful, and flexible military capabilities, the Soviets have sought to establish permanent military relations among three Soviet-inspired security subsystems (the Warsaw Pact, the Middle East/Mediterranean area, and the South Asia/Far East region), as opposed to occasional interactions among the individual states involved. Soviet penetration of the Middle East is designed to confront and offset the US nuclear strike capability deployed on the periphery of the USSR, and to diminish American influence in the area through the denial of local bases and allies to the United States. In the South Asia/Far East region, the Soviets employ their nascent collective security system to weaken the American presence, preempt possible Western military deployment in the Indian Ocean, and to develop a Soviet-sponsored second front against China.

The Soviets have successfully linked, either directly or indirectly, much of the Soviet periphery in a formal alliance system, and have also engaged in the development of an external infrastructure to facilitate the deployment of Soviet forces and enhance their ability to support the security system militarily. At the core of this collective strategy, argues Haselkorn, is the Soviet initiation or encouragement of strategic mutual support functions both within a given subsystem and between the subsystems, comprised of logistical support, military assistance (including the possible threat of direct military intervention by one subsystem in support of another), and the development of expanded offensive options, including the possible use of the security system to institute large-scale military operations against an enemy of the Soviet Union.

The emergent Soviet collective security strategy has repeatedly proven its effectiveness, as Haselkorn demonstrates, both in countering potential threats to Soviet interests and in complicating the political and military position of their adversaries on the Soviet periphery. Within the context of this grand strategy, the Soviets have shown a flexibility and ability to accommodate to shifts in the international milieu, focusing attention and resources on whatever countries or areas present the most immediate danger and/or opportunity. It is therefore crucial that the West develop a macro-view of the Soviet collective security design, for it is only by comprehending the essential outlines of Soviet grand strategy that particular aspects of Soviet behavior can be understood and effectively dealt with. Haselkorn argues convincingly for the development of a coherent Western strategy to match the consistency of Soviet strategic thought and policy, for "without a viable strategy which can resist and hopefully defeat the Soviet effort . . . , the US strategic arsenal may become quite irrelevant."

Mr. Haselkorn, who is an Israeli citizen, holds a B.A. in political science and international relations from the Hebrew University, Jerusalem, and an M.A. in political science from the University of Chicago. He is a candidate for a Ph.D. from the latter institution, and is now working on his dissertation with the Stanford Arms Control and Disarmament Group, Stanford University. Mr. Haselkorn is also a consultant to the Office of the Secretary of Defense, and to several research institutions.

We are especially indebted to Mr. Leo Cherne for his incisive and sobering Foreword to Mr. Haselkorn's study. One of this country's most distinguished publicists and the long-time Executive Director of the Research Institute of America, Mr. Cherne has also served as a member, and subsequently as Chairman, of the President's Foreign Intelligence Advisory Board. His eloquent voice in defense of human freedom has perhaps been most frequently and effectively heard in his capacity as Chairman of the International Rescue Committee since 1953.

Frank R. Barnett, *President*
National Strategy Information Center, Inc.

November 1977

Foreword

Those who seek to understand the Soviet Union's political and military purposes will henceforth disregard only at their peril the extraordinary piece of scholarship and thought that Avigdor Haselkorn has put together here. In describing *The Evolution of Soviet Security Strategy, 1965-1975,* Haselkorn has meticulously assembled a massive and apparently disparate set of actions taken by the Soviet Union, as well as the statements made by those concerned with these actions at the time. From these separate threads, the author has woven an intricate fabric in which he has perceived a remarkably clear design—the creation of a Soviet collective security system in which the Warsaw Pact, the Middle East, and South Asia and the Far East are the vital "subsystem" areas in the Soviet design.

It is impossible to read the detail which has been assembled in this study without observing that the Soviet Union's efforts are as expansive as they are painstaking. The author has selected a period which is not only rich in its display of Soviet ambitions, but one which, in addition, is of critical concern to the collective security efforts of the West. In these pages, one meets the other face of the detente coin, and perceives the essential nature of the post-Khrushchev development of Soviet strategy. Here is the dimension against which the SALT negotiations, the agreements reached at Helsinki, and sudden crises like the Yom Kippur War may be understood with greater clarity and objectivity.

It is not the author's thesis that the Soviet Union is relentlessly seeking world hegemony. He does not assert that the data he has assembled and analyzed enable us to understand definitively Soviet intentions or their central core of ideological purposes. Yet, no one concerned with those questions will henceforth be able to argue his perceptions cogently without reference to the unique and invaluable evidence which Avigdor Haselkorn's effort has produced.

There have been those within recent years who have sought to fathom the ultimate purpose of the Soviet Union. There are others who have concentrated on a more manageable objective—the military ability which the Soviet Union is able to bring to whatever its purposes may be. And the depth of that capability clearly emerges from these pages. There are no discrete separations between military and political capability, and Haselkorn is consistently sensitive to the political increment which flows from the Soviet Union's widening net of interlocking military presences.

This is a sober document. One will search hard to find polemical phrases or value judgments. Nor does Haselkorn overstate the content of the strategic policy he is examining. Note the sobriety—as well as the importance—of these words which appear in the first pages of the study.

> It is not suggested that the Soviet collective security system resembles in every dimension Western conceptions of collective security. Rather, it should be stressed that the *facade* of collective action is of extreme importance to regimes lacking wide popular support. By recruiting many member states, Soviet military moves gain in legitimacy by being able to point to an "international" consensus motivated by a collective desire to restore "peace." Further, collective condemnation by members of the Soviet collective security system makes it politically difficult for the United States to maintain a military presence in affected areas, particularly when the Soviets are able to maintain ambiguity over their presence.

The author does, however, make distinctions between the collective security system of which the United States is a part and that which the Soviet Union has been constructing.

> The United States and its allies have, in general, favored the status quo; its alliances have been defensive. In contrast, the

Soviet Union and its allies, at least in the Middle East and South Asia, are trying to change the status quo: India and Afghanistan with respect to Pakistan; Iraq with respect to Kuwait; Somalia with respect to Ethiopia; and so forth. Alliances based on an anti-status quo principle are, on the whole, more unstable, less controllable, and more subject to divergent forces than the defensive alliances that the United States has fostered.

This is not a document designed for hasty reading or easy conclusions. In fact, there are lengthy tables which carefully chart the movement of Soviet military forces, the delivery of weapons and weapon systems, and the accompanying statements—for us almost totally unobserved at the time—which were made as each of these smaller steps was being taken. Haselkorn has labored with the delicate care of the archeologist who brushes aside the sand and debris which has obscured the unidentified object and hidden it from view.

There is a great deal in his assembly of data which will support those who have seen in the evolving pattern of Soviet capability a fundamental concern with defense. It is clear that much that the Soviet Union has undertaken through this collective security strategy is animated by the historical concern over a danger to the Soviet Union on two fronts. But here, too, it is not the author's intention to settle the question of whether the Soviet Union's purposes are essentially defensive or mask more aggressive goals. It is his objective to unearth and describe a process, a pattern, a developing strength which must be taken into detailed account by scholars and policymakers alike.

The NATO Supreme Commander, General Alexander Haig, observed some months ago that "the relentless growth in sheer Soviet military capability, once confined to Europe, has today become a global capability." One might have expected that from a NATO Commander. In the Brookings Institution study entitled *Settling National Priorities* (one of whose directors, Charles Schultze, is now the Chairman of the Council of Economic Advisors), one finds this echo to General Haig's observation: "The USSR will remain a totalitarian, heavily armed state, determined to continue to dominate Eastern Europe and to extend its influence in the world, whatever we may do." *That* echo was not as readily to be expected.

But toward what end? This, of course, is the ultimate question around which differing opinions will continue to swirl. Haselkorn does not resolve the disputes which are inevitable—and essential—as we try to find the answer. But he does introduce an indispensable body of fact and knowledge which, even at the risk of overschematizing, will give much firmer footing to those engaged in the difficult quest.

Leo Cherne

The Evolution of Soviet Security Strategy

1965-1975

1

The Conceptual Framework

For reasons of academic tradition, most Western scholars have adopted the study of bilateral (and sometimes regional) relations as the preferred mode for assessing Soviet foreign policy and strategy. Rarely does one encounter a macroanalysis of the links, in operational strategic terms, between the various Soviet regional efforts.[1] But it is precisely when taken in their totality that military interactions, within and between the Warsaw Pact, Middle East, and India/Far East regions (that is, the areas where in the past several years Moscow has either concluded or proposed friendship treaties), reveal an emerging structure of a Soviet collective security system. Moreover, it is maintained here that these geographical segments should be viewed as its subsystems.

By demonstrating the performance of various *strategic mutual support* functions between the security subsystems, I expect to show that a Soviet collective security system is far from being an illusive grand design. It is, in fact, largely in place today, and may well be extended in the future.

---

[1] Two notable exceptions are J. C. Campbell, "The Communist Powers and the Middle East: Moscow's Purposes," *Problems of Communism*, September-October 1972, on the theoretical level; and J. A. de Plessis, "Russian Aid to Africa," *Bulletin of the Africa Institute of South Africa*, no. 7, 1974, pp. 277-287, on the operational level.

1

To illustrate the point, we will examine the following interactions:

1. *Type* of mutual support mission performed:
    (a) Logistic support—the supply of military advisors, equip-
        ment, and bases between the above subsystems;
    (b) Defensive support—a threat of direct military interven-
        tion by one subsystem in support of another (obviously a
        mission that could be identified only with regard to cases
        in which a part of the collective security system had been
        put in jeopardy);
    (c) Offensive options—situations in which the security system
        could be utilized to institute large-scale military operations
        against an enemy of the Soviet Union.

2. Mutual support missions according to the *area* of performance:
    (a) *Intrasubsystem*—strategic mutual support activity (of the
        above types) between states (other than the Soviet Union)
        within a given subsystem (for example, the Warsaw Pact)
        either initiated or encouraged by the USSR.
    (b) *Intersubsystem*—strategic mutual support (of the above
        types) performed *between* the subsystems, that is, between
        the Warsaw Pact-Middle East subsystem (and vice versa);
        between the Middle East-India/Far East subsystem (and
        vice versa); and between Warsaw Pact-India/Far East sub-
        system (and vice versa).

It is not suggested that the Soviet collective security system
resembles in every dimension Western conceptions of collective
security. Rather, it should be stressed that the *facade* of collective
action is of extreme importance to regimes lacking wide popular
support. By recruiting many member states, Soviet military moves
gain in legitimacy by being able to point to an "international"
consensus motivated by a collective desire to restore "peace." Further, collective condemnation by members of the Soviet collective
security system makes it politically difficult for the United States to
maintain a military presence in affected areas, particularly when the
Soviets are able to maintain ambiguity over their presence.

There are three main differences between the Soviet experiment
with the establishment of a collective security system and that of the
United States:

1. The Soviets have 25 years of American experience to learn from. While this is no insurance against committing errors, it at least reduces the probability of repeating American blunders.
2. Most importantly, the objective strategic need for such a system is completely different. While the dismantling of the American collective security system would have only a modest effect on US security, *in the Soviet case such a direct link definitely exists;* the health of the system directly affects the level of Soviet security. For example, the loss of India (to an India-China axis) would have drastic effects on the Soviet perception of the hostility of their immediate vicinity. A plausible inference from these geopolitical differences is that the *level* and *duration* of Soviet commitment to such a system is higher than in the American case.
3. The United States and its allies have, in general, favored the status quo; its alliances have been defensive. In contrast, the Soviet Union and its allies, at least in the Middle East and South Asia, are trying to change the status quo: India and Afghanistan with respect to Pakistan; Iraq with respect to Kuwait; Somalia with respect to Ethiopia; and so forth. Alliances based on an anti-status quo principle are, on the whole, more unstable, less controllable, and more subject to divergent forces than the defensive alliances that the United States has fostered.

2

The Point of Origin—1965

New strategic inputs and an abrupt change in leadership, both occurring in late 1964, combined to make 1965 a year of decision for the Soviet Union. The essence of the Soviet problem may be summed up as follows: "Since at least as long as Stalin's time, the Soviet leadership has had a powerful *two-front complex,* in other words a determination to avoid simultaneous crisis in Europe and in the Far East. *A situation of this kind seemed to Moscow to be emerging in the mid-1960s with the establishment of a linkage between its European and its Chinese problems at a time when it was beginning to regard Peking as a military threat.*"[1] Even without subscribing to the "worst case logic" contained in this statement—that is, the assertion not only of the existence of a two-front problem, but also of a degree of "collusion" between the two[2]—it is generally accepted that the emergence by 1965 of a new eastern front for the USSR had a profound impact on the political-strategic perspective of the Soviet leadership.

It is the thesis of this author that, as a consequence, the Soviets

---

[1] H. C. Hinton, *Three and a Half Powers, The New Balance in Asia,* Indiana University Press, Bloomington, Indiana, 1975, p. 203.

[2] Among the signs of "collusion" that Hinton mentions were (1) the exchange of diplomatic recognition between France and China in January 1964, in a move that had anti-Soviet motives on both sides; (2) a series of secret talks between Bonn and Peking in 1964 on a possible trade agreement and consular relations. Soviet obsession with possible collusion between the two fronts has been manifested periodically. Thus, a Soviet government statement (*Pravda,* September 21, 1963) defended its refusal to give nuclear weapons to China on the ground that the United States would then be prompted to do likewise with respect to West Germany and the other Western countries. Further, on February 21, 1967, *Krasnaya Zvezda* (Red Star) carried an article entitled "From Hostility to Collusion," charging that China had taken steps which showed its readiness for collusion with the most aggressive

were laying the groundwork for a major build-up of their forces on both fronts by the end of 1965, as well as reassessing the role of their East European allies. At the same time, they were actively pursuing two outflanking moves designed to safeguard what was probably defined as the defense perimeter of the USSR. The first was into the Middle East/Mediterranean region, with an *immediate* military goal— that is, confronting the US nuclear strike capability deployed on the periphery of the Soviet Union, and a *long-range* political goal—the end of American influence and presence in this area through the denial to Washington of local bases and allies. The other outflanking move, directed at the South Asia-Far East region, had an *immediate* political aim—the containment of China and the end of the American presence in the area; and a *long-range* military aim—laying the infrastructure for confronting possible American nuclear deployments in the Indian Ocean, combined with the development of a Soviet-sponsored second front against China. Since then, concern over what it views as its defense perimeter has remained Moscow's top priority, leading it toward the gradual establishment of a Soviet collective security system designed (at least in the short range) to cope with a Soviet-perceived *multithreat environment* through a *multioptional belt* of allies, air and naval bases, improved lines of communication, and forward force deployments.

The elements that contributed to the creation of a second front

US circles, and that, having disrupted the alliance with the Soviet Union, Peking was now "searching for new allies." It was accompanied by constant propaganda attacks on the "militarists" and "revanchists" of West Germany and frequent charges that Bonn was out to get nuclear weapons of its own. See *Observer* (London), February 26, 1967. *Krasnaya Zvezda* (October 3, 1968) accused China of attempting to stir up Czechoslovak neutralism and anti-Soviet feelings in East European countries. It suggested that there was a united counterrevolutionary front including Washington, Bonn, and Peking. *Literaturnaya Gazeta* (January 8, 1969) reaffirmed the existence of a secret cooperation agreement between China and West Germany. It said that China had opened a recruiting office for aeronautical specialists in West Germany, and claimed that many West German rocket specialists, including Wolfgang Piltz and Berthold Zepiger, were working in China. Further, *Washington Post* (March 7, 1969) reported that the Kremlin had cancelled most of its plans to harass the West German presidential elections (of March 5) because of the Russian-China fire-fight across the Ussuri River, "a reliable Soviet diplomat said." See also P. Mayer, "Why the Ussuri?" *Military Review*, June 1970, pp. 27-29. For general discussions, see J. R. Thomas, *U.S.-East European Relations: Strategic Aspects*, RAC-P-37, Research Analysis Corporation, McLean, Virginia, December 1968, pp. 3, 5-8, 15, note 3. P. Windsor, "Security Seen from the East," in G. Schöpflin, *The Soviet Union and Eastern Europe, A Handbook*, Praeger, New York, 1970, pp. 167-177.

for Moscow were (1) a general recognition that the Sino-Soviet conflict would be a long, bitter struggle,[3] coupled with the fact that in 1965 China began construction of an ICBM testing range and in this way gave notice that it intended to become a major nuclear power.[4] Thus, in August 1967 it was revealed that the Soviet Information Service had been distributing leaflets in Asian capitals warning of the danger of a Chinese nuclear attack in that area. The leaflets, made available by US sources in Washington, said: "Even eight to ten years from now, the Chinese nuclear warheads will hardly be able to deal a 'retaliatory' blow and hit overseas targets. No doubt Peking understands this. Nevertheless, it hastily builds up its own nuclear weapons. Why? This is not a rhetorical question. For many Asian countries, it is of vital importance."[5] (2) The American military build-up in Vietnam, which began in April 1965. For example, some Western analysts had argued that the Soviet decision to deploy IRBMs in Mongolia was a calculated reply to the increased US military presence in Vietnam. The "Buir Noir area (where the missiles were deployed) is 1,450 miles from Okinawa and 1,300 miles from Tokyo. It is in that region that some of America's most important Far Eastern bases lie. Soviet sensitivity to

---

[3] See, for example, W. A. C. Adie, "Possibilities for Regional Defence in the Post-Vietnam Era," *Journal of South-East Asia and the Far East,* no. 2, 1970, p. 148.

   "The Chinese became more and more cognizant after 1965 of the fact that the change of leadership in the Soviet Union had resulted in a shift of Soviet foreign policy goals. Unlike Khrushchev, Brezhnev and Kosygin assumed that repairing of relations with China was not possible until leadership in Peking changed hands. Yet their perception of danger from China was put in a more realistic perspective and was considered more a potential than an immediate threat." I. C. Ojha, "A Comparison of China's Policies toward Western and Eastern Europe," *Asia Quarterly,* no. 2, 1975, p. 113.

[4] Hinton, *op. cit.,* p. 98; also F. Ermarth, "Moscow and the Chinese Missile," *East Europe,* December 1966, pp. 2-6.

[5] *Facts on File,* August 31-September 6, 1967, p. 364. One observer maintains that President Kennedy underestimated Soviet interest in attaining a nuclear test ban treaty "particularly since the Soviets were almost certainly aware of how close the Chinese were in 1963 to a nuclear weapons test. Consequently, agreement on a test ban treaty in 1963 may have been the Russians' last chance to isolate the Chinese in world opinion by an international treaty prohibiting just what the Chinese were about to do." W. B. Bader, *The United States and the Spread of Nuclear Weapons,* Pegasus, New York, 1968, p. 54. See also T. W. Wolfe, *Soviet Military Policy under Khrushchev's Successors,* Rand, Santa Monica, California, P-3193, August 1965, p. 26. Further, it is claimed that as early as 1964, Soviet Premier Khrushchev had given serious thought to an attack against China's budding nuclear capacity. P. Van Ness, "China and the Third World," *Current History,* September 1974, p. 108.

America's build-up has been displayed in a number of ways; for example, the Russians have protested repeatedly to Japan over the regular entry of American nuclear submarines to Okinawa, over the use of Okinawa by B-52 strategic bombers, and over the frequent joint naval exercises in the Sea of Japan by Japanese and American naval units."[6] Russia's anxieties were not allayed by the disclosure in 1965 that the Soviet Union was specified as a "future enemy" of Japan in a secret military contingency plan, named the Three Arrows.[7] Western intelligence sources soon began noting stepped-up Soviet air and sea surveillance operations of Japan. In a development believed to be linked with the Vietnam War, the Russians reportedly were particularly anxious to follow what was going on in the big US naval base at Yokosuka, 40 miles southwest of Tokyo. Soviet Tu-16 Badgers and Mya-4 Bisons, which apparently had taken off from Siberia, flew across Sakhalin Island to the east of the Kurile Islands, proceeding then to the limits of Japanese international waters. Beginning in September 1966, the Soviets reportedly had extended the southern limits of these flights to a point just south of Yokosuka.[8] In May 1967, the US Defense Department also disclosed the collision of a US Navy research vessel, the *Banner,* with a Soviet trawler on June 24, 1966, in the Sea of Japan. The Russian vessel, the *Anemometer,* was described as an intelligence-gathering ship.[9] (3) Another Russian complaint was that Japan's armament program, and in particular its atomic energy industry, were developing too rapidly. *Pravda* (May 7, 1968) said: "Japanese factories have started mass production of missiles and other kinds of nuclear armaments." It also alleged that the United States was delivering uranium to the Japanese in unlimited quantities.

In consequence, many observers have concluded that "the most active and wide-ranging phase of Moscow's Asian diplomacy began in 1965."[10] On December 7, 1964, the Soviets proposed that the

---

[6] *Foreign Report* (Economist), July 6, 1968, pp. 6-7.

[7] This was a joint Japanese-American compilation, the existence of which was officially admitted in Tokyo, amid much embarrassment, in 1965.

[8] *Foreign Report* (Economist), January 1, 1967, p. 6.

[9] *Facts on File,* May 11-17, 1967, pp. 162-163.

[10] *Far Eastern Economic Review,* August 21, 1968, p. 49; *Christian Science Monitor,* November 28, 1964; *Neue Zurcher Zeitung* (Zurich), February 13, 1965. The Chinese commented: "The new leaders of the CPSU came to realize that it was no longer advisable to copy Khrushchev's policy of 'disengagement' in its totality. So they switched to the policy of involvement, that is, of getting their hands in." *Peking Review,* November 12, 1965, p. 15.

Indian Ocean should be denuclearized, that is, that the powers should agree to maintain no forces with nuclear capability (submarines or strike carriers) in it. Geoffrey Jukes claims that both the proposal and Soviet naval expeditions to the Indian Ocean (which began in 1967) were made in the expectation that the US Navy would eventually utilize the Indian Ocean as a deployment area for ballistic missile submarines.[11] The Soviets were probably linking the construction of a US Navy communication station at Northwest Cape in Western Australia (agreed to in 1963, and completed 1967), the Polaris A-3 (operational since 1964), and the Poseidon (operational in 1970) as indicating an operational plan for missile submarine deployment in the Indian Ocean, and decided to pre-empt Western action.

Elsewhere, the Soviets have demonstrated their increased concern over China since early 1965. Indeed, it has been reported that in 1964, Soviet ground forces in the area of Vladivostok conducted maneuvers that assumed a nonnuclear Chinese invasion of the Maritime Province.[12] In the Winter of 1964-65, the Viet Cong shifted from guerrilla warfare to a main force offensive, which in turn implied even greater military dependence upon, and control by, Hanoi. "North Vietnam probably took this decision after it had been assured in November 1964 by the post-Khrushchev Soviet leadership that Soviet SAMs would protect Hanoi and Haiphong against any American air retaliation."[13] On January 4, 1965, Soviet Foreign Minister Andrei Gromyko, in a note to North Vietnamese Foreign Minister Xuan Thuy (published in *Izvestiia*), had reiterated Soviet support for North Vietnam in the event it was attacked. *Tass* (January 31, 1965) announced that Soviet Premier Kosygin would soon visit North Vietnam. "Kosygin was going to Hanoi to woo the North Vietnamese further away from China, and to urge a degree of moderation in their confrontation with the United States in South Vietnam."[14] On Febru-

---

[11] Geoffrey Jukes, *The Soviet Union in Asia,* University of California Press, Berkeley, California, 1973, p. 86.

[12] M. J. Mackintosh, "The Soviet General's View of China in the 1960s," in R. L. Garthoff, ed., *Sino-Soviet Military Relations,* Praeger, New York, 1966, p. 187.

[13] W. E. Griffith, *Sino-Soviet Relations 1964-1965,* MIT Press, Cambridge, Massachusetts, 1967, p. 107.

[14] A. B. Ulam, *Expansion and Coexistence, The History of Soviet Foreign Policy, 1917-1967,* Praeger, New York, 1968, p. 703; *New York Times,* January 31, 1965. In contrast, Soviet economic aid to Ho Chi Minh's government dwindled significantly in the last two years of Khrushchev's rule. D. S. Zagoria, *Vietnam Triangle: Moscow, Peking, Hanoi,* Pegasus, New York, 1967, p. 43.

ary 4, Kosygin left Moscow for a visit to North Vietnam and North Korea, accompanied among others by the head of the Soviet Air Force. In Korea, Kosygin consented in principle to the resumption of military assistance to Pyongyang, and expressed anew the "unbreakable friendship" between the two countries.[15] On February 13, the North Korean Minister of Defense, General Kim Chang-pang, was reported to have held "friendly talks" with Soviet Air Marshal K. A. Vershinin. These talks were probably instrumental in dispatching a high-ranking North Korean military delegation to Moscow less than three months later. The visit of that delegation led to the signing of a Soviet-North Korean military agreement at the end of May 1965.[16] Moscow reportedly agreed to the supply of MIG-21s and SAMs, and resumed the training of North Korean military personnel in Soviet military academies.

As for Kosygin's visit to North Vietnam, the Soviet-North Vietnamese joint statement of February 11, 1965, contained the first public offer of Russian military aid to Hanoi. On February 26, moreover, Kosygin (in a nationwide television broadcast) declared that an agreement to strengthen North Vietnam's defenses was "now being implemented."[17] During North Vietnamese Deputy Premier Le Thanh

[15] Note that in November 1962, a North Korean military delegation seeking aid in Moscow reportedly came away emptyhanded; and by early 1963, references to the Soviet Union had largely disappeared from the North Korean media. North Korea also found itself increasingly snubbed by Moscow's East European allies. A low point was reached in January 1963, when the East German Communist Party refused the North Korean representative permission to address its Party Congress. R. R. Simmons, "The Peking-Pyongyang-Moscow Triangle," *Current Scene,* November 7, 1970, p. 11.

[16] J. C. Kun, "North Korea between Moscow and Peking," *China Quarterly,* July-September 1967, pp. 49-51, and fn. 10-13 therein; Simmons, *loc. cit.,* p. 12. On June 25, 1966, an editorial in the official organ of the Chinese Communist Army, *Liberation Army Daily,* warned the North Koreans against their recent rapprochement with the Soviet Union. "North Korea's drift away from its Chinese ally appears to be causing serious concern in Peking. The Koreans have clearly ignored or perhaps even rejected (China's warnings). The Chinese leadership thus finds itself increasingly isolated even from its erstwhile allies." *Manchester Guardian,* June 29, 1966. Indeed, on August 12, 1966, the North Korean Communist Party (in an editorial entitled, "Let Us Defend Our Independence") rejected both Soviet and Chinese interference in its affairs. Yet its "heavier attack was on Peking's international policy." *New York Times,* August 13, 1966.

[17] "Soviet military aid was said to consist largely of ground-to-air missiles, jet fighters, and technical advisors." *Washington Post,* February 22, 1965. For Soviet-Chinese polemics over Soviet military aid to Vietnam, see A. Parry, "Soviet Aid to Vietnam," *Survival,* March 1967, pp. 77-79; *New York Times,* March 29, 1965, and January 16, 1966.

Nghi's visit to Moscow, *Izvestiia* (June 4, 1965) pledged further Soviet military aid to North Vietnam.[18] On July 2, 1965, the US State Department confirmed that two of four SAM sites being built by the Soviet Union in North Vietnam were completed. By early October 1966, this number had risen to 25 or 30, each with six launchers. There were also some 130 sites from which the batteries could operate; 20 percent were occupied and active at any given time.[19] The use of East European cargo ships for provision of logistic support to Hanoi should also be noted, together with the reported presence of East German officers (employed in SAM training) and a 100-man East German medical mission.[20]

Pakistan's President Ayub Khan had visited the USSR on April 3-4, 1965. During the visit, the first indications were given of a change in Soviet policy toward Pakistan as well.[21] In May Day and anniversary celebrations in Moscow, a new Central Committee slogan appeared: " 'May the friendly relations between the Soviet people and the people of Iran, Pakistan, and Turkey develop and grow stronger.' This greeting was unmistakably linked with the emerging Soviet diplomatic effort on its southern flank."[22] The shift in Moscow's policy became further evident during the Indo-Pakistan War in August-September 1965. Soviet Premier Kosygin expressed concern over the military conflict in Kashmir which, as he put it, "has broken out in an area directly adjacent to the frontiers of the Soviet Union."[23] *Tass* on September 7 announced that the Soviet Union had urged Pakistan and

---

[18] Soviet military aid to North Vietnam between 1955-64 averaged about $35 million per annum. As from 1965, however, it increased to at least $300 million annually. E. Einbeck, "Moscow's Military Aid to the Third World," *Aussen Politik,* English edition, April 1971, p. 466; *Neue Zurcher Zeitung,* October 29, 1967.

[19] Parry, *loc. cit.,* p. 78. *Krasnaya Zvezda,* December 1, 1965, admitted the presence of Soviet SAMs in North Vietnam. An increased Soviet commitment of both military and economic aid seems to have been given during the visit of a high-ranking Russian delegation led by Alexander Shelepin, and including Colonel General V. F. Tolubko, to Hanoi in January 1966. See Zagoria, *op. cit.,* p. 51.

[20] Zagoria, *op. cit.,* p. 80.

[21] M. A. Chaudhri, "Pakistan's Relations with the Soviet Union," *Asian Survey,* September 1966, p. 497.

[22] R. H. Donaldson, *Soviet Policy toward India, Ideology and Strategy,* Harvard University Press, Cambridge, Massachusetts, 1974, p. 204.

[23] S. W. Simon, "The Kashmir Dispute in Sino-Soviet Perspective," *Asian Survey,* p. 177. For a comparison with the Soviet stance during the 1959 and 1962 Sino-Indian wars, see H. Kapur, *The Embattled Triangle, Moscow-Peking-New Delhi,* Humanities Press, New York, 1973, pp. 113-118.

India to stop fighting, and offered its good offices for a settlement of their dispute over Kashmir. The statement added that "present developments in that region play only into the hands of those outside forces that seek to disunite and to get at loggerheads those states that have cut off their colonial yoke." Finally, it expressed "serious concern" over the fighting because it was taking place "in an area directly adjoining the borders of the Soviet Union." On September 10, First Secretary Leonid Breznev repeated the Soviet offer of good offices to end the Indo-Pakistan conflict, and assailed those outside forces "who pour oil on the fire" instead of helping to restore peace.[24] "Soviet policy, which was aimed at extinguishing the conflict as quickly as possible, ran directly counter to that of the Chinese, who followed the traditional Communist line of seeking to exploit to the hilt anti-imperialist contradictions."[25] By adopting such a policy, "Moscow's minimal objective was the containment of both Peking and Washington; its maximum was to detach India from Washington and Pakistan from Peking while moving both closer to Moscow, and finally to improve relations between the Indians and the Pakistanis so that together they might devote their energies to containing China rather than fighting each other."[26] In short, the "Russians were seeking a chance to reduce their total commitment in India in favor of regional influence."[27]

Indian Defense Minister Sardar Swaran Singh admitted for the first time in the Lok Sabha on April 9, 1969, that there had been a shift in the Soviet Union's policy toward Pakistan after the Tashkent Agreement of January 1966.[28] At the same time, the Russians made it plain to the Pakistanis that simultaneous good relations with Mos-

---

[24] *New York Times,* September 12, 1965.

[25] W. Welch, "Containment: American and Soviet Versions," *Studies in Comparative Communism,* Autumn 1973, p. 223.

[26] Griffith, *op. cit.,* p. 117.

[27] W. Wilcox, "China's Strategic Alternatives in South Asia," in T. Tsou, ed., *China in Crisis, America's Policies in Asia and America's Alternatives,* Chicago University Press, Chicago, 1968, p. 416; also T. P. Thornton, "South Asia and the Great Powers," *World Affairs,* March 1970, pp. 353-355.

[28] *Asian Recorder,* New Delhi, April 30-May 6, 1969, p. 8895. Kosygin's opening speech at Tashkent on January 4 reaffirmed the Soviet Union's special interest in the area because India and Pakistan "are our southern neighbors." *Asian Analyst,* London, January 1966, p. 12. "Indeed, at the very time that Kosygin was greeting Ayub and Shastri in Tashkent, Alexander Shelepin was in Hanoi winning the agreement of the North Vietnamese Party to send a delegation to the forthcoming Soviet Party Congress in return for a substantial increase in Soviet aid in the Vietnam War." Donaldson, *op. cit.,* p. 209.

cow and Peking were not possible for Pakistan. Clearly, the "Soviet posture toward the states on China's Himalayan border has changed generally in step with changes in the Soviet posture and conduct toward China's northern border."[29] On November 22, 1965, Indian Defense Minister Y. B. Chavan disclosed in the Indian parliament that India would buy submarines and "other naval craft" from the Soviet Union, and that Soviet experts would help design new shipyards in India.[30] Thus in 1965-66, Moscow became the largest single supplier of military hardware to India.[31]

The abortive Indonesian coup of September 30, which was an attempt by President Sukarno and some elements of the Indonesian Communist Party to remove the last obstacle to full rule (namely, control of the armed forces), demonstrated anew the change in Soviet policy. In January 1965, against Soviet advice, Indonesia pulled out of the United Nations and thus emphasized its solidarity with Peking. This development, plus the pro-Peking stance of the PKI and the existence of a sizeable overseas Chinese community in Indonesia, made the future evolution of the country a source of considerable anxiety in Moscow. There was also a distinct possibility of the development of a Pakistan-China-Indonesia axis directed against India.[32] "The failure of the coup and the subsequent relegation of Sukarno to a figurehead position—indeed, to become a virtual prisoner of the regime—was thus greeted in Moscow with relief and in Peking with anguish, since its success would have meant Indonesia becoming a full satellite of Communist China . . . Soviet reactions to the India-Pakistan War and to the repression of the Indonesian Communists were thus directed almost entirely by the Sino-Soviet conflict and the fear that any further expansion of communism in

---

[29] Welch, *loc. cit.,* p. 222.

[30] "Moscow has agreed to accept rupees, not scarce foreign exchange in payment." *Baltimore Sun,* November 23, 1965; also *Manchester Guardian,* August 4, 1965.

[31] A. Stein, "India and the U.S.S.R.: The Post-Nehru Period." *Asian Survey,* March 1967, pp. 167, 173-174. In September 1964, Moscow also agreed to supply India with 44 MIG-21s, 50 ground-to-air missiles, 70 tanks, and an assortment of infantry weapons. Kapur, *op. cit.,* p. 118.

[32] *Foreign Report* (Economist), October 21, 1965, p. 1. During the Indo-Pakistan War of 1965, "at least one Indonesian submarine had turned up in Pakistan." R. G. C. Thomas, "The Indian Navy in the Seventies," *Pacific Affairs,* Winter 1975-76, p. 507.

Asia would rebound to China's advantage and not be in Russia's interest."[33]

King Mohammed Zahir Shah of Afghanistan visited the Soviet Union between August 3-14, 1965. On August 6, the two countries signed a protocol prolonging the Soviet-Afghan Treaty of Non-aggression,[34] while the Soviet media carried charges that the CENTO powers were plotting to divide Afghanistan between Iran and Pakistan.[35]

The NATO-Mediterranean Front

Although we started our discussion with the emergence by 1965 of a new eastern front for the Soviet Union, it is by no means suggested that the traditional Soviet defense orientation—that is, preoccupation over its western front—had somehow changed.[36] On the contrary, it increased during the same period. Thus, it seems probable that the Soviets tried to calm the Chinese and devote their attention to the NATO-Mediterranean front immediately after Khrushchev's fall (between November 1964 and March 1965). "The Soviet plan was to improve Sino-Soviet state relations on a pragmatic basis . . . ,

---

[33] Ulam, *op. cit.*, p. 718; also H. C. Hinton, "The Foreign Policy of Communist China," *Journal of South-East Asia and the Far East,* no. 2, 1970, p. 148. For recent developments in Soviet-Indonesian relations, see R. C. Horn, "Moscow's Southeast Asian Offensive," *Asian Affairs,* June 1975, pp. 224-229.

[34] "The visit of the Afghan King and Queen had been preceded by a visit in April of the Afghan Prime Minister, Mr. Mohammed Yusef . . . a joint communique of the Afghan Premier with Mr. Kosygin stressed (Soviet aid for such) projects as the road tunnel through the Hindu Kush . . . and the 465-mile motor road linking the Soviet frontier town of Kushka in Turkmenia with Kandahar via Herat." *Neue Zurcher Zeitung,* August 8, 1965. The Kushka-Herat-Kandahar Highway was opened to traffic on November 15, 1965. *World* (Hong Kong), August 1, 1971, p. 3. It was described by one source as "a tank-proof concrete road." Einbeck, *op. cit.*, p. 467.

[35] S. Y. Dai, "China and Afghanistan," *China Quarterly,* January-March 1966, p. 228.

[36] Since the first official "Statement by USSR Ministry of Foreign Affairs on Security in the Near and Middle East" in April 1955 (text in *Pravda,* April 11, 1955), the USSR had constantly stressed its direct geopolitical interest in the region, in view of its physical proximity, as not only justifying the Soviet penetration but also invalidating the American presence. For early military indications of Soviet concern, see J. W. Lewis, *The Strategic Balance in the Mediterranean,* American Enterprise Institute, Washington, D.C., 1976, pp. 57-58. See also U. Ra'anan, *The U.S.S.R. Arms the Third World, Case Studies in Soviet Foreign Policy,* MIT Press, Cambridge, Massachusetts, 1969, pp. 16-20.

(but) the Chinese response was substantively at least as negative as before Khrushchev's fall."[37]

On March 30, 1963, the United States announced that a Polaris SSBN was on patrol in the Mediterranean. On April 12, the Pentagon stated that a second Polaris SSBN had taken station there, and that a third would arrive later in the month.[38] Soviet warships, on the other hand, were first stationed in the eastern Mediterranean on a sustained basis in September 1963, when the United States opened negotiations with Spain for the establishment of a Polaris base at Rota.[39] The introduction of Polaris missile submarines into the Mediterranean "seriously undermined the Soviet Navy's attempt to establish meaningful forward deployments, since its existing resources were still insufficient to check even the lesser strategic threat posed by the Sixth Fleet's attack aircraft carriers. In order to maintain a permanent naval presence in the Mediterranean to meet this challenge (both SSBNs and CVAs), the USSR needed access to naval facilities in the region itself."[40] Consequently, Russian pressure on Egypt for port facilities increased precipitously.[41]

"The greatly increased range of seaborne nuclear systems means that in many ways the eastern Mediterranean is now of greater defensive concern to the Soviet Union than her Arctic seas. Moscow lies midway between the two, but whereas the population and industry thin out to the north, to the south and east of the capital lies a large part of Russia's industrial strength. This new maritime interest reinforces the traditional requirement to prevent maritime intervention

---

[37] Griffith, *op. cit.*, p. 63; Ulam, *op. cit.*, p. 697. *Foreign Report* (Economist), February 4, 1965, p. 7.

[38] *New York Times,* April 13, 1963.

[39] G. Jukes, *The Indian Ocean in Soviet Naval Policy,* Adelphi Paper No. 87, International Institute for Strategic Studies, London, May 1972, pp. 5-6.

[40] S. Dragnich, *The Soviet Union's Quest for Access to Naval Facilities in Egypt Prior to the June War of 1967,* Professional Paper No. 127, Center for Naval Analyses, Arlington, Virginia, July 1974, pp. 24-25.

[41] *Ibid.*, pp. 23-27. Thus, during his visit to Egypt, Khrushchev in a speech in Port Said on May 19, 1964, condemned the introduction of Polaris submarines into the Mediterranean as a "great danger" to the *Arabs* and said the use of missile-equipped aircraft carriers in the area was aimed at "restoring reactionary and obsolete regimes to the countries of Asia and Africa." For an analysis of Khrushchev's 1964 visit to Egypt, see O. M. Smolansky, *The Soviet Union and the Arab East Under Khrushchev,* Bucknell University Press, Lewisburg, 1974, pp. 263-289.

in the Black Sea area."[42] Soviet Mediterranean deployment thus "fits squarely into (the) general pattern of extending the Soviet Union's maritime defense perimeter. Admiral Gorshkov explained the need for this shift to forward deployment in February 1963. Commenting on the West's increasing investment in seaborne strategic delivery systems, he concluded that the maritime defense of the Soviet Union would henceforth depend on naval engagements fought far from her shores. As he said in 1966, one third of the US strategic strike weapons were seaborne, adding (in 1967) that by 1970 this proportion would have risen to half."[43] Consequently, ever since

FIGURE ONE

The Soviet Mediterranean Fleet

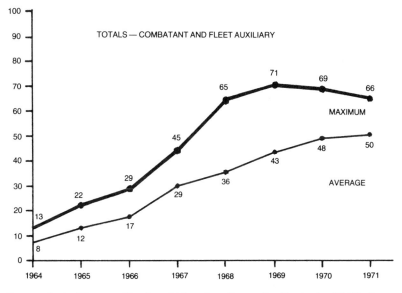

Source: L. L. Whetten, *The Canal War, Four-Power Conflict in the Middle East,* MIT Press, Cambridge, Massachusetts, 1974, p. 392.

---

[42] M. MccGwire, "The Mediterranean and Soviet Naval Interests," in MccGwire, ed., *Soviet Naval Developments, Capability and Context,* Praeger, New York, 1973, p. 355.

[43] *Ibid.*, pp. 352-353.

1964, "the Mediterranean has clearly been the focus of Soviet naval operations, accounting for over 50 percent of all such activity (in terms of ship operating days) for five of the ten years (up to 1973) and over 40 percent for four of the remaining five years."[44]

On March 10, 1965, Soviet Navy Commander Admiral Gorshkov arrived in Egypt at the head of a Soviet naval delegation. The visit took place just before the start of the second year's partial deployment of Soviet warships in the Mediterranean, which still relied on open anchorages. Gorshkov might have sought Egyptian permission for the Soviet Navy to use the anchorage at the Gulf of Salum. In April 1966, the *New York Times* reported that Soviet naval vessels had made covert calls at Salum in the past.[45] In September, Soviet warships made the first naval visit to Egypt in ten years; and in December 1965, Soviet Defense Minister Marshal Grechko went to Egypt at the head of a military delegation which included Admiral Sergeyev, Chief of Staff of Soviet naval forces. "One of the areas of the Red Sea coast which the delegation visited was Ras Banas, where the USSR had helped develop a fishing port under a March 1964 agreement. Khrushchev had visited the area in May 1964, and it had been subsequently closed to Western diplomats. Grechko's visit there increased speculations that the Soviets wanted to use it to support intelligence trawlers (AGIs) in order to monitor Western fleet movements in the Indian Ocean."[46] The Soviets were also accelerating at that time the completion of Hudeida's harbor in Yemen and the extension of pre-existing airfields there;[47] while on May 10, 1965, an agreement for the provision of Soviet technical aid to Algeria was

---

[44] R. G. Weinland, *Soviet Naval Operations—Ten Years of Change,* Professional Paper No. 125, Center for Naval Analyses, Arlington, Virginia, August 1974, p. 2.

[45] Dragnich, *op. cit.,* pp. 28-29. Soviet ship operating days in the Mediterranean in 1965 totaled 4,000. B. M. Blechman, *The Changing Soviet Navy,* Brookings, Washington, D.C., 1973, p. 13, Table 4.

[46] Blechman, *op. cit.,* p. 30. Other indications of a heightened Soviet interest in Egypt included increased economic aid; more frequent visits of high-ranking officials (for example, Nasser visited the USSR in August 1965, and Premier Kosygin made his first trip to Egypt in May 1966); and major arms agreements in November 1964 and a year later. See A. Z. Rubinstein, *Red Star on the Nile, The Soviet-Egyptian Influence Relationship Since the June War,* Princeton University Press, Princeton, 1977, p. 7.

[47] M. Abir, "Red Sea Politics," in *Conflicts in Africa,* Adelphi Paper No. 93, International Institute for Strategic Studies, London, December 1972, p. 26.

signed by Defense Ministers Rodion Malinovsky for the Soviet Union and Houari Boumedienne for Algeria.[48]

Shah Mohammed Reza Pahlavi of Iran visited the Soviet Union from June 21 to July 3, 1965. At a reception on June 26th, Soviet President Anastas Mikoyan stated that the Soviet Union "appreciates the Iranian government's statement that Iran will not allow foreign missile bases of any type to be set up on her territory and will never be a means of aggression against the Soviet Union."[49] On June 25, 1965, Soviet Premier Kosygin (in an interview with the correspondent of the Turkish weekly newspaper *Akis*—his first with a foreign newsman in Moscow) called for a Soviet-Turkish nonaggression pact. Turkish Premier Suat Hayri Urguplu had started a visit to the Soviet Union on August 9. "Turkish-Russian reconciliation, which has been going on for a year, is a political event of the first order, increasing Moscow's influence in the eastern Mediterranean and providing 'relief' for the Soviet Union on her southern flank. After Pakistan, Iran, and Afghanistan, the Kremlin leadership is taking on Turkey."[50]

On the strategic level, one may also assume that in 1965 the Brezh-

---

[48] *Washington Post,* May 11, 1965.

[49] In an exchange of notes on September 12, 1962, the Iranian government undertook not to allow "any foreign power to establish rocket launching sites of any kind on Iranian territory." It also declared that Iran would never be a party to any aggression against the USSR, *Christian Science Monitor,* June 5, 1975; *Pravda,* September 17, 1962.

[50] *Die Welt* (Hamburg), August 9, 1965. Note that regarding the Montreux Convention of 1936, which controls the Straits, the United States took the view that destroyers equipped with SAM missiles but otherwise meeting the restrictions on tonnage and caliber of armament specified in the convention should be allowed to pass into the Black Sea. In fact, American ships armed with missiles were permitted to enter the Black Sea until as late as January 1966. By September 1966, however, Ankara had shifted its interpretation of the restrictions imposed by the Montreux Convention. The Turks no longer were disposed to accept the American contention that SAMs did not fall under the category of arms limited by the convention. "In part, this new stance represented the growing Turkish anxiety not to give offense to the Soviets, who had complained loudly at the visits of US naval vessels." G. S. Harris, *Troubled Alliance, Turkish-American Problems in Historical Perspective, 1945-1971,* Hoover Policy Studies, American Enterprise Institute, Washington, D.C., June 1972, pp. 171-172. By early 1970, it was reported that Turkey had acceded to Moscow's request that Soviet submarines en route to the Mediterranean be allowed to enter the Bosphorus an hour or more before first light, although the Convention restricts passage of submarines to daylight hours. *New York Times,* January 27, 1970; *FBIS* (PRC), January 21, 1976, p. A1, for a recent example. See also B. Buzan, "The Status and Future of the Montreux Convention," *Survival,* November/December 1976, p. 245.

nev-Kosygin regime found it prudent to "conduct a running reappraisal of its military planning to take into account a potential 'two-front' threat in Europe and the Far East . . . It no doubt would have raised the question whether Soviet theater forces in the regions bordering China should be permanently strengthened, and if so, whether this requirement might be met by shifting some forces from the European theater to the Far East. The answer apparently was that the Soviet Union should indeed bolster its military garrisons in Asia, but not at the expense of the general purpose forces deployed in Europe."[51] Indeed, "the enormous increase in Soviet forces, which started after 1965, was initially a response to developments along the Sino-Soviet frontier. Since 1969, however, this increase has, in large measure, been associated with a substantial improvement in the capability of these forces in Eastern Europe, opposed to NATO."[52]

Thus, after Khrushchev's dismissal, the argument for multiple options was made explicit, a form of Soviet "flexible response" which envisaged Soviet forces being prepared and trained for general nuclear war, for conventional operations, and for operations in which nuclear weapons were employed on a limited scale.[53] By July 1965, "following evidence of considerable internal debate over allocation of resources for defense and other requirements, a consensus was apparently reached among the leadership which favored those opposing any policy of economizing on defense."[54] Further, aside from the shift toward a forward naval deployment, several other indications testified to Soviet efforts to acquire more mobile and flexible military capacities. In the Summer of 1964, Soviet marine forces (the Naval Infantry) were reactivated and put through special landing exercises with a good deal of attendant publicity. An interest in long-range

---

[51] T. W. Wolfe, *Soviet Power and Europe, 1945-1970,* Johns Hopkins Press, Baltimore, 1970, p. 461.
[52] US Secretary of Defense James R. Schlesinger in *US Forces in Europe,* Senate Committee on Foreign Relations, Hearings, Subcommittee on Arms Control, International Law and Organization, 93rd Congress, 1st Session, July 27, 1973, p. 59.
[53] J. Erickson, *Soviet Military Power,* Royal United Services Institute, London, 1971, p. 8; Wolfe, *op. cit.,* p. 451.
[54] T. W. Wolfe, *The Soviet Union and the Sino-Soviet Dispute,* P-3203, Rand, Santa Monica, California, August, 1965, pp. 36-37. Erickson, *op. cit.,* maintains that the above Soviet operational assumptions did not mark a radical break with Khrushchev's policies. "There has been no 'new' strategic policy in this sense, but the great and growing difference with the early 1960s has been the magnitude of the military effort devoted to implementing these goals."

airlift capability was also indicated through programs to develop long-range transports like the An-22, which made its first appearance at the 1965 Paris show and went into production in the Fall of 1966.[55] At the same time, Soviet military writings pointed out that airborne landing operations in conjunction with amphibious operations would take on increasing significance in the future, and increased emphasis was given to airborne operations and airlift reinforcements in connection with various Warsaw Pact field exercises.[56]

Finally, several other indications relate to Soviet reassessment of the strategic role of the Warsaw Pact.[57] Brezhnev declared in mid-September that "the current situation places on the agenda the further perfection of the Warsaw Pact organization";[58] and on September 29, he declared that the complex international situation made it mandatory to give special attention to questions of military cooperation among the Socialist countries. In a speech in Kiev at the end of October 1965, the First Secretary indicated that the Warsaw Pact organization must be strengthened.[59] Soviet Defense Minister Marshal Grechko in 1964 and again in 1965 stated that "the great importance" of Warsaw Pact joint exercises "lies in their contribution to

---

[55] T. W. Wolfe, *The Soviet Quest for More Globally Mobile Military Power,* RM-5554-PR, Rand, Santa Monica, California, December 1967, pp. 5-6. In the Moscow air show of July 1967, the Soviets demonstrated new air landing equipment and the landing of batteries of Frog-3 rockets and SA-4 Ganef SAMs on tracked launchers. *Aviation Week and Space Technology,* August 14, 1967, pp. 52-53; also G. Turbiville, "Soviet Logistic Support for Ground Operations," *Journal of the Royal United Services Institute for Defence Studies,* September 1975, p. 68.

[56] *Ibid.* In the Warsaw Pact maneuvers of September 1964, for example, Soviet marines made a landing on the Bulgarian coast while paratroopers were dropped behind the "enemy" lines. R. F. Staar, *The Communist Regimes in Eastern Europe,* Hoover Institution Press, Stanford, California, 1971, p. 228.

[57] Thus, unlike the case of the 20-year Soviet-Czech friendship treaty of 1943, which, on December 27, 1963, was simply extended by a protocol prior to its expiration, an entirely new mutual assistance pact was concluded on April 8, 1965, between Poland and the Soviet Union. Pre-1965 mutual assistance pacts "were exclusively directed against Germany and her allies. They came into being because of Germany and against Germany. The new accords reached since 1965, by contrast, principally governed the basic question of relationship between the two signatories." D. Frenzke, "New Czech-Soviet Alliance Treaty," *Aussen Politik,* English edition, March 1970, p. 323; A. Wschakow, "Der Erneuerte Bindnisvertrag Zwischen der Sowjetunion und Polen Von 8 April 1965 im Lichte des Volkerrechts," *Osteuropa-Recht,* December 1966, pp. 281-304.

[58] Cited in T. W. Wolfe, *The Evolving Nature of the Warsaw Pact,* RM-4835-PR, Rand, Santa Monica, California, December 1965, p. 22.

[59] *Pravda,* October 24, 1965; also *Neue Zurcher Zeitung,* October 27, 1965.

further growth of the combat might of our joint armed forces, to higher standards of training, to better coordinations of forces and staffs, and to the elaboration of common views on methods of nuclear and conventional warfare."[60]

In the following chapters, an effort is made to describe the evolution since 1965 of a long-range, coherent Soviet strategy aimed at establishing a multioptional collective security system. This strategy is based on four elements: (1) political-strategic moves; (2) internal military build-up; (3) external deployment; and (4) strategic mutual support activity.

The reader should be aware that although I describe these elements in a sequence, they are at work simultaneously; and that different mixes between them may produce different tones of Soviet policy. Nevertheless, the main theme has remained largely unchanged. Partial discussions of Soviet strategy which are usually focused on one or two of the above elements should be abandoned in favor of a macro-view of the Soviet collective security design. Further, it is recognized that past failures to grasp Soviet strategy were partly due to the fact that until now we have largely seen segments of this system operating together, rather than a unified operational structure. This, in turn, has to do with the fact that during the past decade the conflicts along the Soviet periphery have been limited in nature and geography. The closest we came to a demonstration of a unified collective security system performing militarily was during the Yom Kippur War of 1973.[61] This could signal that a new phase in Soviet strategy is about to commence, if it has not done so already.

---

[60] Cited in Wolfe, *op. cit.,* December 1965, p. 8. Note that there is little evidence that when established (1955) the Warsaw Pact served, or was intended to serve, as a means for speeding up military integration of Soviet-East European armed forces. Thus, it was only in October 1961 that the first Warsaw Pact maneuvers took place. See R. L. Garthoff, "The Military Establishment," *East Europe,* September 1965, p. 14. The integration of the Warsaw Pact into Soviet military planning in the early 1960s was probably associated with Khrushchev's policy of stressing Soviet nuclear weapons and reducing the place of conventional armaments, which led to increased emphasis on the conventional forces of the Warsaw Pact member states. Although it seems that in this respect there has been little change in Soviet strategy since Khrushchev's downfall, the rationale behind Moscow's emphasis on better military integration within the Warsaw Pact has changed.

[61] See A. Haselkorn, "The Soviet Collective Security System," *Orbis,* Spring 1975, pp. 232 ff.

3

Political-Strategic Moves

Even though Leonid Brezhnev had formally proposed the creation of a collective security system for Asia on June 7, 1969,[1] it is apparent by now that the establishment of such a system has proceeded through a network of bilateral friendship treaties between Russia and several countries on its periphery. In addition, a process involving the renegotiation of bilateral friendship treaties between Moscow and its Warsaw Pact allies, which has taken place in parallel, may contain significant implications for that system.

It has become almost customary among Western analysts to complain about the ambiguity of Brezhnev's proposal. Few have understood the proposal as a signal or clue to a possible Soviet solution for what is usually termed in Moscow as "the complex international situation"[2]—that is, the quasi-permanent potential two-front environment. Bhabani Sen Gupta was probably closest to the truth when he wrote:[3]

---

[1] On this occasion, Brezhnev also charged the "Mao group" with making preparations for conventional as well as nuclear war against the Soviet Union. *Pravda*, June 8, 1969. In fact, "the Soviets for the first time—in Brezhnev's collective security proposal—publicly coupled conduct toward China's Himalayan and other borders with that toward the Soviet border." Welch, *op. cit.*, p. 224.

[2] See H. Goldhammer, *The Soviet Union in a Period of Strategic Parity*, R-889-PR, Rand, Santa Monica, California, November 1971, p. 52.

[3] "Soviet Thinking on Asian Collective Security," *Institute for Defense Studies and Analyses Journal*, October 1972, p. 173.

21

Soviet writers point out that security is indivisible, and that there cannot be a collective security system in Asia that is not structurally and functionally linked with security systems in other conflict regions, notably Europe. The Soviet leaders, then, are thinking in terms of a global security system based on, and supported by, regional collective security subsystems in the conflict zones. Africa and Latin America are at present excluded from the list of conflict-prone regions. The emphasis is, therefore, on Europe and Asia.

Further, in his report to the 24th CPSU Congress, Brezhnev stated that "for its part, the Soviet Union invites those countries which accept our approach to collective security to conclude appropriate bilateral or regional treaties."[4] Soon after, the cornerstones of this system were laid down in both the Middle East and the India/Far East subsystems. On May 27, 1971, Egyptian President Sadat and Soviet President Podgorny signed a 15-year Treaty of Friendship and Cooperation in Cairo[5] which was heralded in the Soviet media as an "historical event" and the "dawn of a new era."[6]

Addressing the People's Assembly on June 2, Sadat said: "We wanted this treaty and we signed it with conviction," adding that the new element in Soviet-Egyptian relations was contained in Article 8 referring to military cooperation.[7] Admittedly, the military aid obligation in this clause also exists for the period after a peaceful solution of the Middle East question has been reached. "The military presence of the USSR . . . in Egypt, and the Arab claim to military cooperation are, therefore, detached from the causal case of conflict and only linked to the period of validity of the friendship treaty."[8]

---

[4] Cited in A. L. Horelick, *The Soviet Union's "Asian Collective Security Proposal," A Club in Search of Members*, P-5195, Rand, Santa Monica, California, March 1974, pp. 7, 9. Radio Peace and Progress, March 15, 1972, urged countries which rejected the use of force to conclude "corresponding bilateral or regional treaties."

[5] The treaty was unilaterally abrogated by Egypt on March 15, 1976.

[6] See I. Diamant-Kass, "The Soviet Military and Soviet Policy in the Middle East, 1970-73," *Soviet Studies*, October 1974, p. 515.

[7] *Arab Report and Record* (London), June 1-15, 1971, p. 330.

[8] T. Schweisfurth, "U.S.S.R. Treaties with Third World States," *Aussen Politik*, English Edition, August 1972, p. 313. The treaty "will help retain for Soviet warships their docking, supply, and repair facilities in the harbors of Alexandria and Port Said." A. Hottinger, "The Soviet Fleet in the Mediterranean," *Swiss Review of World Affairs*, August 1971, p. 4.

Nevertheless, from the Soviet point of view, Article 2 of the treaty is of much greater importance. This article, which calls for cooperation to preserve social and economic gains, and so forth, "could be read as an implicit extension to the Middle East of the Brezhnev Doctrine that had been invoked against Czechoslovakia in 1968, claiming for the USSR the right to intervene in a Socialist state to protect the domestic system."[9] At the ratification sitting of the Presidium of the Supreme Soviet on June 28, Soviet Foreign Minister Gromyko called Article 2 a "very important regulation."[10] As one observer noted at the time: "In the Soviet Union's world political overall concept, the Soviet-Egyptian treaty detaches Egypt from the conglomeration of states loosely hovering around between the world political poles of the Third World and transfers it to the threshold of the 'Socialist Community of States.' "[11]

Less than three months later, on August 9, 1971, Soviet Foreign Minister Gromyko signed a 20-year friendship treaty with India. After the signing, Swaran Singh, India's Foreign Minister, claimed that the treaty had been under discussion soon after Brezhnev made his Asian security system proposal in June 1969.[12] Many observers point out, therefore, that the treaty was probably conceived as part of Brezhnev's security design; "its resemblance to the Soviet Union's treaty with Egypt . . . also suggests that it was originally drafted in Moscow."[13] In fact, Radio Peace and Progress (August 2, 1972) and

---

[9] M. H. Kerr, "Soviet Influence in Egypt, 1967-1973," in A. Z. Rubinstein, ed., *Soviet and Chinese Influence in the Third World,* Praeger, New York, 1975, p. 102.

[10] *Izvestiia,* June 29, 1971.

[11] Schweisfurth, *loc. cit.,* pp. 314-315.

[12] G. Jukes and I. Clark, "The Soviets and Asian Collective Security, 1969-74," in R. E. Kanet and D. Bahry, eds., *Soviet Economic and Political Relations with the Developing World,* Praeger, New York, 1974, p. 149; Donaldson, *op. cit.,* p. 225 and fn. 39 therein.

[13] *Far Eastern Economic Review,* October 16, 1971, p. 14. Also T. W. Robinson, "Soviet Policy in East Asia," *Problems of Communism,* November-December, 1973, p. 44; A. O. Ghebhardt, "The Soviet Collective Security System," *Asian Survey, December* 1973, p. 1089. It is also claimed that, as a part of this new security strategy, Moscow decided in 1971 to supply North Vietnam with the weaponry necessary to conquer the South. F. C. Parker, "Vietnam and Soviet Asian Strategy," *Asian Affairs,* November-December 1976, p. 105. Moreover, in 1971 the Soviets offered to renew the supply of spare parts for the Indonesian Navy and Air Force, as well as to train personnel of Malaysia's armed forces in Russia. *Soviet Activities in South East Asia, June 70 - July 71,* SEATO, Bangkok, 1971, pp. 8-9.

Radio Moscow (August 9, 1972), in broadcasts to Asia on the first anniversary of the Indo-Soviet friendship treaty, confirmed that it was regarded as a step toward creating a collective security system and as an example for other countries.

Under the treaty, "India—though she had not denied herself the option of unilateral military action—had solemnly declared her intention to consult the Soviets in the event of any threatened attack, thus formalizing and displaying for the benefit of third parties the strong Soviet political influence in Subcontinent affairs."[14] All India Radio on August 9, 1971, said: "The threats to India are very clear. The President of Pakistan, taking considerable encouragement from recent statements by China, has twice threatened general war upon India. China has held out vague threats . . . directly in its statements as well as through Pakistan. The Soviet Union has had an armed conflict on its borders with China. *Therefore, there can be little ambiguity about what the Soviet Union and India mean when they talk of a threat to either of them and pledge to consult with each other in order to remove the threat.*" One Indian commentator had raised the possibility that under Article 9 of the treaty, the Soviets may press for facilities on Indian soil, on the ground that deployment of American Poseidon missile submarines in the Indian Ocean would constitute a threat to Soviet security.[15] Moreover, under the pact, "Indian antisubmarine warfare forces might . . . be used against US Polaris/ Poseidon submarines in the Arabian Sea or Bay of Bengal."[16] Other more cautious observers say the treaty appears to provide the Soviet Union with access to Indian facilities in the event of East-West hostilities.[17]

On April 9, 1972, Soviet Prime Minister Kosygin signed a 15-year Treaty of Friendship and Cooperation with Iraq. "It was apparently the Iraqis who took the initiative when government and Ba'ath Party delegates, visiting in Moscow in February, proposed a treaty based

---

[14] Donaldson, *op. cit., pp.* 227-228.
[15] B. Vivenkanandan, "Naval Power in the Indian Ocean: A Problem in Indo-British Relations," *Round Table,* January 1975, p. 69.
[16] W. A. C. Adie, *Oil, Politics, and Seapower, The Indian Ocean Vortex,* Crane, Russak, New York, 1975, p. 46.
[17] *German Tribune,* April 30, 1975; also M. K. Chopra, "Zunehmender Macht Kampf im Indischen Ozean," *Wehrkunde,* February 1975, p. 72.

upon the Soviet-Egyptian model."[18] It should be noted, however, that Radio Hamburg on December 15, 1971, indicated that a Soviet-Iraqi friendship treaty was already being negotiated during the visit of Marshal Grechko to Iraq at the end of 1971 "for talks on bases." If true, it further highlights this treaty as being a part of a general Soviet security strategy process. Indeed, one Soviet commentator saw it as promoting the Soviet collective security effort. "The treaties which the Soviet Union has concluded recently with the Arab Republic of Egypt, India, and Iraq, the USSR's relations with a number of other Asian countries, create a political climate more conducive for stepping up efforts in safeguarding security."[19] In fact, "the chance contained in the Soviet-Arab friendship treaties of the Soviet pulling Egypt and Iraq into the 'Socialist community of states' was the reason why Gromyko described both treaties as historical documents. This would mean that extension of the Soviet-dominated 'Socialist world system' to the developing countries has thus manifestly got under way."[20]

This last observation proved to be highly accurate, since the expansion of the Soviet collective security system has also brought a 20-year friendship treaty with Somalia signed on July 11, 1974, by President Podgorny and Somali President General Mohamed Siad Barre. Following a visit by the Soviet Defense Minister Marshal Grechko to Somalia, for the February 1972 signing of a military

---

[18] *Strategic Survey 1972*, International Institute for Strategic Studies, London, 1972, p. 27; A. Kelidar, *Iraq, The Search for Stability*, Conflict Studies No. 59, Institute for the Study of Conflict, London, July 1975, p. 16.
[19] V. Pavlovsky, "Collective Security: The Way to Peace in Asia," *International Affairs*, Moscow, July 1972, p. 24. A CENTO Ministerial Council, which met in Teheran in June 1973, said, on the other hand, that the Soviet-Iraqi treaty was a threat to CENTO powers. Vivekanandan, *loc. cit.*, p. 62, fn. 11. Prior to the March 6, 1975, Iran-Iraq agreement, it was further reported that the Shah was demanding renunciation by Iraq of its friendship treaty with the Soviets as a precondition for normalizing relations with Iran. *Washington Post*, February 1, 1975.
[20] Schweisfurth, *loc. cit.*, p. 323. It should be further noted that while the Iraqi-Soviet treaty was being signed, a National Liberation Front (NLF) delegation from Aden, led by its Secretary General, Mr. Ismail, was in Baghdad. "It might mean either a close cooperation between Iraq and Aden in the future which would have its repercussions in the Persian Gulf area, especially upon the liberation movements there, or it can mean that the USSR and Aden may also sign a friendship treaty in the near future." K. R. Singh, *Politics of the Indian Ocean*, Thompson Press, New Delhi, 1974, p. 145.

agreement between the two countries, an increase in Soviet use of facilities at Berbera was noted, as well as the arrival of a Soviet barracks ship (which has remained ever since) and the opening in December of that year of two Soviet naval communications sites there.[21] Further, it is believed that Soviet pressure for the conclusion of a friendship treaty began during Grechko's visit.[22] Recent statements by President Barre asserting that the economic and social progress of Somalia depended "upon the support of the countries of the Socialist community"[23] testify to the fact that the Somalis themselves recognize they are participants in a Soviet alliance system. The use of an identical verbal code by various Soviet clients is, in general, a reliable indicator of membership, and should caution us against an overoptimistic assessment of the prospects for winning away Soviet allies.

Although the recent conclusion of a 20-year friendship treaty with Angola on October 8, 1976,[24] may lead us to assume that the Soviets have a global design in mind, it is apparent that most Russian offers of such treaties—up to now, at least—have involved countries situated on the Soviet periphery. In fact, an examination of the various Soviet approaches leads one to conclude that the Soviet leadership may have decided to proceed with the treaty network until the entire periphery of the Soviet Union is linked, either directly or indirectly, in a formal alliance system to Moscow. This does not mean that the

---

[21] Statement by US Defense Secretary James R. Schlesinger in *Disapprove Construction Projects on the Island of Diego Garcia,* Hearings, Committee on Armed Services, US Senate, 94th Congress, 1st Session, June 10, 1975, p. 7. Also J. B. Bell, *The Horn of Africa, Strategic Magnet in the Seventies,* Crane, Russak, New York, 1974, p. 42. There have been reports that the Soviet Union has deployed nuclear-powered hunter-killer submarines in the Indian Ocean, and Soviet communication facilities near Berbera may indicate a capability to communicate with them while submerged. *World Armaments and Disarmaments, SIPRI Yearbook 1975,* Stockholm International Peace Research Institute, Stockholm, 1975, pp. 65, 76.

[22] B. Crozier, *The Soviet Presence in Somalia,* Conflict Studies No. 54, Institute for the Study of Conflict, London, February 1975, p. 4. A little more than a week after the conclusion of the Soviet-Somali friendship treaty, a South Yemeni delegation arrived in Moscow headed by the General Secretary of the ruling National Front, Fatah Ismail. *Christian Science Monitor,* August 15, 1974. In late 1974, Israeli sources reported that Somalia and the USSR had signed a secret appendix to their friendship treaty, allowing Moscow to build additional facilities for the Soviet fleet in the Indian Ocean. *Middle East Intelligence Survey* (Tel Aviv), November 15, 1974, p. 128.

[23] *FBIS* (USSR), October 4, 1976, p. H8.

[24] Text in *Pravda,* October 9, 1976.

Soviets will never reach for global targets, but only that in the short to medium future, Moscow's strategic design is clearly focused on its periphery.

A Radio Peace and Progress commentary said on March 23, 1972, for example, that the search for peace had been a major topic in talks between Soviet Premier Kosygin and Sheikh Mujibur Rahman of Bangladesh and Pakistani President Bhutto during their recent visits to Moscow; and added that the principles embodied in the Indo-Soviet friendship treaty were applicable "for other people of the Asian continent," thus reinforcing the impression that both Bangladesh and Pakistan were being encouraged to emulate India.[25]

Subsequent Soviet offers for the conclusion of friendship treaties went to Turkey and Syria, leading a Turkish observer to note: "It is true that the USSR has now turned to the sea, but she has by no means given up the traditional Russian geostrategic postulate of 'contiguous land power,' that is, the demand that her borders be surrounded by states which are subject to her influence."[26] A recent Soviet offer was also made to Japan designed to block a possible Japanese-Chinese peace treaty. Foreign Minister Gromyko, during his visit to Tokyo, January 9-13, 1976, is said to have told his hosts that Moscow might have to reconsider its relations with Japan if it signs a peace treaty with Peking containing an antihegemony clause. "Instead, he proposed Japanese acceptance of Moscow's anti-Chinese Asian security pact proposal, and was refused."[27] Further, on December 10, 1975, the Soviet Union and Afghanistan signed a protocol extending their treaty of neutrality and nonaggression for ten years.[28]

---

[25] Prior to his May 1974 visit to Moscow, Pakistan's President Bhutto was reported to be considering the conclusion of a friendship treaty "like that of the Indo-Soviet treaty of 1971" with the USSR. But "Bhutto was reported to have received warning from his generals against having any ventures which might jeopardize Pakistan's friendship with China." G. W. Choudhury, "Pakistan and the Communist World," *Pacific Community,* October 1974, p. 137.

[26] F. A. Vali, *The Turkish Straits and NATO,* Hoover Institution Press, Stanford, California, 1972, p. 130. For Soviet pact offers to Syria in 1972, see *Events* (London), May 6, 1977, pp. 15-16; also, Syria's President Assad on Radio Damascus, August 11, 1972.

[27] *Soviet World Outlook,* February 13, 1976, p. 6. *Izvestiia* on December 17, 1969, stated that Japan's participation in an Asian collective security system would require, as a prior step, the formation of a new parliament which would support "democracy," neutrality, and the liquidation of the US-Japan security pact. Tokyo's renunciation of nuclear weapons was also seen as a crucial precondition by the paper.

[28] *Pravda,* December 11, 1975.

"Equally significant, however, is that Mr. Podgorny's visit to Kabul yielded a joint communique that was supportive of the Soviet concept of collective security in Asia."[29]

The process involving the renegotiation of bilateral friendship treaties between Moscow and its Warsaw Pact allies, which has been paralleled by an increasing number of Eastern bloc statements concerning the alleged emergence of a "Socialist community" or "Socialist commonwealth," should be viewed as complementary to developments promoting the Soviet collective security systems described above. To begin with, it is important to note that the separate bilateral treaties between Russia and the East European countries "have been kept up to date and 'in reserve,' so to speak, in the event that the Warsaw Pact itself should ever be dissolved." It should be considered "a standby or substitute network through which the Soviet Union's policy preferences might be promoted and implemented."[30] Moreover, to maintain Soviet hegemony in the East-Central European area "the bilateral pact system in its new form (that is, post-1965) shows many advantages over the Warsaw Pact system. In the first place, assistance stemming from the bilateral treaties will be forthcoming 'automatically,' that is, without prior consultations, and, according to the texts, with all available means. Secondly, a portion of the treaties provides for preventative measures that go beyond the right of self-defense. Thirdly, only in them is the principle of 'proletarian Socialist internationalism' outranking that of 'peaceful coexistence' firmly established."[31] While these "second generation" treaties of the East European nations among one another contain only a simple consultation clause in the matter of foreign policy (exception: the treaty between East Germany and Bulgaria of September 7, 1967), toward the Soviet Union itself there exists a qualified obliga-

---

[29] *Christian Science Monitor,* January 26, 1976. For a similar Soviet-Afghan joint communique from June 8, 1974, following a visit by Kabul's Premier Mohammed Daud to Moscow, see *Soviet Analyst* (London), July 4, 1974.

[30] T. W. Wolfe, *Role of Warsaw Pact in Soviet Policy,* P-4973, Rand, Santa Monica, California, March 1973, pp. 3, 15. Thus, recent Eastern bloc proposals that would have both NATO and the Warsaw Pact agree to limit themselves to current members (*see Christian Sciance Monitor,* November 30, 1976) were intended not only to block the possible addition of Spain into NATO. If accepted, it would have left open new additions to the Warsaw Pact by way of bilateral friendship treaties concluded between new and veteran members of the Warsaw Pact.

[31] B. Meissner, "The Soviet Union and Collective Security," *Aussen Politik,* English edition, March 1970, p. 281.

tion on the part of Poland, Hungary, Bulgaria, Czechoslovakia, and East Germany to hold consultations on international matters and to *"act in conformity with agreed positions."* These nations have thus undertaken to "forfeit their own permanent foreign policy as far as the Soviet Union is concerned, but not among themselves. This means a partial limitation of sovereignty. In this point, the 'Brezhnevized' Moscow Doctrine *is valid in law.*"[32]

Further, the stipulation concerning the geographical extension of the post-1965 Warsaw Pact bilateral friendship treaties beyond Europe, which was imposed by Moscow, is of extreme importance. The alliance clause of Article 4 of the Warsaw Pact unequivocally shows that an assistance obligation is acknowledged only in the event of an armed aggression in Europe. In this regard, there is a limitation of the territorial applicability of the Warsaw Pact to Europe. This is not the case, however, with recent bilateral friendship treaties between Russia and its Warsaw Pact allies.

The May 6, 1970, friendship treaty between Czechoslovakia and the Soviet Union specifically pledges each state to regard an attack upon the other from *any* direction as an attack on itself. Further, Article 10, Section 1, of this pact obliges both to offer the attacked party "instantaneous assistance of every variety, including military assistance, and sending it support likewise with all measures at its disposal." Little wonder, then, that Soviet Foreign Minister Gromyko, in an address to the Foreign Affairs Commission of the Supreme Soviet, described the treaty as "a forward step toward the development of a *new type* of relations between the Soviet Union and Czechoslovakia." *Manchester Guardian* on May 19, 1970, commented on the treaty. "If this new clause had not already been spotted as a device for widening the pact's traditional European focus, the Rumanians did their best to point it out. In the space of a week, they took three opportunities to say that the Warsaw Pact was a defensive alliance against an imperialist attack in Europe." *Pravda* on May 28, 1970, further underscored the change. "The boundaries of the Soviet Union and other Socialist states are boundaries of a new type . . . these brothers-in-arms see that their international duty lies in the reliable safeguarding of their states' frontiers as component parts of the whole Socialist camp's boundaries . . . the idea of brotherhood-in-

---

[32] T. Schweisfurth, "Moscow Doctrine as a Norm of International Law?" *ibid.,* January 1971, p. 95. Emphasis added.

arms runs like a red thread through all these (second generation) treaties."

The renegotiation of similar bilateral friendship treaties with Rumania on July 8, 1970, and East Germany on October 7, 1975, also contained no geographical restrictions as far as the mutual assistance obligations are concerned, and further proved that "Germany as an object of political and strategic planning and of contractual agreements has in increasing measure fallen out of view in the bilateral pact system of the East European nations."[33] Instead, China has captured its place as a major input into Soviet strategic calculations. On May 14, 1970, a week after the new Soviet-Czech pact, *Krasnaya Zvezda* called attention to the "violent anti-Soviet campaign which has been building up for several years" in China, and warned: "All this demands that Soviet soldiers as well as our comrades in armies in the fraternal Socialist countries should be more vigilant and constantly ready selflessly to defend Socialist gains."

Already on March 17, 1969, immediately following the Sino-Soviet clashes along the Ussuri River, it was reported that the USSR had asked Warsaw Pact countries to send military experts to the Sino-Soviet border;[34] and on April 12, 1969, press reports quoting Western intelligence sources said that token contingents of Polish, Hungarian, Bulgarian, and East German troops were on their way to various points on the Soviet-Chinese frontier. "These troop movements are thought to be primarily of 'symbolic value' . . . as the expression of a united front of participating East bloc states with the Soviet Union."[35] The same day, the Rumanian government issued a statement that the Warsaw Pact had been established as a defense against "imperialist aggression," and in no case "can (its) actions be expanded to other areas."[36] Bulgarian Foreign Minister Ivan Bashev

---

[33] Frenzke, *loc. cit.*, p. 327.

[34] *Asian Almanac* (Kuala Lumpur), May 17, 1969, p. 3331; *East Europe,* April 1969, p. 35.

[35] *Frankfurter Allgemeine Zeitung,* April 12, 1969; *Baltimore Sun,* April 13, 1969; *Le Monde,* April 14, 1969. By September, reports indicated that air force units from Poland, Hungary, and Bulgaria had been transferred to Soviet Central Asia within striking distance of China. *East Europe,* October 1969, p. 36. For reports of Hungarian aviation units in Tashkent, see also S. T. Possony, *Threat to U.S. Security Posed by Stepped-Up Sino-Soviet Hostilities,* Hearings, Subcommittee to Investigate the Administration of the Internal Security Act and Other Internal Security Laws, Committee on the Judiciary, US Senate, 91st Congress, 2nd Session, March 17, 1970, p. 46.

[36] *Facts on File,* April 10-16, 1969, p. 211. See also Wolfe, *op. cit.,* 1970, pp. 497-498.

publicly declared in April, however, that the Soviet Union and its Warsaw Pact allies would intervene in other Communist countries "should developments like these in Czechoslovakia take place. Such a joint action is also possible (against China) should the border incidents between the Soviet Union and China endanger the Socialist camp."[37] An indication that Poland might also have responded to Soviet requests for cooperation against China was given by Polish Defense Minister Jaruzelski during a visit to the USSR in April. In a speech at Volgograd, he noted that in view of the "anti-Soviet madness of Mao Tse-tung's group," each "fraternal Socialist state" should make its own contribution to "the arsenal of political weapons and armaments which consolidate our combined strength."[38]

In February 1974, it was reported that, according to East European sources, the Soviet Union had redoubled its efforts to have Warsaw Pact operations extended from Eastern Europe to Russian territory adjacent to China. Pact members were reportedly asked to station forces along the Chinese borders and Pact maneuvers were to be held there at regular intervals. A mid-January 1974 account in the Polish Army newspaper *Zolnierz Wolnoci* seemed, in fact, to support this report. It said that units of the Polish Air Force and the Kracow Airborne Division had held maneuvers in the Soviet Union several thousand miles from the Polish border. In all likelihood, that meant east of the Urals, in the Asian territory of the USSR.[39] Another observer maintains that "each recent Summer appears to have witnessed maneuvers by selected East European as well as Soviet units near the Chinese border."[40]

From this perspective, the recurring Communist theme concerning

---

[37] H. Ray, "China's Initiatives in Eastern Europe," *Current Scene,* December 1, 1969, p. 5.

[38] Cited in Wolfe, *op. cit.,* 1970, p. 498, fn. 119. Subsequent to the renegotiation of the friendship treaties, it was reported that Mongolia's Party Secretary Y. Tsedenbal participated in the August 2, 1971, and July 31, 1972, meetings of the Party heads of the Warsaw Pact member states. L. T. Caldwell, "The Warsaw Pact: Direction of Change," *Problems of Communism,* September-October 1975, Table 1, pp. 4-5. The Mongolian leader reportedly also attended the April 1974 meeting of the Warsaw Pact Political Consultative Committee. *Far Eastern Economic Review,* June 24, 1974. p. 31. Note also that Mongolia's Defense Minister has been a regular observer at recent Warsaw Pact exercises. See, for example, G. H. Turbiville, "Warsaw Pact Exercise Shield-72," *Military Review,* July 1973, p. 17.

[39] Cited in *Christian Science Monitor,* February 4, 1974.

[40] H. C. Hinton, "The Soviet Campaign for Collective Security in Asia," *Pacific Community,* January 1976, p. 155.

the "borders of the Socialist community"[41] acquires a special strategic significance. "The Socialist community is not meant simply to comprise the COMECON and Warsaw Pact nations situated within the closer confines of Soviet hegemony. A number of references make it evident that the Soviets conceive of it as being the entire 'Socialist world system' from Cuba to Red China, North Korea, and North Vietnam. African nations and other developing countries, according to the degree of 'socialization' and commitment to the Soviet Union, presumably will be included into the 'Socialist world system.' "[42] Internally, within the sphere of the "Socialist community," according to the Brezhnev Doctrine, only "limited sovereignty" and a limited right of "self-determination" is granted to the various "Socialist states." Moreover, "withdrawal from the 'Socialist community' is forbidden since, in the latest Soviet version, it is to be regarded as the common 'Socialist fatherland.' "[43] Externally, nonmember states situated on the Soviet periphery can expect, during crisis periods, to be confronted with "systemic wars"—that is, military cooperation between two or more Soviet security subsystems in case of conflict.[44]

---

[41] See, for example, comments by the Mongolian Defense Minister, General Batyn Dorj, during a 1974 visit to East Germany, in *FBIS* (Eastern Europe), April 4, 1974, p. E6.

[42] Schweisfurth, *loc. cit.,* 1971, p. 92. In 1972, in fact, Brezhnev declared that Cuba was an "integral part of the Socialist community," and added in 1974 that it "will never be alone." Meanwhile, a closer Cuban relationship with the Warsaw Pact is indicated by high-level East European military visits to Cuba. In addition to Soviet Defense Minister Marshal Grechko, the head of the Polish Air Force and Bulgaria's Deputy Defense Minister appeared in Cuba in March 1973, and the Hungarian Defense Minister in April 1974. L. Gouré, & M. Rothenberg, *Soviet Penetration of Latin America,* University of Miami, Center for Advanced International Studies, Washington, D.C. 1975, pp. 31-32. The Bulgarian Defense Minister, Dobri Dzurov, stopped in Algeria in February 1977, on his way to Cuba. *Marches Tropicaux et Mediterraneens,* February 12, 1977. Further, a joint communique following the visit of Egyptian Presidential Advisor Hafiz Ismail to Moscow in February 1973, stressed the need for firm Soviet ties, "for a decisive checking of any attempt at weakening the Soviet-Egyptian friendship and the close relations which *bind Egypt and the other countries of the Socialist community.*" Rubinstein, *op. cit.,* 1977, p. 227. On the economic aspect of this concept, see R. Lowenthal, "Soviet 'Counterimperialism,' " *Problems of Communism,* November-December 1976, pp. 52-63; *Soviet World Outlook,* September 15, 1976, pp. 10-12.

[43] Meissner, *op. cit.,* p. 282.

[44] Haselkorn, *loc. cit.,* p. 253.

4

Internal Military Build-Up

Three major aspects of the Soviet internal military build-up program which commenced in 1965 are of particular importance as far as the Soviet collective security system is concerned. The first relates to developments in the Soviet arsenal designed to confront American nuclear deployments on the Soviet periphery, especially aircraft carriers and Polaris/Poseidon submarines. Though a detailed description of Soviet capabilities in this field is beyond the scope of this study, several important developments deserve closer scrutiny.[1] In his address to the 23rd Communist Party Congress on April 1, 1966, Soviet Defense Minister Marshal Malinovsky declared: "The creation of the Blue Belt of Defense has been completed for our state." Subsequently, Communist sources were quoted in the *New York Times* as saying that the term Blue Belt referred to the capabilities for global submarine operations reflected by Malinovsky's simultaneous revelation that a group of Soviet nuclear-powered submarines had just completed the USSR's first submerged circumnavigation of the earth. Less than two months later, East German Defense Minister Hoffman talked about "the nuclear submarines of the Blue Defense Belt which can operate in every sea in the world." Later in the Summer, an AP

---

[1] The interested reader may refer to N. Polmar, *Soviet Naval Power, Challenge for the 1970s*, Crane, Russak, New York, 1974; D. Fairhall, *Russia Looks to the Sea, A Study of the Expansion of Soviet Maritime Power*, Andre Deutsch, London, 1971, pp. 179-261; E. Wegener, *The Soviet Naval Offensive* (translated from the German), Naval Institute Press, Annapolis, Maryland, 1975; MccGwire, *op. cit.*, pp. 125-236.

report from Moscow revealed that some unidentified Soviet admirals had indicated that nuclear submarines composed only a part of Blue Belt. The report went on to suggest that the Soviet Naval Air Force might also be included, among other elements.[2]

Late in April 1967, an article in the Hungarian Communist Party newspaper *Nepszabadsag* identified Blue Belt unequivocally as the Soviet Union's missile defense system. "Had the piece not gone unnoticed by the Western news media, it probably would have led to a much broader view of Blue Belt as a unified effort by all branches of the Soviet armed forces to contribute to protection of the USSR from nuclear atacks from any sources, whether land- or sea-based."[3] During the Soviet worldwide naval maneuvers in May 1970, which were code-named *Okean-70,* a further reference to Blue Belt was made. A commentary on East Berlin Radio on the exercise stated: "Strategic tasks were assigned to all units of the socalled Blue Belt of Defense, that is to say, to nuclear submarines, ASW surface ships, Naval Air Force units, missile-firing destroyers, and helicopter carriers."[4]

Faithful to this concept, the increased mobility of American aircraft carriers, and the correspondingly more difficult problem of detecting them, enforced a change in Soviet tactics whereby Russian missile-carrying ships were to make contact with the American carrier strike groups. In this way, it was hoped that, in case of war, these Soviet ships could be in position to eliminate with their missiles at least part of the nuclear threat posed by American aircraft carriers before being destroyed themselves. In pursuit of such a tactic, however, the long-range surface-to-surface missile Shaddock no longer was necessary; and the switch to the short-range SS-N-10 missile, which first appeared in 1970 on board the Kresta-II-class guided missile cruisers, also permitted a doubling of the number of launch tubes.[5] As Admiral Gorshkov stated in his recent book *Sea Power of the State* (1976): "The imperialists are converting the ocean into a

[2] For a comprehensive analysis, see R. W. Herrick, *The USSR's "Blue Belt of Defense" Concept, A Unified Military Plan for Defense against Seaborne Nuclear Attack by Strike Carriers and Polaris/Poseidon SSBNs,* Professional Paper No. 111, Center for Naval Analysis, Arlington, Virginia, May 1973.
[3] *Ibid.,* p. 2.
[4] Cited in *ibid.,* p. 3.
[5] J. Rowher, *Superpower Confrontation on the Seas, Naval Development and Strategy since 1945,* Washington Paper, vol. 3 (26), Center for Strategic and International Studies, Georgetown University, Washington, D.C., 1975, p. 66.

vast base for launching sites for ballistic missile submarines and carrier-borne aircraft aimed at the Soviet Union and the countries of the Socialist community. In their opinion, these bases are less dangerous for their countries than land bases. And our Navy must be capable of countering this real threat."[6]

It appears that the Soviet Union has developed a regional or "zone" approach to antisubmarine warfare. For the noncontiguous Mediterranean and Norwegian Seas, which were operational areas for Polaris submarines with A-1 and A-2 missiles, the Soviet Navy developed surface warships such as the Kashin guided missile frigates, Kresta-II and Kara guided missile cruisers, and the Moskva-class helicopter carriers—vessels with the necessary endurance and antiair defenses—as well as longer-range maritime reconnaissance/ASW aircraft such as the IL-38 May, and possibly attack submarines and bottom-anchored acoustic detection devices.[7] The recent introduction of the Backfire bomber into the Soviet long-range naval aviation arsenal, with "a deeply disturbing capability against US fleets at sea,"[8] further strengthens Soviet capabilities in this respect. In fact, these

[6] Cited in *Norfolk Virginia-Pilot,* August 10, 1976. In a speech following the 1967 Middle East War, Brezhnev declared that the strong US presence in the Middle East and the Mediterranean represented a threat to the USSR. *Pravda,* July 6, 1967. Soon after, Gorshkov stated that the United States was attempting to use the Mediterranean as a "springboard for an attack on the USSR, and that the Soviet Navy could help to meet the challenge represented by the US Sixth Fleet." *Pravda,* July 30, 1967. Soviet Vice Admiral Smirnov stated that the Soviet naval build-up in the Mediterranean was defensive, because "the Sixth Fleet (was) stationed in the area . . . to be prepared to strike at enemy targets from sea and air with nuclear and conventional weapons, and the Soviet Union and other Socialist countries are designated as the principal enemy." *Krasnaya Zvezda,* November 12, 1968. For similar statements, see *Izvestiia,* November 11, 1968; *Pravda,* November 17, 24, 25, 1968.

[7] N. Polmar, "Thinking about Soviet ASW," *U.S. Naval Institute Proceedings,* May 1976, pp. 19-20. Since 1965, two classes of Soviet nuclear cruise missile submarines (Charlie and Papa) have been deployed, as well as two new classes (Victor and Alpha) of nuclear attack submarines. It appears, however, that neither the Papa SSGN nor the Alpha SSN have entered production. Nevertheless, there has been continued growth in terms of submarine armaments: cruise missile launchers at an 18 percent annual rate from 1965 to 1975, and torpedo tubes at 13 percent. A. Moore,"General Purpose Forces: Navy and Marine Corps," in W. Schneider, Jr., and F. P. Hoeber, eds., *Arms, Men, and Military Budgets, Issues for Fiscal Year 1977,* Crane, Russak, New York, 1976, p. 65.

[8] US Research and Development Chief Dr. M. Currie in *Armed Forces Journal International,* December 1974, p. 19. For a general account, see G. Panyalev, "Backfire—Soviet Counter to the American B-1," *International Defense Review,* October 1975, pp. 638-642.

bombers have already been spotted flying over the mid-Atlantic as far south at the Portuguese Azores from a base on the Kola Peninsula west of Murmansk, near 70 degrees north latitude.[9]

Evidently, there is only a short doctrinal "distance" between the Blue Belt of Defense concept and the overall Soviet strategic design as presented here, that is, the establishment of a collective security system designed to cope with a potential two-front situation. In fact, it may be argued[10] that due to the seaborne strategic-nuclear threat directed against the Soviet Union, the Soviets have decided to extend their maritime defense zones to cover the sea areas whence such nuclear strikes could be launched, and to establish an increasingly active naval presence in these areas (for example, the Mediterranean) to contest and perhaps deny their use by the West for the deployment of strategic systems. Furthermore, economy in numbers of naval units required naval facilities in forward operating areas, and the new Soviet policy was predicated upon their availability. This was such a fundamental assumption that in several key areas the requirement for bases evidently became a major determinant of Soviet foreign policy. For example, in a commentary on President Nixon's 1974 visit to the Middle East, the Budapest Domestic Television Service asserted on June 11 that America's Middle East policy was guided by the hope of regaining influence in some Arab countries and pushing the Soviet fleet back, to restore Mediterranean hegemony to the Sixth Fleet. It added: "An important fleet needs ports and sources of supply. NATO always had that, for example at Cyprus and Malta; while the Soviet fleet has had this only since it extended full support to the Arab countries by making good the losses inflicted by Israeli aggression."[11]

Some 400 planes of the Soviet Naval Air Force took part in the

---

[9] *Defense Space Business Daily,* July 30, 1976. The Backfires were probably refueled by a Bison tanker during the flight. It is estimated that the Russians have built at least 90 Backfires, and US intelligence sources have forecast an eventual force of about 400 Backfires armed with the new AS-6 Kerry standoff air-to-surface missile, with a maximum range of some 800 km. *Chicago Tribune,* November 20, 1976. Some 16 Backfires were reported to be operational with the Black Sea Fleet, capable of flying into the Mediterranean. *Aviation Week and Space Technology,* January 17, 1977, p. 48.

[10] M. MccGwire, "The Evolution of Soviet Naval Policy, 1960-74," in MccGwire, et al., *Soviet Naval Policy, Objectives and Constraints,* Praeger, New York, 1975, pp. 532-535.

[11] *FBIS* (Eastern Europe), June 12, 1974, pp. F1-2.

Okean-75 maneuvers; IL-38s based near Berbera, Somalia, and other planes flying from South Yemen worked with the Soviet Navy's Indian Ocean squadron. It is believed that the important role played by Soviet air power symbolized the attention given to ASW in the exercise. The ASW phase was followed by what appeared to be simulated anticarrier attacks by surface ships and a large number of Tu-16 Badger bombers based in Eastern Europe and the Soviet Union. In addition, an attack force of two missile-armed cruisers conducted what were believed to be anticarrier operations in the Mediterranean.[12]

More recently, Admiral Noel Gayler, who commands US forces in the Pacific, disclosed that the Soviet Navy has been moving into new areas "where previously it had not been very much," for maneuvers and the build-up of its intelligence capabilities. Japanese defense officials reported in early July 1976 that four Soviet warships were conducting what appeared to be large ASW exercises about 120 miles east of Okinawa. At one stage, the ships were accompanied by six Soviet Tu-95 Bear bombers and IL-38 ASW surveillance planes.[13] This expansion of Soviet maritime operations along the periphery of the USSR explains the reported Soviet interest in building a submarine base at Haiphong in Vietnam, and in obtaining the right to use the huge base at Cam Ranh Bay for its air and naval forces in the Pacific.[14]

A strategically-oriented Soviet forward deployment posture which, as a prerequisite of its effectiveness, relies on an external basing structure, logically presupposes some form of Soviet alliance system. Once in place, the strategic utility of such a system from Moscow's point of view is determined by its ability to deal with threats posed to the USSR proper rather than to its security subsystems. But to the extent that an effective Soviet defense of the subsystems complicates, and hopefully terminates, the political and military presence of its enemies on the Soviet periphery, it serves Moscow strategically. Further, in the real political world it is obvious that the strategic goal of the Soviet collective security system could not be attained without the Russians demonstrating they could "service" their system effectively.

[12] *New York Times,* April 28, 1975; *Financial Times,* July 18, 1975; *Christian Science Monitor,* December 30, 1976. For general accounts, see "Okean 75," *Armées d'Aujourd'hui,* July 1975, pp. 34-35; J. Labayle-Couhat, "Das Sovjetische Seemanover OKEAN 75," *Marine Rundschau,* August 1975, pp. 452-454.
[13] *Baltimore Sun,* July 10, 1976.
[14] *New York Times,* January 4, 1977; see also below.

A second major aspect of the Soviet military build-up relates to the Sino-Soviet border. The dramatic build-up of forces on the border with China that has taken place since 1965 reflects the reality of the Soviet second front perception. Moreover, as might have been expected, the Soviet build-up in the Far East was not accomplished by transferring forces from the European front, but rather by a mobilization which had raised the overall number of Soviet divisions from about 140 to 160.[15] In fact, at the same time that the Soviet Union was shoring up its forces in Asia, it also was apparently on the verge of sending more occupation troops into Czechoslovakia.[16]

Clear indications of a new Soviet strategic outlook were evident as early as 1966. On January 15 of that year, the Soviet Union and Mongolia renewed their 20-year friendship treaty; and secret clauses in it are believed to have provided for the stationing of Soviet Army units on Mongolian soil. "Earlier Soviet treaties with Mongolia had been directed against the threat of Japanese aggression and second against Nationalist China. But Ulan Bator's new treaty with the Soviet Union also set itself to the task of 'constantly strengthening the defensive might of the Socialist community' . . . Within a month, large numbers of Soviet troops and armored units were moving into Outer Mongolia. Provisions for the troop movement were believed to have been made in secret clauses of the treaty. Estimates regarding the size of the Soviet forces varied from 2,000 to more than 10,000."[17]

This was followed by the introduction of a Soviet East Europe-

---

[15] T. W. Wolfe, *Worldwide Soviet Military Strategy and Policy,* P-5008, Rand, Santa Monica, California, April 1973, p. 30; C. Stockell, "Soviet Military Strategy: The Army View," *Military Review,* October 1973, pp. 76-77.

[16] Wolfe, *op. cit.,* 1970, p. 468. Thus, by early December 1968, following the first announced withdrawal of some occupation units several weeks earlier, it became known that the number of Soviet divisions in Eastern Europe had risen to 31 (16 armored and 15 motorized infantry), compared with 26 divisions (13 armored and 13 motorized infantry) stationed there before the invasion.

[17] W. C. Clements, Jr., *The Arms Race and Sino-Soviet Relations,* Hoover Institution Press, Stanford, 1968, p. 72; *Far Eastern Economic Review,* April 3, 1969, p. 18. "After 1965, it became increasingly clear to Mongolia that the Soviet Union would not tolerate a neutral stance. This was probably connected with Mao's now famous statement to a visiting delegation of the Japanese Socialist Party (JSP), that China had not presented the Soviet Union with a bill for the territories stolen from China, and included Mongolia among them. Mongolia responded by signing a new defense agreement with the Soviet Union in 1966." *Far Eastern Economic Review,* April 17, 1971, p. 27; see also November 21, 1970, pp. 35-36. For text of the treaty, see *Pravda,* January 18, 1966.

Far East troop rotation plan using airlifts.[18] In general, the Soviets in early 1966 began to bring their existing forces along the border— some 12 to 14 divisions—to a higher state of readiness and to equip them with better and more weaponry, including the deployment of surface-to-surface nuclear-tipped missiles. In September 1966, Moscow was said to have delegated responsibility and authority for handling border incidents to local commanders. The Soviets apparently also stepped up the size of the border guard by possibly 20,000, and Soviet media began to emphasize the importance of paramilitary training by citizens of the border regions.[19]

A year later, the Soviets had restored the separate command of the Soviet Ground Forces, which had been abolished in 1966 (when they were subordinated directly to the General Staff in the Ministry of Defense as part of Khrushchev's effort to streamline the military establishment).[20] *Pravda* on January 20, 1968, emphasized that, among recent military assignments, the new Commander-in-Chief of the Soviet Ground Forces, Army General I. G. Pavlovskii, had been the Commander of the Far East Military District.

On October 10, 1967, a new draft conscription law was submitted to the Supreme Soviet for approval. It reduced compulsory military service from three to two years in the Army and Air Force, and from four to three years in the Navy. At the same time, the call-up age was lowered from 19 to 18 years of age. As a result "half instead of one third of the conscript strength (the seagoing Navy, and the like, excepted) comes into the armed forces every year and half likewise goes to the reserve, so that the strength of the reserve is increased . . . the theoretical number of reservists after ten years on the reserve, that is, up to the age of 30) would be about five million at end of 1971. At present, it is less because up to 1967 the annual conscription intakes (500,000), and hence the additions to the reserve, were less. On this basis, the figure at end 1971 was one million less, at about four million. That will grow to five million after six years when all reservists up to 30 will have been conscripted under the 1967 law . . . The figures do illustrate the very great potential of young trained

---

[18] T. W. Robinson, *The Sino-Soviet Border Dispute: Background, Development, and the March 1969 Clashes,* RM-6171-PR, Rand, Santa Monica, California, August 1971, pp. 27, 29; *New York Times,* October 9, 1966; *Foreign Report* (Economist), November 1, 1966, p. 1; *Washington Post,* February 19, 1967.
[19] Robinson, *op. cit.,* pp. 27-29.
[20] Wolfe, *op. cit.,* 1970, pp. 464-465.

manpower in the Army reserve and the effect of the reduction from three to two years' service. They contrast with the figure of two million reservists for the whole armed forces, which seems to have found credence in some circles in the West."[21] In addition, the new law called for preconscription training to be introduced. A system of compulsory military training was to be set up in schools beginning in the ninth grade, and there would also be training periods for youths already employed. One expert saw the law as having "an obvious bearing on the *Soviet Union's ability to meet the manpower requirements of any 'two-front' situation calling for the simultaneous use of theatre forces in Europe and the Far East.*"[22]

By 1968, it was estimated that the Soviets kept 15 to 17 regular divisions along the Sino-Soviet border, of which ten were fully combat ready and the remainder in a lower state of readiness, but capable of full combat deployment in 30 days. This force was supplemented by contingents of nondivisional forces and border guards.[23] This relatively modest deployment was quickly reinforced following the Sino-Soviet border clashes of 1969. *Krasnaya Zvezda* reported on March 8 that Soviet military units had been put on alert in the Far East. (According to Western intelligence sources, this was the first time that the USSR's military deployment in the Far East had been connected publicly with a possible confrontation with China.) The *Christian Science Monitor* (March 27, 1969) said that "as a result of the Ussuri (clashes), Mongolia's military forces now have been placed on permanent alert." Further, it was estimated that some 27 Soviet divisions were stationed along the Sino-Soviet border and two more were deployed in Mongolia.[24] The *Times* (June 23, 1969) reported that Soviet Army field headquarters had been es-

---

[21] For an elaboration, see J. H. C. Currie, "A Background to the Soviet Army, Part II: Manpower and Mobilization," *Army Quarterly and Defence Journal*, April 1973, pp. 342-345. See also J. Erickson, "The Military Potential of the Warsaw Pact Countries," in Schöpflin, *op. cit.*, p. 182.

[22] Wolfe, *op. cit.*, 1970, p. 466. Emphasis added.

[23] Robinson, *op. cit.*, p. 26. One source claims that by 1968, the Soviets already had 22 divisions along the Chinese border. See A. H. S. Candlin, "The Sino-Soviet Situation," *Army Quarterly and Defence Journal*, January 1974, p. 151.

[24] *The Military Balance, 1970-1971*, International Institute for Strategic Studies, London, 1970, p. 6; *Strategic Survey, 1969*, International Institute for Strategic Studies, London, 1970, p. 71. Compare with *Strategic Survey, 1971*, London, 1972, p. 56, and *Strategic Survey, 1973*, London, 1974, p. 67, both indicating 21 Soviet divisions along the border. For the higher estimate, see also Robinson, *op. cit.*, p. 31, fn. 65.

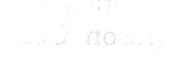

tablished near exposed border points, and that the Maritime Military District remained on the highest state of alert. In August, a Soviet missile specialist, Colonel General Vladimir Tolubko, was appointed to command the Far Eastern Military District, a move widely interpreted as signalling Soviet readiness to use nuclear missiles if necessary.[25] In November 1969, a new Soviet command known as the Central Asian Military District was created to control the Soviet Republics of Kazakhstan, Kirghizia, and Tadzhikistan.[26] "The highest ranking Military District commanders are now Army generals, and there are only four of them. Of these, three (Tolubko, promoted in 1970, Lyashchenko, and Army General P. A. Belik of the Transbaikal Military District) command the districts which between them cover the whole Sino-Soviet border."[27] During the year, there were also frequent reports regarding the construction of new airfields and miltary installations of various kinds, and large-scale civil defense efforts, especially in Kazakhstan.[28]

It should be further noted that on March 2, 1969 (the day Chinese troops ambushed a Soviet unit on the disputed island of Damansky), Soviet Defense Minister Marshal Grechko, heading a nine-man delegation, arrived in India for a one-week tour; and before leaving, he reportedly held talks with Indian officials on the coordination of policy against China.[29] "Grechko received assurances that New Delhi will not make up with Peking behind Moscow's back."[30] In return, he reportedly pledged "full military support in the

---

[25] See, for example, N. Brown, "The Myth of an Asian Diversion," *Military Review,* January 1974, p. 36; *New York Times,* November 19, 1969. On June 3, a Radio Peking dispatch claimed that the USSR had installed launching pads for nuclear-tipped missiles along China's Soviet and Mongolian borders "for use against China."

[26] *Mizan,* November-December 1969, p. 323. With headquarters in Alma Ata, this new command borders Sinkiang Province in China for 1,000 miles.

[27] G. Jukes, "Political and Military Problems of the Sino-Soviet Border," *New Zealand Slavonic Journal,* Summer 1972, p. 27.

[28] H. Gelber, "Strategic Arms Limitations and the Sino-Soviet Relations," *Asian Survey,* April 1970, p. 267. In an article in *Pravda,* August 14, 1969, Vitlay N. Titov, General Secretary of the Kazakhstan Communist Party, said that large-scale defense preparations were being taken in the Republic. Titov added that the civil defense preparations were designed to protect people against "imperialist" nuclear, biological, chemical, and other mass destruction attacks. On August 15, a Radio Peking broadcast charged that Moscow had constructed a 12-mile-wide "no-man zone" at the border, and was building military roads and railroads along the border.

[29] H. C. Hinton, *The Bear at the Gate, Chinese Policy Making under Soviet Pressure,* American Enterprise Institute, Washington, D.C., 1971, p. 24.

[30] *Manchester Guardian,* March 11, 1969.

event of aggression of China."[31] Further, the Soviet delegation proceeded to Pakistan for a five-day visit to confer with Pakistani civil
and military leaders.

On January 21, 1970, *Krasnaya Zvezda* admonished the Soviet
people to take China's war preparations seriously; and on February 4,
the Soviet news agency *Tass* reported that Soviet military and political
leaders had met in the military command bordering China's Sinkiang
Province to discuss "combat readiness." *Pravda* (March 19, 1970)
accused China of resorting to threats in the border talks between the
two countries, and warned that any attack on the Soviet Union would
be met with a firm rebuff. Again, on March 31, *Krasnaya Zvezda*
charged that China was building military roads to the Soviet border
while Soviet Defense Minister Marshal Grechko made demands for
defenses in the east as strong as those in the west.[32]

Subsequently, press reports quoting US intelligence sources said
that the Soviets had 35 combat-ready divisions on the Sino-Soviet
border with a capability to reinforce rapidly with an additional 25
divisions. For the first time, the Soviets reportedly deployed the
new solid-fuel mobile missile SS-12 Scaleboard on the border.
They also added a fourth company to each of their Frog nuclear
rocket battalions in the Far East. (In Europe, such battalions have
only three companies.) Expansion of existing border air bases and
construction of "several dozen" new landing strips that "remain un-
occupied" was also reported. [33] In mid-year, the Soviets held military
exercises in Kazakhstan.[34]

---

[31] *Asian Analyst,* April 1969, p. 13; *Neue Zurcher Zeitung,* March 20, 1969.
Note also that subsequently, between March 27-30, Indian Premier Gandhi
had visited Burma and conferred with the Burmese head of state, General Ne
Win. "The Indians have for some time urged on the Burmese the need for a
common military strategy along their frontiers where (the hill tribes) are rely-
ing on the Chinese for their revolts." *Times,* March 30, 1969. All-India Radio
reported on March 13, 1969, soon after the Sino-Soviet border clashes, that
P. Reshetov, a member of the Praesidium of the Soviet Peace Committee, had
proposed the formation of a common front of the "peace-loving people of the
Soviet Union, India, and Burma against the adventurist policies of the Chinese
government." Cited in *Mizan,* March-April 1969, p. 135.
[32] C. L. Sulzberger, *The Coldest War, Russia's Game in China,* Harcourt Brace
Jovanovich, New York, 1974, p. 97. Radio Moscow, on June 19, 1970, said
that the portion of the Soviet defense budget covering "allocation for the defense of our border areas" had been increased by 12 percent over the 1969 figure.
[33] *New York Times,* July 22, 1970; *Times,* July 23, 1970; Candlin, *loc. cit.,* p.
151; Erickson, *op. cit.,* 1971, p. 73.
[34] *Far Eastern Economic Review,* January 16, 1971, p. 46.

Although several private sources claim that by 1971 there were 46 Soviet divisions along the Chinese border[35] and that this figure had risen to 49 in 1972 with the addition of three Soviet motorized infantry divisions,[36] official US estimates which were released in 1975 say the Soviets are maintaining about 40 divisions there, along with some 1,000 tactical aircraft, half of them nuclear armed.[37]

Latest additions to the Soviet arsenal along the border include the deployment of the new SS-20 solid fuel IRBM, which carries three warheads. Sites for this missile have been spotted on the Kamchatka Peninsula.[38] Further, on March 31, 1976, the Japanese Defense Agency disclosed that the Soviet Union has deployed MIG-23 Flogger aircraft in the Vladivostok area.[39] Nevertheless, it is claimed, that although being modernized, equipment of Soviet Army units along the Sino-Soviet border remains below the standard of Eastern Europe.[40]

A third aspect of the Soviet build-up concerns Soviet power projection capabilities. The establishment of an alliance system, such as

---

[35] Candlin, *loc. cit.*, pp. 151, 152. Of these, 11 were claimed to be noncombat ready.

[36] *New York Times,* September 10, 1972; also F. Sagner, "On Both Sides of the Soviet-Chinese Border," *Aussen Politik,* English Edition, vol. 23 no. 2, 1972, pp. 165-174. F. O. Miksche, "UdSSR: Rot-China," *Wehr und Wirtschaft,* October 1974, pp. 424-428.

[37] Testimony of CIA Director William E. Colby before the Joint Economic Committee, Subcommittee on Priorities and Economy in Government, June 18, 1975, in *Washington Post,* October 27, 1975; Secretary of Defense James R. Schlesinger in a letter to Senator John L. McClellan, Chairman of the Senate Appropriations Subcommittee on Defense, *Air Force Times,* November 19, 1975, p. 5. Lieutenant General Eigil Wolff of Denmark, Chief of the NATO Defense College in Rome, said the Russians now have 11 armored divisions and 32 mechanized infantry divisons along their border with China. *Atlanta Constitution,* November 13, 1975. See also General George S. Brown, Chairman of the Joint Chief of Staffs, *US Military Posture for FY 1977,* Washington, D.C., January 1976, p. 51. Nevertheless, recent private estimates still claim over 45 Soviet divisions, including about seven armored, along the Sino-Soviet border. Of these, it is claimed that three armored and at least six mechanized infantry divisions are stationed in Mongolia. Other concentrations exist on the Ussuri and Amur Rivers, and opposite Sinkiang. Approximately one third of these divisions are category one (between three-quarters and full strength, with full equipment); one third are category two (half to three-quarters strength with complete combat vehicle establishment); and one third are category three (one-third strength, possibly with full combat vehicle establishment of older types). R. D. M. Furlong, "China's Evolving National Security Requirements," *International Defense Review,* August 1976, p. 558.

[38] *Aviation Week and Space Technology,* May 31, 1976, pp. 12-13.

[39] *FBIS (PRC),* April 5, 1976, p. A12; *Daily Telegraph,* May 17, 1976.

[40] Furlong, *loc. cit.*

the Soviet collective security system, presupposes the simultaneous development of the capabilities required to support it. Hence, Soviet airlift capability and its airborne forces, together with its sealift resources and naval infantry units, should be of particular interest. The trend has been recently summarized by the Commander-in-Chief of the Soviet Navy, Admiral Gorshkov:

> Despite the fact that vast regions of the World Ocean have become basic regions of activity by our Navy under present-day conditions, unflagging attention continues to be given to improving cooperation with the ground forces, the factor which was determining in the combat action of all our fleets during the last war. As during that war, so *today the highest form of such cooperation is marine landings.*
> During the Great Patriotic War, one marine landing was carried out every two weeks on the average. Preparation for them was made more complicated by the fact that we did not have adequate numbers of special landing equipment. Nevertheless, the high level of operational ability shown in preparing for and carrying out marine landings is worth study today, even though the mobility of action of ground forces in coastal areas has increased substantially in comparison with the last war. (During the war) . . . we created our own national school of marine landings, and *our duty today is to continue improving this very complex type of combined actions by naval forces, ground forces, and the Air Force.*[41]

Starting in 1966, the 4,000-ton Alligator LST, a landing ship which has accommodations for an entire marine battalion below deck, and space for 20 to 25 tanks, APCs, or vehicles on deck,[42] began delivery. Later, during the 1967 Navy Day, growing Soviet amphibious force capabilities were first openly demonstrated in mock amphibious maneuvers (Polnocny craft, each carrying two amphibious tanks and four amphibious armored personnel carriers). The number of Soviet naval infantrymen was estimated at the time at 8,000.[43] A Soviet

[41] "Historical Experience and the Present Day," *Voprasy Filosofii,* May 13, 1965, pp. 26-38 (pp. 9-10 of *Translations on USSR Military Affairs,* no. 1167, JPRS-65314, July 25, 1975).
[42] C. G. Pritchard, "The Soviet Marines," *U.S. Naval Institute Proceedings,* March 1972, p. 21.
[43] C. G. Jacobsen, "The Soviet Navy: Acquiring Global Capabilities and Perspectives," *Naval War College Review,* March 1972, pp. 44, 51, fn. 30.

admiral subsequently asserted that the "naval infantry has special armament and various types of amphibious equipment. Landing ships with naval infantrymen can surmount vast spaces of water and quickly put the men ashore."[44]

A building program of Soviet aircraft carriers (Kiev class) was apparently approved in early 1969,[45] and construction of the first of these carriers, in the naval shipyard at the Black Sea port of Nikolayev, became evident in early 1970.[46] US Secretary of the Navy J. William Middendorf predicted recently that Russia will field at least eight such carriers, "although Washington knows only of three that are built, and that one eventually may operate from Cuba." By introducing the Kiev carrier into service, the Secretary added, "the Soviets move from a navy without sea/air power to a formidable force with sea/air cover, and for the first time they have the ability to project air power from isolated areas."[47]

By 1970, the number of Soviet naval infrantrymen had grown to 15,000 men;[48] and in late August of that year, a unit of these forces conducted an amphibious landing on the island of Socotra, which belongs to South Yemen.[49] "Four days (after the landing), strong patrols of (Soviet marines) fanned out (to) the adjacent tiny islands of Abd al-Kuri, Kal Farun and 'The Brothers.' "[50] More recently, an Alligator-class tank landing ship with some 100 to 150 Soviet marines aboard was reportedly involved in the Angolan war of 1975-76. *Le Monde* of February 17, 1976, quoting diplomatic sources, said in this connection that three Soviet ships gave artillery support during an amphibious assault of Cuban troops on Mocamedes. One of the participating Soviet ships was reportedly identified as of the Alligator class.

It was estimated by 1975 that the Soviet naval infantry totaled

---

[44] Cited in J. T. Howe, *Multicrises, Sea Power and Global Politics in the Missile Age,* MIT Press, Cambridge, Massachusetts, 1971, p. 309.

[45] U. Ra'anan, "The USSR and the Middle East: Some Reflections on the Soviet Decision-Making Process," *Orbis,* Fall 1973, p. 959.

[46] *Time Magazine,* January 31, 1972, pp. 10-11; also *Times,* January 18, 1972.

[47] Interview with *Norfolk Virginia-Pilot,* August 1, 1976.

[48] Jacobsen, *loc. cit.,* p. 51, fn. 30.

[49] *Sunday Telegraph,* August 30, 1970; *Time Magazine,* October 5, 1970, p. 33; *Africa Report* (Washington), April 1971, pp. 8, 10; R. F. Staar, "Soviet Weapons for the Third World," *Allgemeine Schweizerische Militarzeitschrift,* January 1974, p. 16. A Soviet landing craft of the Alligator class was used by the landing force. *Daily Telegraph,* August 31, 1970, said that Defense Ministry spokesman in London had confirmed that a Soviet landing craft was in the area of Socotra.

[50] *Africa Confidential* (London), October 16, 1970, p. 8; November 13, 1970, p. 7.

18,000 to 20,000 men; and as demonstrated below, this steady expansion has been accompanied by the growth in the carrying capacity of the Soviet naval infantry fleet.[51]

TABLE ONE
The Naval Infantry Fleet as of July 1, 1974

	Pacific	Baltic	Black Sea	North Sea
Polnocny	15	20	20	10
LSM	(20)	(9)	(15)	(6)
Alligator	4	4	3	3
LST	(3)	(2)	(2)	(—)
MP2, 4, 6, 8				
LSM	10 ⎤	10 ⎤	10 ⎤	10 ⎤
Vydra MP	⎬(40)	⎬(31)	⎬(35)	⎬(19)
10 LCT	45 ⎦	40 ⎦	30 ⎦	15 ⎦
Total	74	74	63	38
	(63)	(42)	(52)	(25)

(Figures within brackets reflect estimates as of July 1, 1972.)

Further, a new amphibious LST (designated the Ropucha class) was introduced in 1974,[52] and "ships of this class have already been transferred to the Pacific fleet."[53]

The other naval dimension concerning possible support for member states of the Soviet collective security system has to do with its growing sealift capability. A recent estimate says: "The USSR operates 1,500 merchant ships totaling about 12.5 million deadweight tons. Of this total, there are some 370 cargo ships and 112 tankers which appear to be equipped and suitable for long-range military sealift. All are less than 20 years old, are capable of speeds in excess of 14 knots, and have the required heavy lift booms and hatch size. In 1973, it was noted that Soviet shipbuilding facilities have been

---

[51] E. P. Takle, "Soviet Naval Infantry," *Journal of the Royal United Services Institute for Defence Studies,* June 1975, p. 30; also R. Berman, "Soviet Naval Strength and Deployment," in MccGwire, *op. cit.,* 1975, pp. 419-423.
[52] *Warship International,* no. 3, 1975, p. 235.
[53] W. H. J. Manthorpe, "The Soviet Navy in 1975," *U.S. Naval Institute Proceedings,* May 1975, p. 206.

expanded so significantly that they retain the option to double their current capability by 1980."[54] Of particular importance are the "RO/RO" (roll-on roll-off) ships designed so that vehicles can be driven directly onto the ship and off at destination. The Russian ships, entering the Soviet merchant fleet in 1973, have decks and ramps strong enough for carrying heavy equipment, and have been used to sealift tanks to Angola and Middle East trouble spots (see Figure Two). In fact, the *Okean-1975* exercise included the participation of merchant shipping in a convoy as well as what may have been the first ocean convoy escort operations for the Soviet Navy.[55]

It is usually asserted that compared to the United States, Soviet capabilities for amphibious operations are relatively limited. But while this may be so, it should be stressed that these forces are supplemented by seven Soviet airborne divisions, totaling some 50,000 paratroops. In fact, the Soviets make it abundantly clear that both expeditionary forces are part of the same strategic concept.[56] General Yakubovsky, the late Soviet commander of the Warsaw Pact forces, summed up this concept when he remarked that "contemporary landings represent a good combination of sea and air landings, complementing one another."[57]

In 1945, no airborne forces existed in the Soviet Union; and not until 1960, during a military organizational reform, were new concepts come upon which supported reorganization. Since then, the airborne units have been constantly expanding, with large-scale airborne maneuvers in Central Asia and the Ukraine in the Fall of 1967 and early Summer of 1968, and with two more divisions being authorized in 1969.[58] In April 1967, Colonel General Margelov, chief of the airborne troops, indicated that airborne units may be

[54] Admiral Thomas H. Moorer, Chairman of the Joint Chiefs of Staff, "General Purpose Forces Compared," *Commander's Digest,* April 18, 1974, p. 5. Since 1965, the Russian merchant fleet has grown at an average of 600,000 tons per year. R. T. Ackley, "The Soviet Merchant Fleet," *U.S. Naval Institute Proceedings,* February 1975, p. 30.
[55] "Soviet Naval Activities 1971-1976," *NATO Review,* December 1976, p. 10.
[56] For more on cooperation between the naval infantry and Soviet reinforced motorized rifle battalions in amphibious landings, see G. H. Turbiville, "A Soviet View of Heliborne Assault Operations," *Military Review,* October 1975, pp. 12-13.
[57] Cited in J. F. Meehan, "The Soviet 'Marine Corps,'" *ibid.,* October 1972, p. 92.
[58] "Soviet Airborne Forces," *Aerospace International,* March/April, 1973, p. 10.

FIGURE TWO

US and USSR RO/RO Ships

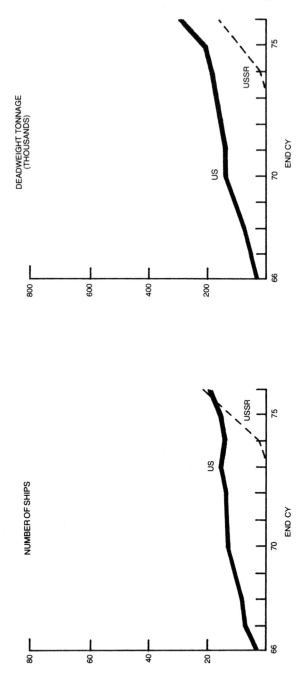

Source: Commander J. G. Roche, "The Soviets' Growing Reach: Implications of Comparative Capabilities to Project Military Power," Paper Presented at the European-American Workshop, May 1977, Belmont, Md., p. 14.

transported to the "operational radius of modern aircraft."[59] Further, exercise *Dvina* (March 1970) had included a full-scale test of Soviet logistics with a significant use of airlift for reinforcement and mobility. A force of 8,000 parachute troops with 160 vehicles was dropped in some 22 minutes (using daylight) during the maneuvers.[60] A combination air-assault air-landing operation was also conducted during exercise *Yug* (June/July 1971). "Press reports give rise to the possibility that the airborne troops may have had a sensitive strategic mission which the Soviets are reluctant to talk about."[61] In Warsaw Pact exercise *Shield-72*, a new element had been introduced. The Soviets used a massive airlift to transport units to *prepositioned* equipment in Eastern Europe. For this purpose, mobilization of a large segment of the Soviet civilian airline fleet, Aeroflot, was conducted.[62] Similarly, reports in early 1973 concerning the increased use of airlifts for troop rotation between the USSR and forward areas in Eastern Europe indicated that the aircraft involved came from Aeroflot.[63]

It is estimated that the Soviet Air Force can currently move three airborne divisions in one lift over short or medium range[64] and some sources say this capability is being expanded to handle the rapid deployment of five airborne divisions.[65] This will probably be achieved by the introduction of the new Il-76 Candid, which has a nominal range of 3,100 miles with a maximum payload of 88,500

---

[59] Cited in G. H. Turbiville, "Soviet Airborne Troops," *Military Review*, April 1973, p. 69.

[60] Erickson, *op. cit.*, 1971, p. 95; *Ha'aretz* (Tel Aviv), January 17, 1971.

[61] Turbiville, *loc. cit.*, 1973, p. 69.

[62] See J. Erickson, "Soviet Shield '72," *Journal of the Royal United Services Institute for Defence Studies*, December 1972; G. H. Turbiville, "Warsaw Pact Exercise Shield—'72," *Military Review*, July 1973, pp. 17-24. It is estimated that between 20 and 25 percent of the Aeroflot potential of 600 to 800 aircraft is available for military lift purposes. See R. Meller, "Europe's New Generation of Combat Aircraft," *International Defense Review*, April 1975, p. 185. J. Erickson, "Soviet Military Capabilities in Europe," *Journal of the Royal United Services Institute for Defence Studies*, March 1975, p. 67. See also J. T. Reitz, "Soviet Civil Aviation in Peace and War," *East Europe*, July 1974, pp. 10-13; *Neue Zurcher Zeitung*, March 18, 1970. Note the applicability of such a procedure to non-European contingencies.

[63] *Aviation Week and Space Technology*, April 2, 1973.

[64] *Military Review*, April 1973, p. 100. Some estimates put this number at three to four divisions. Erickson, *op. cit.*, 1971, p. 63. For more conservative estimates, see J. L. Moulton, "Seaborne and Airborne Mobility in Europe," *U.S. Naval Institute Proceedings*, Naval Review 1974, p. 129; *The Military Balance 1970-1971*, London, International Institute for Strategic Studies, 1970, p. 8.

[65] *Military Review*, April 1973, p. 100.

lbs.[66] One hundred of these craft, which can carry 250 troops, reportedly have been ordered.[67] In 1975, the Il-76 made its first operational appearance outside the USSR when it participated in the Soviet military airlift to Angola.[68] Shortly before, Western military analysts were said to have been concerned over an increase in airborne strength in Soviet Central Asia, deployed in the Turkmen Republic north of Iran, within range of the Middle East. Some estimates said at the time that there were four or five airborne divisions in the area.[69]

Soviet airlift capability has been tested time and again in missions involving logistic and defensive support for member states of its collective security system. For example, as early as November 1967 it was reported that the Soviets flew 24 MIG-19s and 40 to 50 Soviet aviation technicians into Sana'a airport (North Yemen) to help fight the royalists.[70] Subsequent flights were also made to Hudeida[71] using the Vinnitsa (USSR)-Luxor (Egypt)-Hudeida route.[72] In December 1967, Western diplomats confirmed that the Soviet Union had completed a three-week emergency arms airlift to Yemen which began in the last week of November and had comprised from 75 to 100 flights of Soviet transport planes.[73] Further, a royalist broadcast said on December 3 that royalist antiaircraft guns near Sana'a had shot down a Soviet-built military aircraft piloted by a Russian.[74]

---

[66] *Aviation Week and Space Technology*, May 31, 1971, p. 29. Subsequent to its appearance, Soviet military officials declared that the aircraft will be given Air Force cargo missions. *Aviation Week and Space Technology*, May 28, 1973, p. 49; *Air Force Magazine*, March 1975, p. 68. *Komsomo-l'skaya Pravda* on August 17, 1975 (Air Force Day), carried a picture showing a line-up of five Il-76s being boarded by paratroops.

[67] *Aviation Week and Space Technology*, June 11, 1973, p. 57; *Ha'aretz*, June 2, 1971. Further, the "civil" versions of the Il-76 assigned to Aeroflot nevertheless carry all the necessary installations for a radar-controlled turret at the rear of the fuselage. J. Erickson, "Soviet Military Capabilities," *Current History*, October 1976, fn. 21.

[68] *New York Times*, January 22, 24, 1975.

[69] *Ibid.*, February 9, 1976.

[70] W. Joshua and S. P. Gibert, *Arms for the Third World, Soviet Military Aid Diplomacy*, Johns Hopkins Press, Baltimore, 1969, p. 27.

[71] *New York Times*, July 16, 1968.

[72] *Neue Zurcher Zeitung*, February 4, 1968.

[73] *Middle East Record, 1967*, Shiloah Center for Middle Eastern and African Studies, Tel Aviv, 1971, p. 30; *New York Times*, December 15, 1967.

[74] *Arab Report and Record*, December 1-15, 1967, p. 382; *New York Times*, December 13, 1967. Note that shortly thereafter, the Russian pilots were reportedly replaced by Syrians. Joshua and Gibert, *op. cit.*

A massive Soviet arms airlift had also taken place during and after the 1973 Yom Kippur War. In an address to the Knesset on October 16, 1973, Prime Minister Golda Meir said: "The Soviet planes and ships carry military equipment, including missiles of various types; and it may be assumed that the planes are also bringing in advisors and experts on operational matters, as well as equipment and armament. The Soviet airlift up to October 15 included: to Syria, 125 Antonov-12 planes; to Egypt, 42 Antonov-12 and 16 Antonov-22 planes; to Iraq, 17 Antonov-12 planes. Intelligence reports indicate the Soviet Union has succeeded in involving other countries of the Soviet bloc in the supply of aid to Egypt and Syria."[75]

More recently, in July 1974, Somalia received seven MIG-21s from the Soviet Union, of which three were airlifted and the rest brought in crates and assembled by Soviet technicians already in the country.[76] The airlift probably necessitated the utilization of various landing sites within the Middle East subsystem (for example, Egypt) for refueling. Further, this somewhat strange and expensive delivery procedure may be best explained by Soviet interest in testing their system's quick reinforcement potential.

In summary, it is obvious that from the perspective of the security system, "Soviet land and sea forces have an overall coherence and logic which is fitting for their geopolitical situation. Too close a focus upon the elements of the Soviet armed forces as discrete entities is misleading. They are in fact independent parts of the whole. The ultimate purpose of the combined forces is the seizure and consolidation for defense of the World Island."[77] Indeed, there is a certain irony in all the efforts to understand the particular aspects of Soviet military policy when we fail in general to grasp or identify the essentials of its security strategy.

---

[75] G. Meir, *My Life*, Putnam, New York, 1975, p. 434.

[76] *Facts on File*, August 24, 1974, p. 695, citing a July 8 broadcast from Addis Ababa; *Africa Research Bulletin* (London), July 1-31, 1974, p. 3315; *To the Point International* (Brussels), July 27, 1974, p. 27; *Christian Science Monitor*, August 15, September 3, 1974; *Washington Post*, August 26, 1974.

[77] E. B. Atkeson, "Hemispheric Denial: Geopolitical Imperatives and Soviet Strategy," *Strategic Review*, Spring 1976, p. 35.

5

External Deployment

The third element of the Soviet collective security system concerns the development of an external infrastructure capable of supporting the *de facto* stationing of Russian forces in each of the security subsystems, that is, the Warsaw Pact, Middle East, and India/Far East. As the series of tables presented in Annex A demonstrates, only in a few geographical sites along the Soviet periphery have the Russians refrained from efforts to erect, modernize, or propose new harbors, port facilities, air bases, and improved overland communications.

Some of the more recent examples of Soviet infrastructure development include the reported servicing of a large part of the Soviet force of submarines operating in the Mediterranean in Yugoslav ports.[1] The Russians have made use of a Yugoslav law (amended April 30, 1974, following persistent Soviet pressure for port facilities), permitting any nation to berth no more than two warships at a time at a Yugoslav repair dock, with no single ship permitted to remain more than six months. A major new Yugoslav naval dockyard at Tivat in Kotor Bay, near Albania, went into operation in 1974. In December 1974, the first Soviet warship entered its berth at Tivat; and since then, the Soviet fleet has used the port up to the maximum permitted. Moreover, Soviet ships repaired at Tivat (mostly F-class submarines) reportedly stay for much shorter periods than the stipulated six-month maximum, so that many more than the mini-

---

[1] See *New York Times,* February 7, 1977.

mum of four Soviet warships are serviced by Yugoslavia each year. The Commander-in-Chief of the Soviet Navy, Admiral Sergei Gorshkov, paid an official visit to Yugoslavia from August 18 to 24, 1976, and the Yugoslav news agency *Tanjug* said that he was expected to tour the Adriatic coast and visit Yugoslav naval units and installations. Further, it was reported that Gorshkov tried to persuade the Yugoslavs to cooperate more closely with the Soviet Mediterranean fleet to increase the number of foreign naval vessels that may be repaired simultaneously in Yugoslav ports, and to accord priority to Soviet naval units in using them.[2]

Meanwhile in Libya, on the southern shores of the Mediterranean opposite to Yugoslavia, large shipments of unidentified Soviet goods have been passing through Tobruk lately. This has led to speculation that "the USSR may be building up the Libyan port of Tobruk as a major staging port and possibly a base for Soviet naval activity in the western Mediterranean."[3] Egyptian President Sadat said recently that although there were no Soviet bases in Libya, "the Russians are starting to send MIG-25s there. Libya is buying them, but they will be flown by Soviet pilots, because no Libyan is up to it."[4]

A military mission from East Germany recently arrived in Mozambique, which borders on the Indian Ocean, to undertake the planning, establishment, and operation of a logistical system for the Frelimo military forces.[5] At the same time, it was reported that Equatorial Guinea's army was controlled by Soviet specialists and advisors to President Francisco Macias.[6] The 200 Soviet military experts in the country (together with some 200 Cubans and 60 North Korean military advisors) were reported also to be running the port of Luba and two main airports.[7]

---

[2] For details, see Z. Antic, "Soviet Naval Commander Visits Yugoslavia," *Radio Free Europe Research,* Background Report No. 193, September 6, 1976.

[3] *Armed Forces* (Johannesburg), October 1976, p. 5.

[4] Interview with *New York Times,* January 16, 1977. Further, "the Soviets had just finished building three radar stations near the Egyptian border. These (would) cover all of Egypt's airspace, as well as naval and air activity in the Mediterranean. The Soviets have also set up a very large communications center in Tobruk, providing a communications network for Africa and the Middle East." *National Review Bulletin,* August 26, 1977.

[5] *Armed Forces,* April 1976, p. 3. See also H. von Löwis of Menar, "Solidarität und Subversion: Die Rolle der DDR im Südlichen Afrika," *Deutschland Archiv,* June 1977, pp. 644-645.

[6] *Christian Science Monitor,* June 23, 1976.

[7] *To the Point International,* January 10, 1977, p. 22.

The development of an infrastructure abroad has, of course, facilitated the external deployment of Soviet forces and contributed to Soviet strategic goals, as well as enhancing Russia's ability to support the security subsystems militarily. In fact, the analysis (in Annex A) of a decade of Soviet *de facto* external stationing highlights the dynamics of the USSR's forward deployments.

First, it is important to note that this external military presence has been growing steadily during peace times. Moreover, from the systemic perspective, existence of proxy contingents in various points along the Soviet periphery (for example, North Korean pilots in Syria, Cubans in South Yemen, and so forth) should be included in our calculations if we are to get an accurate measure of the Soviet presence in the subsystems. Indeed, one can make the case that the utilization of proxies enables the Soviets to reduce their own military presence abroad, thus creating an "optical error" in Western perceptions. Second, time and again the Soviet military presence has peaked quickly during wars related to the periphery. This, in turn, emphasizes the dynamic dimension of the concept; that is, even if we were to observe a temporary decline in Soviet deployments in a certain member state or region during peacetime, this would not necessarily mean a reduction of Soviet interest, commitment, and/or capability to reappear there in force during a crisis. Instead, the peaking of the Soviet external presence during wartime should be perceived as a *function* called for by the Soviet security system—that is, for the provision of either intrawar logistic or defensive support—rather than as a random phenomenon.

In fact, this function has been clearly recognized by the Soviets. The late Soviet Defense Minister, Marshal Grechko, in an article in May 1974, stated: "At the present stage, the historic function of the Soviet armed forces is not restricted merely to their function in defending our Motherland and the other Socialist countries. In its foreign policy activity, the Soviet state actively (and) purposefully opposes the export of counterrevolution and the policy of oppression, supports the national liberation struggle, and resolutely resists imperialist aggression in whatever distant region of our planet it may appear."[8]

Moreover, the emergence of this new function was used by some

---

[8] Cited in W. F. Scott, "The USSR's Growing Global Mobility," *Air Force Magazine,* March 1977, p. 57.

Russian military commentators as an argument for expanding further Soviet defense capabilities. "The intensification and expansion of the *international* task of the Soviet armed forces also objectively condition the need for their further strengthening. The situation requires increasing attention to questions of Soviet military construction."[9] Additionally, the Soviets were recently hinting that they will not tolerate any outside interference in their quest to accomplish these strategic support missions. A recent article by Captain V. Serkov in the Soviet naval journal *Morskoi Sbornik* argued: "As thorough analysis of the Montreux Convention shows, one can consider from a legal point of view that passage through the (Turkish) straits by *any* ships of states on the Black Sea does not contradict the letter and the spirit of the Convention."[10] This seemed to some analysts "to point to a wholesale abandonment of the Montreux Convention, rather than just a stretching of categories."[11]

It follows that we need to recognize that the "moment of truth," in so far as collective security arrangements are concerned, comes during wars. During peacetime, one may be confronted with a hazy picture involving frequent friction between the Soviets and their allies. Some member states may even drop out of the system, while others may join in. But in the final analysis, what counts is the shape of this "picture" during wartime. It should be stressed that ever since 1970, all wars fought along the Soviet perimeter have had systemic (that is, nonbilateral and nonregional) parameters. Soviet security strategy, in turn, has repeatedly proven its effectiveness.

---

[9] Colonel V. Serebriannikov and Colonel M. Iasiukov, "Peaceful Coexistence and Defense of the Socialist Fatherland," *Comunist Voorushennykh Sil,* August 1972, pp. 15-16. Emphasis added.

[10] Cited in *Washington Post,* August 13, 1976. Emphasis added. The article followed the passage of the first Soviet aircraft carrier, the *Kiev,* into the Mediterranean through the Turkish Straits.

[11] Buzan, *loc. cit.,* p. 246.

6

Strategic Mutual Support

The prime mechanism linking the three security subsystems—the Warsaw Pact, Middle East, and India/Far East—among themselves consists of strategic mutual support missions. The operational outcome involves a process through which the subsystems actually reinforce each other. In addition, this mechanism has the main responsibility for the "collective" character of the Soviet security strategy.

As stated earlier, demonstrations of the system's related logistic and defensive mutual support activity during the last decade have been abundant. It is hoped that the few examples listed below support this contention, even if the list is far from exhaustive.

Intrasubsystem Strategic Mutual Support

Obviously, indications of intrasubsystem strategic linkage are most widespread in the Warsaw Pact subsystem. In addition to regular joint military exercises, the following developments should be noted. On September 7, 1967, the first 20-year friendship treaty between Bulgaria and East Germany was signed, providing for joint military defense between the countries against *any* "imperialist, militarist, and revanchist" aggression. Bulgaria's Party Secretary Zhivkov said that the treaty "expresses our decision to strengthen the power of our defense organization, the Warsaw Pact."[1]

Following the August 1968 invasion of Czechoslovakia, Moscow urged the countries of the "Socialist commonwealth" to strengthen their military alliance, and stressed that joint maneuvers would continue to have "an important place" among various "practical measures for improving collective defense."[2] In fact, Soviet attempts to portray the invasion as a Warsaw Pact affair should be noted, even though this position has never been taken in a formal Warsaw Pact document. Moscow thus "stressed the *multilateral* nature of the intervention, and begged the question of decisionmaking."[3]

Subsequently, it was reported that Moscow was applying pressure on Rumania, insisting that Budapest participate in Warsaw Pact military activities.[4] In June/July 1971, the Warsaw Pact launched joint military exercises with the significant code name *Yug* (South), on the Black Sea, in the Ukraine, and in the Moldau Republic. The fact that the maneuvers were conducted "on Rumania's frontiers (as well as in the eastern Mediterranean, that is, at Yugoslavia's front door) . . . can be construed as a hint from Moscow to Rumania . . . The fact that official notice of the *Yug* maneuvers came only a few days prior to the announcement that Ceausescu . . . would travel to Peking only strengthens this assumption, since these travel plans had been known to the Soviets in advance."[5]

Little wonder, therefore, that by early 1972 Rumania had signalled its readiness to get back in line. Thus, on February 24, Hungary and Rumania signed a friendship treaty. The terms of the pact are virtually identical with the one Bucharest concluded with Bulgaria on November 19, 1970, which contains in Article 7 a mutual pledge for military assistance "in case of an armed attack against one of the High Contracting Parties by a state or group of states." The Rumanian-Hungarian pact was thus "believed to resemble the Soviet-Rumanian Treaty of 1970."[6] Further, on May 12, 1972, Rumania and East Germany

---

[1] *East Europe*, October 1967, p. 35.
[2] Wolfe, *op. cit.*, 1970, p. 482.
[3] R. A. Remington, "The Warsaw Pact: Communist Coalition Politics in Action," *The Yearbook of World Affairs, 1973*, London Institute of World Affairs, London, 1973, p. 166. Emphasis added.
[4] *New York Times*, February 9, 1970.
[5] D. Schlegel, "Romania's Position Vis-à-Vis Moscow," *Aussen Politik*, English Edition, April 1970, p. 452; *International Herald Tribune*, August 4, 1971.
[6] *Facts on File*, March 12-18, 1972, p. 193.

also concluded a friendship treaty, "the first such document between the two countries."[7] Article 8 of the treaty pledges mutual military assistance in the event of an armed attack by *any* state or group of states against one of the parties. It should be stressed that this treaty has completed the series of bilateral treaties concluded between the Warsaw Pact countries. *Krasnaya Zvezda* on February 22, 1973, was thus able to report that the Warsaw Pact countries had completed a ten-day staff exercise in Rumania.[8]

Facilitation of intrasubsystem strategic mutual support missions is by no means limited to bilateral friendship treaties concluded between the Warsaw Pact members. East Berlin's ADN International Service, for example, said on January 13, 1973, that the GDR and Czechoslovakia had signed a military cooperation pact with the "objective of consolidating the existing links in all spheres of the military system."[9] Further, a plan for cooperation between GDR's NVA (Nationale Volksarmee) and the Group of Soviet Armed Forces in Germany was signed on January 24, 1975, by East Germany's Defense Minister General Heinz Hoffman and Soviet Army General Y. Ivanovsky. Hoffman (in *Neues Deutschland,* May 14, 1975) hailed the military integration of the Warsaw Pact countries. "When we speak about the military superiority of the Warsaw Pact in regard to NATO, then we refer first of all to the uniformity of our armed forces from its class character and its political task, armament and equipment, tactical and operational concepts, from the level of training, to the unshakable fighting morale and the fine relations of the Socialist brotherhood of arms."

At the same time, the physical aspects of intrasubsystem mutual

---

[7] *Yearbook on International Communist Affairs, 1973,* Hoover Institution Press, Stanford, California, 1973, p. 67.

[8] This was reportedly the first time since 1962 that Rumania had allowed military maneuvers to take place inside the country. Further, there were reports on August 22, 1974 (during Soviet Premier Kosygin's visit to Rumania), that Bucharest had allowed the Soviet Army transit rights through Dobrudja to join Warsaw Pact maneuvers in Bulgaria earlier that Summer. Indeed, *Frankfurter Allegemeine Zeitung,* June 20, 1974, said (in a dispatch from Belgrade) the Rumanian State Council has ratified a law on "the special rights and the immunity of the General Staff and other leadership organs of the United Armed Forces of the Warsaw Pact." The paper added: "This legal stipulation appears necessary because Rumanian defense laws prohibit the presence of foreign, even allied, troops in peacetime (on Rumanian soil)."

[9] *FBIS* (Eastern Europe), January 15, 1973, p. 19.

support were indicated by reports concerning the improvements of transportation systems in western Russia and several Pact countries. Roads, rail networks, and airports were reportedly upgraded, and single track rail lines became double track. Standardization of track width was also under consideration in order to avoid time-consuming transfers at the Soviet western border.[10]

Turning to the Middle East subsystem, one finds intrasubsystem mutual support a constant theme in both Soviet statements and operations directed at their Arab allies. *Pravda,* on October 25, 1975, summed up the strategy as follows: "There has been no meeting between Soviet and Arab leaders, there has been no Soviet-Arab document, in which the Soviet side has not emphasized the importance of the solidarity of the Arab states and of strengthening the unity of their actions in the struggle against Israel's continuing aggression. In its practical activity, the Soviet Union is doing everything it can do to facilitate the solidarity of the Arab states on an anti-imperialist basis." For instance, during his visit to Cairo in May 1966, Soviet Prime Minister Kosygin had publicly and privately urged President Nasser to drop the line of all-Arab cooperation and to concentrate on building an alliance of "progressive forces." "Such an alliance had been a specific aim of Soviet policy in the Middle East since the Syrian coup of February 1966."[11] Thus, on May 17, Kosygin called for a united front of progressive states "such as the United Arab Republic (Egypt), Syria, Algeria, and Iraq to confront imperialism and reaction and strengthen the front against

---

[10] *Military Review,* April 1973, p. 45; see also R. D. Lawrence and J. Record, *US Force Structure in NATO, An Alternative,* Brookings Institution, Washington, D.C., 1974, p. 16.
[11] *Middle East Record, 1967,* p. 8. "The core and center of the new Soviet initiative in this region was the attempt to form a 'bloc of progressive Arab states' closely linked to the 'Socialist Community,' proclaimed by Premier Kosygin in his address to the Egyptian National Assembly in Cairo in the Spring of 1965—in contrast to Khrushchev's traditional policy of backing individual Arab states in their conflicts with 'Imperialism and Zionism,' but of opposing 'Pan-Arabism' . . . This amounted to the transition from a strategy of denial of this region to Western control, to the attempt to establish a positive sphere of Soviet influence there, and the Kremlin must have been aware that this meant a vast increase in its political and military commitments, not only its economic ones." R. Löwenthal, "Changing Soviet Policies and Interests," in *Soviet-American Relations and World Order, The Two and the Many,* Adelphi Paper No. 66, International Institute for Strategic Studies, London, 1970, p. 17.

colonialism."[12] Further, "the Moscow-inspired Cairo-Damascus rapprochement culminated in a new (Egyptian)-Syrian defense pact
signed in November 1966."[13]

During 1968, there were a number of indications that the Soviets
were particularly interested in effecting military cooperation between
Syria, Jordan, and Iraq.[14] Indeed, it is known that Syria sent a force
of 2,000 troops to Iraq as a gesture of defensive support in the conflict between Iraq and Iran over the Shatt-al-Arab.[15] Yet there is an
abundance of evidence to suggest that Soviet policy has not been
limited to these countries. Rather, the real scope of Soviet intentions
was clearly derived from an overall collective security conception.

South Yemen's Premier Faisal Abad al-Latif, for instance, revealed in 1969 that South Yemeni troops were preparing to go to
the Suez Canal front to assist Egypt in its war of attrition against
Israel. The Soviet Union, he added, "supplies us with all we need,
including MIGs and rockets, and our pilots are now trained in Egypt,
Algeria, and the Soviet Union."[16] Further, the Beirut newspaper,
Al Hayat on July 27, 1970, reported an agreement reached in early
May 1970 between Syria and South Yemen whereby the latter was
allowed to recruit Syrian pilots on a contract basis to man South
Yemen's Soviet-made MIG fighters. The paper added that Aden had
recently received new arms shipments from the USSR. This followed
an earlier report that a number of retired Syrian Air Force pilots had
been reactivated "at the request of the Soviet Union."[17] In December
1970, Arab pilots at a number of "strategically located harbors" were

---

[12] *Times,* May 18, 1966; *New York Times,* May 19, 1966.
[13] A. S. Becker and A. L. Horelick, *Soviet Policy in the Middle East,* R-504-FF,
Rand, Santa Monica, California, September 1970, p. 44.
[14] *Middle East Record, 1968.* Shiloah Center for Middle Eastern and African
Studies, Tel Aviv, 1973, p. 25. Note that in the changed circumstances brought
about by the Six-Day War, Soviet emphasis shifted from the unity of the
"progressive" states to unqualified Arab unity. However, a Soviet shift back-
ward, stressing "progressive Arab unity," occurred after the Soviet expulsion from Egypt in July 1972. See, for example, *Pravda,* August 19 and
September 15, 1972, the latter quoting Soviet President Podgorny.
[15] *Military Review,* November 1969, p. 103.
[16] Interview in *Al Anwar* (Beirut), April 10, 1969.
[17] *Al Hayat,* February 15, 1970. Note that *Le Monde* (February 5, 1970) had
reported that newly trained Syrian pilots had returned to Syria from the
Soviet Union, which may indicate the Soviet request was intended, in fact, to
meet South Yemen's needs.

reportedly replaced by Russians presumably freeing them in this way for defensive support missions in Egypt.[18] A similar procedure was applied by the Soviets to Israel's northern borders. The Beirut paper, *Al Kifah,* which is known for its close contacts with the Iraqi regime, said on May 18, 1970, that a high-ranking delegation led by Vice Chairman of the Revolutionary Council Saddam Husein Takriti was about to visit Moscow. It added that the delegation would discuss Iraqi-Soviet cooperation in the military field "in light of the new commitments Iraq has taken up in the eastern front" against Israel.

Moreover, in a manner resembling the Warsaw Pact's collective defense tradition, it was announced in Damascus on August 15, 1971, that a Soviet military delegation led by the deputy commander of the Caucasus Military District, General Karlov, and an Egyptian military delegation led by General Saad Shazli, were observing, with Syrian President Assad, the final phase of military maneuvers in southern Syria.[19] It was also reported that officer candidates of the Syrian Navy were being trained at the Egyptian Naval Academy,[20] a procedure evidently preconditioned upon the existence of similar Soviet equipment and doctrine in the navies of both countries. Such an infrastructure is, obviously, a major stipulation for effective intra- and intersubsystem logistic support. For instance, *Al Nahar,* the Beirut daily, said March 6, 1972, that it had learned from reliable Arab diplomatic sources that Libya and the Soviet Union had agreed to conclude an arms deal under which Libya would buy sophisticated weapons for eventual delivery to Egypt. *Akhbar al-Yawm,* from Cairo, quoted Sadat on March 30, 1974, as disclosing that Algeria among others had sent 100 tanks to Egypt during the Yom Kippur War. Soviet approval of this procedure could be detected when *Krasnaya Zvezda* pointed out on October 20, 1973, that Iraq, Algeria, Jordan, Morocco, Saudi Arabia, and Kuwait supplied military units to Egypt and Syria.

Subversion and guerrilla warfare along the Soviet periphery are also frequently fed by intrasubsystem logistic support. Aside from the political convenience for Russia of such a procedure—that is, of not

---

[18] *Evening Standard* (London), December 14, 1970. According to the paper, ten Arab pilots at Aden had been thus replaced and similar changes were underway at Hudeida.
[19] *Arab Report and Record,* August 1-15, 1971, pp. 419-420.
[20] *Military Review,* November 1970, p. 102.

being formally involved—it virtually guarantees that when the final takeover occurs, the new regime will already be linked, at least indirectly, with the Soviet system. For instance, the Eritrean Liberation Front (ELF), which established its headquarters from about 1965 in Damascus, benefited at second hand from the large post-1967 flow of Soviet and East European arms to the Arabs. Further, in May 1969 Osman Saleh Sabbe, Secretary of the ELF, said the organization was exchanging expertise with Palestinian "resistance groups," and some of its members were training with them. An ELF delegation led by Tedla Bairu, Deputy Chairman of the ELF's Executive Committee, visited Al Fatah bases in November 1969.[21]

In 1972, it was reported that South Yemen was giving valuable support to the insurgent ELF, whose units used the Kamaran Islands as a base for operations against Ethiopian forces.[22] Azzein Yasir, the foreign relations chief of the National Congress of the Revolutionary Council (ELF-RC), said in 1974 that "provisions (for the ELF) were mainly shipped across the Red Sea from South Yemen." He further indicated that "one idea now under consideration . . . is to airlift supplies

---

[21] *African Review* (London), July 1969, p. 12; May 1970, p. 17. See also Sabbe's interview with *Al Takika* (Tripoli), June 16, 1972. The Lebanese newspaper *Bayrut* said on June 15, 1971, that it had received information that Palestinian guerrillas who attacked the Israeli oil tanker *Coral Sea* in the Red Sea, came from a position on Hamish Island, which belongs to Ethiopia and is situated several miles north of Perim Island. The paper added that it was likely that guerrillas of the ELF helped to establish this position. Further, on November 22, 1975, a passing-out parade of trainees from the ELF was held at a camp of the Popular Front for the Liberation of Palestine (PFLP-GC), the "17 September Camp" in Syria.

[22] *Al Nahar*, May 4, 1972; *Le Monde*, May 31, 1972; *Ha'aretz*, October 11, 1972; *Jerusalem Post*, October 18, 1972, and March 22, 1973; *Strategic Survey, 1972*, p. 30. It should be noted that Cuban military personnel began arriving in South Yemen during the year. *Washington Post*, June 25, 1973; *Soviet Analyst*, August 15, 1974, pp. 5-6; *Christian Science Monitor*, September 9, 1974. South Yemen's Foreign Minister, Saleh Mouti, confirmed recently the presence of Cubans as well as Russians in South Yemen. Interview with *Le Monde*, December 10, 1976. See also the Shah of Iran's interview with the Kuwait daily *Al Siyassa*, January 29, 1977. Further, a small group from the Southern Liberation Front, directed at the Gala areas of Ethiopia, has been sent to North Korea for training. C. Clapham, "Ethiopia and Somalia," in *Conflicts in Africa*, p. 16. It should be stressed that after Ethiopian Emperor Haile Selassie's visit to Peking (October 6-11, 1971), China stopped its arms supplies and training for the ELF. In fact, in 1974 reports said the Ethiopian government was debating an appeal to Peking for arms to fight the ELF. *Washington Post*, December 7, 1974, and April 15, 1976; Adie, *op. cit.*, 1975, p. 34.

into Eritrea from the Middle East."[23] In a series of eyewitness reports published in October 1975 in *Financial Times,* it was said: "The key to the coming battle (for Asmara, the Eritrean capital) may be with the new arms consignments currently being shipped across the Red Sea from South Yemen. These weapons originated in Syria and Iraq and are being moved down to Aden . . . Guerrilla leaders told me that the Soviet Union had made no overt approaches to them. If the rebels achieve success, however, they would probably align with Moscow through Damascus or Iraq."[24]

On May 24, 1972, the Turkish military authorities announced that 14 Turkish terrorists had been caught in a Fatah boat in Turkey's southern waters, near the Syrian border. The terrorists were returning to Turkey after having been trained at a Fatah camp. The announcement by the Turkish authorities stated that "these anarchists were trained by Fatah agents to undermine the Turkish Republic and its national unity, and to serve Marxist-Leninist aims." It should be noted that for years a clandestine radio station, the Turkish "Our Radio," has been operating from Leipzig, East Germany. Turkish Communist activities also include groups in Sofia and Baku, and an ideological department which operates from Prague. Subsequently, the Beirut weekly *Falastin al-Thaura* stated on March 15, 1973, that in Israeli defense forces actions against the Fatah camps Nahar El-Bard and El Bakouni, nine Turkish terrorists were killed. The Turkish news agency *Haber* stated on May 30, 1973, that 18 Turks had been killed in battles in Lebanon during May 1973. Further, on May 21, 1973, the Lebanese newspaper *Al Usbua al-Arabe* reported that the Lebanese Foreign Ministry had officially requested that the Turkish Ambassador remove the Turkish nationals who were volunteers in the terrorist organizations in the Palestinian camps.

In a similar way, Al Fatah received its first *direct* Soviet arms

---

[23] *Financial Times,* August 1, 1975; *African Development,* May 1975, p. 23.
[24] Cited in *Brief* (Tel Aviv), December 16-31, 1975, p. 3. For earlier reports concerning Iraqi and South Yemeni support for the ELF and the Somali Liberation Front, see *Al Kifah,* November 6, 1971; *Middle East News Agency,* April 21, 1972. See also M. Abir, *Oil, Power and Politics: Conflict in Arabia, the Red Sea and the Gulf,* Cass, London, 1974, p. 173. This, of course, does not mean that the Soviets will not drop the ELF if better opportunities to establish themselves in Ethiopia appear, in much the same way as they did with the Kurds in Iraq.

shipment in September 1972 through Syria.[25] Israeli Defense Minister Shimon Peres told the Knesset in July 1974 that the Soviet Union was supplying the Palestinian guerrilla organizations with arms and equipment from ships unloading in Algerian, Syrian, and Iraqi ports.[26] Further, it was reported that a number of guerrillas belonging to the Popular Front for the Liberation of Oman (PLFO) had recently joined the Frente Polisario guerrillas in the Spanish Sahara. Muscat Radio on February 5, 1976, said that the decision to send guerrillas to the Sahara had been taken during the visit to Hungary of PFLO leader Muhammed Ahmed Qahtani. The USSR and Hungary agreed to provide "badly needed" funds for the PFLO on the condition that some fighters joined the Polisario, the broadcast added.

Earlier, in 1973, the Soviets used landing ships based on Berbera, Somalia, to sealift supporters of the Dhufari rebellion, including South Yemeni troops, to Oman. Moreover, the Iraqi *Baghdad Observer* on June 12, 1975, had stated: "The Arab Ba'ath Socialist Party has always regarded the Omani revolution as a great detachment of the Arab revolution throughout the Arab homeland, and consequently it has unlimitedly supported it in facing various attacks launched by reaction and imperialism."

This pattern of intrasubsystem mutual support operations repeats itself in the India/Far East security region. In December 1971, the

---

[25] The Soviet promise of direct arms aid had reportedly been made to Yasser Arafat, the Fatah and PLO leader, when he visited Moscow in July 1972. *International Herald Tribune,* September 19, 1972. The arms shipment was also confirmed by sources in Beirut, September 21. *Facts on File,* September 24-30, 1972, p. 756. "By the end of 1968, Moscow agreed to supply the Palestinian organizations with weapons and other equipment via Eastern European countries. The conduit was Bulgarian, Czech and East German . . . There were also reports of Soviet and East European intelligence aid such as the assistance extended by the Czechs to the guerrillas who overpowered a train in September 1973 carrying Russian Jews from Czechoslovakia to Austria." M. Ma'oz, "Soviet and Chinese Influence on the Palestinian Guerrilla Movement," in Rubinstein, *op. cit.,* 1975, p. 119. *Al Anwar* (April 23, 1970) quoted the Bulgarian Ambassador in Baghdad, Nicolai Boyadzhev, as saying that his country has been providing the Palestinian commandos with arms, ammunition, and other aid. He added that a number of commandos were now receiving treatment in Bulgarian hospitals. Amman Radio reported on March 24, 1973, that jailed Al Fatah leader Abu Daoud told investigators that the 1972 attack on Israeli Olympic athletes in Munich had been planned by Fatah leaders in Sofia, Bulgaria. On the treatment of wounded PLO members in East German hospitals, see *Neues Deutschland* (East Berlin), September 25, 26, 1976; *ADN* (East Berlin), April 4, 1977.

[26] *Arab Report and Record,* July 16-31, 1976, p. 309.

Soviets turned down an Indian suggestion that they sign a friendship treaty with the newly-born nation of Bangladesh. Instead, the Soviets presumably promoted and later publicly welcomed a 20-year friendship treaty between Bangladesh and India, which was modeled largely on the Indo-Soviet pact of August 9, 1971. The terms of the India-Bangladesh treaty were arranged between the late Mujibur Rahman and Mrs. Gandhi during a four-day meeting of the two prime ministers in New Delhi in February 1972. Interestingly enough, however, the text was not announced until March, after Rahman returned from his state visit to Moscow. India's Foreign Minister, T. N. Kaul, said on All India Radio, March 22, 1972, that the treaty was not a military pact, but had taken account of the fact that the security of the two countries was "interlinked"; it was the "best guarantee" against any external aggression, he added. The exact meaning of this observation was made evident shortly after. During Rahman's March 1972 visit to Moscow, Soviet assurances were given of military assistance to Bangladesh. Ten MIG-21s arrived from Russia in April 1973 to form the country's first fighter squadron.[27] It was later learned, however, that the jets were stationed in Calcutta, India, rather than Bangladesh.[28]

During 1974, arrangements were made for military training of Afghan officers in the Indian defense establishment. (Until then, the Afghan officer corps had been trained entirely by the Soviets.) Consideration was also given for setting up a cadet school by the Indians in Afghanistan, and reports said there were plans for sending Indian personnel to serve as advisors.[29] Afghan President Daud, in an interview in May 1976, refused to say whether a military pact with India was "contemplated."[30] There has been recent speculation, however, that India and the Soviet Union may jointly guarantee the integrity

[27] *Asian Almanac,* June 16, 1973, p. 5851; *Asian Recorder,* June 11-17, 1973, p. 11433.
[28] G. W. Choudhury, "Dismemberment of Pakistan, 1971: Its International Implications," *Orbis,* Spring 1974, p. 198. On the India-Bangladesh friendship treaty, see B. S. Gupta, "Moscow and Bangladesh," *Problems of Communism,* March-April 1975, p. 61.
[29] D. Mukerjee, "Afghanistan Under Daud: Relations with Neighboring States," *Asian Survey,* April 1975, pp. 208-209; also M. Ahamad, "Iran—Ambitions and Capabilities," in R. Kaul, ed., *The Chanakya Defense Annual, 1973-74,* Chanakya Publishing House, Allahabad, 1974, p. 143; *Economist* (London), July 19, 1975, p. 34.
[30] *Impact International* (London), May 10-25, 1974, p. 2.

and sovereignty of Afghanistan.[31] Further, in early 1975 it was reported that Iran and Pakistan were concerned because of overflights by long-range Soviet remotely-piloted vehicles (RPVs) coming from the direction of Afghanistan on reconnaissance missions. Quoting "reliable sources," the report said the RPVs overflying Pakistan "are coming out of Afghanistan and then flying on to Indian territory." Those going over Iran were reportedly flying over "strategic positions before flying back over Afghan soil."[32]

It should be further recalled that India was the first to recognize (in April 1975) the new Provisional Revolutionary Government of South Vietnam. Shortly afterwards, the Soviet Union and North Vietnam gave strong and unqualified support to India's Prime Minister Gandhi when the latter declared a state of emergency in India and introduced press censorship. *Komsomo-l'skaya Pravda* said, for example, that attempts were made to create chaos in India, but "the resolute actions of the Indian government put a stop to the designs of the reactionary parties and met with the support of all the patriotic, democratic, and progressive forces of the country."[33] Further, the Hanoi army newspap*er Quan Doi Nhan Dan* expressed support for Premier Gandhi in what it described as her fight against "reactionary rightists."[34]

New Delhi's External Affairs Minister Y. B. Chavan stated recently that "the Indian Government and people are glad of good achievements made so promptly by the Vietnamese people in national reunification and national reconstruction." Chavan went on to say that he "very much wanted to see the friendly relations between his country and Vietnam develop more and more."[35] Similarly, a joint

---

[31] *Far Eastern Economic Review,* March 28, 1975, p. 7.
[32] *Defense and Foreign Affairs Daily,* March 13, 1975.
[33] Cited in *Los Angeles Times,* June 30, 1975, and also in *Christian Science Monitor,* June 18, 30, 1975; *New York Times,* June 27, 1975.
[34] Cited in *New York Times,* June 28, 1975. "North Vietnam alone in Asia supported Gandhi . . . probably act(ing) in concert with Moscow on this issue." S. Fujii, "Peking's Post-Indochina Diplomacy Vis-à-Vis Southeast Asia," *Review* (Tokyo), January 1977, p. 18. Note that *People's Daily* delivered a stinging denunciation of Mrs. Gandhi from Peking, saying that "in the face of an imminent 'nationwide struggle' to throw Indira Gandhi out of office, the sanctimonious Indira Gandhi government did not hesitate to discard the last shred of the fig of 'democracy' and nakedly laid bare its ferocious features." The newspaper also charged India with siding with Moscow. Cited in *Los Angeles Times,* June 30, 1975; *New York Times,* June 28, 1975.
[35] *FBIS* (Asia and Pacific), March 1, 1976, pp. K7-8.

communique issued January 19, 1977, at the end of an eight-day visit by Laotian President Prince Souphanouvong to India, called for the dismantling of the Diego Garcia base in the Indian Ocean. It recorded firm support for the Arab people and their cause, and welcomed the liberation of Vietnam, Laos, and Cambodia.

Intersubsystem Strategic Mutual Support

(1) *Between Warsaw Pact-Middle East Subsystems (and vice versa):*
Many studies have been conducted on Soviet penetration of the Middle East, especially with regard to Egypt, and need not be repeated here. Instead, the examples of intersubsystem logistic and defensive support provided below are designed to expose a recurring pattern of performance, one which supports the hypothesis about the existence of a Soviet collective security system (or, at least, its design).

Following the Six Day War, on July 10, 1967, some 12 Soviet warships, including two guided missile cruisers, two submarines, a destroyer, a cruiser, and a landing craft arrived at the Egyptian ports of Alexandria and Port Said. Fleet Commander Rear Admiral Igor Nikolayevitch Moloshov declared on arrival: "We are ready to cooperate with Egypt's armed forces to repel any aggression." On July 29, Moscow Radio quoted Admiral Grishanov as indicating the defensive support mission of the Soviet Navy: "Our Navy men are engaged in voyages abroad protecting the countries with whom the Soviet Union maintains friendly relations."

The logistic support facilities which have been put at Soviet disposal by various Arab countries ever since soon revealed the strategic *mutual* support character of Soviet-Arab relations. The presence of Soviet warships in Egyptian ports, one newspaper observed at the time, "indicates that the Russians have achieved their longstanding aim of a safe naval base in a Mediterranean port."[36] As a result, "there was a sharp increase in the scale, quality, and effectiveness of Soviet operations (in the Mediterranean)."[37] Further, on October 27, 1967, seven Soviet warships, including two submarines, a destroyer, and a troopship arrived at Port Said and Alexandria. "It may be significant that two submarines were present during all three known Soviet naval visits to Egypt (the first in August 1966). The Soviet Navy's most

[36] *Al Hamishmar* (Tel Aviv), July 16, 1967.
[37] M. MccGwire, "The Mediterranean and Soviet Naval Interest," in MccGwire, *op. cit.,* 1973, p. 354.

pressing need for naval facilities was probably, as it had been in Albania before, its submarine use."[38]

A squadron of ten Soviet Tu-16 bombers visited Egypt during the period December 3-10, 1967, under the command of a Colonel Semeonov. The planes flew over Cairo and carried out live bombing exercises in the desert from bases at Luxor and Aswan. "Western observers said the military significance of the visit lay in the fact that it demonstrated that facilities for Soviet military aircraft were available in Egypt."[39] Subsequently, in an interview with *Ha'aretz* on January 19, 1968, Israeli Defense Minister Moshe Dayan said: "My assessment is that the Russians are now (in Egypt) on the operative level . . . I believe they are . . . involved in operational planning." President Nasser in an interview with *Die Welt* on May 21, 1970, admitted that Soviet pilots had been in Egypt since 1968.

Shortly thereafter, the Soviets were granted "staging rights" in Syrian and Iraqi airfields as well.[40] Moreover, both Soviet military and civilian aircraft have been allowed to use normal ground installations and to make repairs using stocks of spare parts designed for the support of the *Soviet-supplied commercial airlines in these countries.* "The Soviet air elements have thus enlarged their sphere of operations without having to build up a major logistical system."[41]

Another good example of intersubsystem strategic mutual support relations is contained in a four-point long-range military and political pact that had been reached in July 1968 in Moscow between Egyptian President Nasser and Soviet leaders. It assured (1) Soviet military supplies to the Egyptian armed forces "sufficient to help retrieve, within two to five years, all territory lost to Israel since 1967"; (2)

---

[38] Dragnich, *op. cit.,* p. 38. In the wake of President Sadat's recent ouster of the Russian Navy from the port of Alexandria, Pentagon officials were quoted as saying that the Soviets would have to take extra measures to keep their force of ten diesel-powered subs operating in the Mediterranean. "They would have to rotate their subs more frequently from home bases in the Black Sea or send additional support vessels into the Mediterranean to service the submarines at deep water anchorages. Customarily," the sources added, "Soviet submarines have docked at Alexandria in mid-patrol for provisions and upkeep. Three or four submarines often have been in Alexandria at the same time." *Baltimore Evening Sun,* March 23, 1976.
[39] *Middle East Record, 1967,* p. 26; also *Krasnaya Zvezda,* December 14, 1967.
[40] R. E. Hunter, *The Soviet Dilemma in the Middle East, Part I: Problems of Commitment,* Adelphi Paper No. 59, International Institute for Strategic Studies, London, 1969, p. 13.
[41] Whetten, *op. cit.,* 1974, p. 398.

agreement to collaborate in seeking a political solution that would, in effect, constitute an Arab victory, and would "essentially" bring "no real peace for Israel"; (3) permission for the Soviet Union to use Egyptian territory as a base for political and military expansion in the Middle East-Mediterranean area; (4) continuation of pressure by the Arabs—backed by Moscow—against Israel, including long-range guerrilla penetration and espionage.[42]

On July 23, 1968, Nasser stated: "All the liberated states in the region welcome the appearance of the Soviet Navy in the Mediterranean as an element to balance the US Sixth Fleet, which sought to turn the Mediterranean into an American Sea."[43] *Pravda* on November 27, 1968, declared that US domination of the Mediterranean was over and that the presence of Soviet warships there had the approval of the Arab states. Time and again, Moscow has thus displayed its utilization of collective legitimization as a measure to free its hands militarily while simultaneously complicating its opponent's countermoves.

Soviet defensive support intentions were also manifested in 1969. In February, the Chief of the Russian Navy Staff, Admiral Nikolai Sergheev, stated that "Russia cannot leave her friends, the Arab states, in the lurch in the face of the danger of reinforcement of Israeli aggression."[44] Joint exercises by Bulgarian and Soviet ships in the Mediterranean started in late Spring of 1969. According to the Greek press on May 12, 1969, four Bulgarian warships participated in the first exercise.[45] "By introducing Bulgarian warships into the Mediterranean in exercises with Soviet naval units, the USSR is now in a position to claim that (NATO) naval forces in the Mediterranean are now opposed not by the USSR alone but by 'Warsaw Pact' forces."[46] Subsequently, a Bulgarian military delegation headed by Defense Minister Dobri Dzurov arrived in Damascus on June 20 for an eight-day visit. "Military contacts between Bulgaria and Syria have

---

[42] *Middle East Record, 1968,* pp. 33-34. In January 1971, Sadat confirmed that Nasser had granted the Soviet Navy access to Egyptian naval facilities in 1968. Dragnich, *op. cit.,* p. 53; Whetten, "The Military Consequences of Mediterranean Super Power Parity," *New Middle East,* November 1971, p. 16.
[43] *Middle East Record, 1968,* p. 7
[44] Cited in Howe, *op. cit.,* p. 317, fn. 87.
[45] *East Europe,* October 1971, p. 40. The Bulgarian press later confirmed the joint maneuvers.
[46] Radio Liberty Research, quoted in *Military Review,* November 1969, p. 101.

been frequent since 1967";[47] and *Israelski Far,* the Bulgarian-language daily published in Israel, reported that the Syrian army had Bulgarian military advisors and technical personnel.[48]

In an interview published on September 15, 1969, the Iraqi Chief of Staff, Lieutenant General Hammad Shihab—who had completed a one-week visit to Poland the day before—said that Poland and Iraq had similar views about "the aggressive role of American, West German, and Israeli imperialism."[49] In November 1969, at a meeting of members of the Warsaw Pact, Soviet representatives mentioned the plan to send Soviet military elements to take over a portion of actual combat duties in Egypt, "probably because it was originally intended to stage this operation as a Warsaw Pact rather than purely Soviet action, perhaps by including some symbolic East European contingents."[50] Indeed, a Hungarian military delegation led by the Minister of Defense, Colonel General Lajos Czinege, visited Cairo from April 29 to May 5, 1970, leaving afterwards for Syria for a four-day visit.[51] On May 24, *Observer* reported that Hungary had sent military personnel and technicians to Egypt "in the past few weeks" to train pilots and serve at the Soviet missile sites. Articles published in several Sofia newspapers on August 8, 1971, revealed that in the second half of June and the first half of July of that year, Bulgarian warships had again joined the Soviet fleet in the Mediterranean and carried out joint naval maneuvers, in what seemed to be the third such cooperative exercise. Although nothing was reported during 1970, some of the phrases used in the 1971 articles made it almost certain that Bulgarian warships entered the Mediterranean at least once a year. Further, the Soviet commander of the exercises, Admiral Proskunov, was quoted in a Bulgarian journal as saying that "our joint exercises in the Mediterranean will continue to be held."[52]

For his part in the strategic mutual support equation, it was re-

---

[47] *East Europe,* August-September, 1969, p. 46.

[48] June 2, 1969.

[49] *Arab Report and Record,* September 1-15, 1969, p. 359.

[50] Ra'anan, *loc. cit.,* 1973, pp. 959-960. It should be further noted that in Spring 1970, Soviet military journals began stating unequivocally that the Arab "progressive" regimes were included in the Soviet defense sphere. See Y. Ro'i and I. Diamant-Kass, *The Soviet Military Involvement in Egypt, January 1970-July 1972,* Research Paper No. 6, Soviet and East European Research Center, Jerusalem, Hebrew University, February 1974, p. 5.

[51] *Arab Report and Record,* May 1-15, 1970, p. 274.

[52] *East Europe,* October 1971, p. 40; *Strategic Survey, 1971,* p. 30.

ported by the *Daily Telegraph* on April 21, 1970, that President Nasser had suggested to Libya's Qaddafi that he should invite the USSR to use the former British naval facilities at Tobruk and the air base at El-Adem. *Al Hayat* on May 17, 1970 disclosed that the Soviets had asked Nasser to persuade his Libyan allies to grant them naval facilities in Tobruk. Further, Nasser's successor, President Sadat, pointed out in January 1971 that the Soviet presence in Egypt was not a negotiable part of a peace settlement with Israel.[53] Subsequently, he added that the Soviet Union would be permitted to retain its naval bases in Egypt even after a possible peace agreement. Sadat said he intended also to keep Soviet advisors attached to the Egyptian Army "because war is science now."[54]

Although it is usually argued that the Soviet position in the Middle East has deteriorated considerably ever since their expulsion from Egypt in July 1972, and that by now Sadat may have totally defected to the West (a debatable argument at best),[55] this does not necessarily mean that the overall state of Warsaw Pact-Middle East intersubsystem strategic mutual support relations has been adversely affected in a significant manner. As far as the Soviet collective security system is concerned, examination of these strategic mutual interactions provide a much more accurate insight into its "health." As a practical measure of logistic support, for example, one can trace the frequency, number, composition, type, and duration of stay of military delegations going between the two subsystems. (See Table Two below.) The possibility of secret missions should also be kept in mind.

Further, if the hypothesis about the existence of a Soviet collective security system is correct, similar military interactions are bound to occur between the Middle East and the Indian/Far East subsystems. Although these will be discussed later, it is nevertheless appropriate at this point to examine the exchange since 1972 of military delegations between the two subsystems as a partial test of this proposition. Table Three lists these exchanges.

Even if one accepts the notion of an Egyptian defection, it is important to understand that this has occurred not because of the

---

[53] Interview with Walter Cronkite on CBS Television, January 10, 1971.
[54] Interview with *New York Times*, December 9, 1971.
[55] For example, Sadat declared on Cairo Radio (October 24, 1975) that the expulsion of Soviet advisors from Egypt in 1972 served as "a strategic cover-up . . . a wonderful strategic diversion of attention from our intention to go to war (in October 1973)." See also below.

TABLE TWO
Logistic Support: Exchange of Military Delegations Between Warsaw Pact and Middle East Subsystems, 1972-75

1972	1973
A Czechoslovak Army delegation led by General Baroslav Machik, Commandant of the Brno Military College, arrived in Baghdad on February 18 for a fortnight's stay. The Bulgarian Defense Minister, General Dobri Dzurov, arrived in Baghdad for a visit on March 29. In July, a Somali military delegation headed by Defense Minister and Army Commandant General Mohammed Ali Samantar, and including the Air Force Commander, Lieutenant Colonel Yusef Hassan Ibrahim, visited the Soviet Union. Further, a Soviet military delegation headed by Marshal Babajatian, Commander-in-Chief of the Soviet Armored Forces, arrived in Baghdad September 23. A Polish military mission headed by Poland's Defense Minister and Army Chief of Staff General Boleslaw Chocha arrived in Iraq on November 22 for a week's visit; and on the same day, a Hungarian military delegation led by the Defense Minister, Colonel General Lajos Czinege, arrived for five days. The Hungarian delegation proceeded to Aden, South Yemen, on November 28, after concluding its visit to Iraq. The Iraqi Defense Minister, Lieutenant General Hammad Shihab, left on November 29 for a visit to Sofia and Prague. A joint statement on December 4, at the end of the visit to Sofia, said that Iraq appreciated the aid offered by the Bulgarian people and government, and Bulgaria welcomed "the readiness of the Iraqi leaders to build a Socialist society." An East German military mission led by General Heinz Hoffman, Minister of Defense, arrived in Algiers on June 5. During its eight-day stay, the mission visited Algerian military installations.[56] Egyptian Prime Minister Sidqi visited Russia October 16-18 (that is, after the expulsion of Soviet advisors from Egypt), accompanied by Ahmad Ismail Ali, Chief of General Intelligence and Major General Husni Mubarak, Commander of the Air Force. General Mubarak led another Egyptian military delegation to Moscow November 16-29.	*Al Ahram* reported on February 2 that a Soviet military delegation arrived in Egypt, while General Ahmad Ismail Ali, War Minister and Commander-in-Chief of Egypt's armed forces, went to Moscow February 26-March 2. A high-ranking Egyptian naval delegation visited Russia June 19-26. South Yemen's Premier and Defense Minister, Ali Nasir Muhammad Hasani, visited Hungary in late February. He toured armored units of the Hungarian People's Army stationed in Transdanubia, and the Janos Kossuth Military High School. Hasani then left for Czechoslovakia, Poland, and the USSR. In Poland, he visited the military high school of communication at Zegrze.[57] A Soviet military delegation led by Colonel General Ogarkov, First Deputy Chief of Staff, arrived in Algiers on March 22.[58] An Algerian military delegation led by Colonel Ahmed Ben Cherif arrived June 12 on an official visit to East Germany. The delegation "acquainted itself with the high standard of training in the GDR People's Navy" by visiting the Karl Liebknecht Higher Officer's School of the People's Navy and the VEB People's Shipyard at Stralsund. "Aboard a naval vessel, the Algerian military delegaion had an opportunity to observe the combat training of Navy units." A Syrian military delegation led by Mohammad Ibrahim al-Ali, Commander of the People's Army, arrived in East Germany on June 13.[59] In late November, the Commander of the Iraqi Navy, Brigadier Abdu Al-Deri, visited East Germany, heading a military delegation.[60]

1974	1975

The Polish Chief of Staff visited Libya in May in order to discuss arms deliveries and the dispatch of Polish military advisors to Libya. These contacts were started in February when Prime Minister Abd al-Salam Jalloud visited Poland at the head of a delegation which included, among other military men, the heads of Libya's Navy and its air defenses.[61] A Polish military delegation led by General Josef Baryla, First Deputy Chief of the Polish Army Political Board, returned to Warsaw from Syria on March 6. On April 12, a Bulgarian military delegation led by Deputy Defense Minister General Benlavic Travix arrived for a week-long visit. Another Bulgarian military delegation visited Syria in early May. Soviet Defense Minister Grechko held talks in Algeria May 27-31. *Le Monde,* May 31, 1974, commented: "The Defense Minister began his visit while Mr. Gromyko was in Damascus, while the Libyan Premier Mr. Jalloud was returning from Moscow, and while for the first time a Soviet destroyer made a 'friendly visit' to Tunisia. Three Soviet vessels made a similar visit to Algeria recently." A Syrian military delegation headed by the Commander of the Army, General Ibrahim al-Ali, arrived in Poland on September 1. The Hungarian Army Chief of Staff, Lieutenant General Istvan Olah, arrived in Syria on November 10 for a five-day visit. A military delegation led by the Deputy Defense Minister of South Yemen, Ali Ahmed Nassir Antar, arrived in Prague on November 11, and the Commander-in-Chief of the Soviet Navy, Admiral Gorshkov, began a four-day visit to South Yemen on December 12, Aden Radio reported. In early December, the Soviet Chief of Staff, General Viktor Kulikov, was in Iraq ostensibly for observing army exercises on a large scale.[62] A Hungarian military delegation led by the Defense Minister, Colonel General Lajos Czinege, visited Algeria December 9-13. The Polish Deputy Defense Minister, Eugeniusz Malczyk, arrived in Damascus on December 16 for a five-day visit.[63] The Commander of the Soviet Mediterranean Fleet, Rear Admiral Ilich Akimov, visited Alexandria December 12-17, during a port call by two Soviet guided missile ships (the *Groznyy* and the *Krasny Kavkaz*); and Admiral Gorshkov arrived in Cairo a week later.[64]

A Somali military delegation of political commissars headed by the Chief Political Commissar of the Somali Armed Forces, Muhammad Hussein Daud, visited the Soviet Union July 21-26.[65] Syrian Defense Minister Mustafa Tlass arrived in Hungary on October 26.[66] Soviet Defense Minister A. Grechko met on November 14 with a military delegation from the YAR, headed by the commander of its paratroops.[67] It should be further noted that General Shanshal, the Iraqi Chief of Staff, was in Belgrade in early October, where Marshal Tito reportedly "assured him that . . . 150 Yugoslav officers would be in Baghdad by December 1, and that (an) additional 350 (Yugoslav military advisors) would arrive before the end of January 1976.[68] *Tass,* December 11, 1975, reported that a Yugoslav military delegation ended a visit to Iraq. *Krasnaya Zvezda,* December 24, 1975, reported that Soviet Defense Minister Grechko met with Lieutenant General M.A. Bashir, Chief of the General Staff of the Sudanese People's Armed Forces.

TABLE THREE
Logistic Support: Exchange of Military Delegations Between the Middle East and India/Far East Subsystems, 1972-75

1972	1973
The Indian Navy's flagship *Mysore* anchored at Basra, Iraq, on May 25, at the start of a five-day courtesy visit. Admiral E. C. Kuruvila, Commander of the Western Indian Fleet, who was aboard, flew to Baghdad on May 26 for a meeting with the Iraqi Defense Minister, Lieutenant General Hammad Shihab.[69] A North Korean military delegation arrived in Aden, South Yemen, on June 16 for a week's visit, while the Iraqi Defense Minister, Lieutenant General Shihab, after a visit to Moscow and Prague, told reporters on August 29 that "a temporary indisposition had prevented him from visiting North Korea as he had planned."[70]	During the visit of the Egyptian Chief of Staff, Lieutenant General Shazli, to Pyongyang, April 6-13, arrangements for the dispatch of North Korean pilots to Egypt were made.[71] In June, a Syrian military delegation, after a one-day stop in Moscow, arrived in Hanoi to seek North Vietnamese military experts in the use of SAMs.[72] In August, the Chief of the Iraqi Naval Force, Brigadier Abdu Al-Deri, arrived for a nine-day visit at the invitation of India's Chief of Naval Staff, Admiral S. N. Kohli.[73]

1974	1975
On June 10, a North Korean Military delegation headed by General O Chin-u, Chief of the North Korean Army General Staff, arrived in Egypt.[74] On June 18, the North Korean delegation left Egypt for a one-week visit to Syria.[75] An Algerian armed forces delegation led by Lieutenant Commander Muhammad Bin Musa, Commander of the Algerian Navy, arrived in Pyongyang on September 4, and was received by President Kim Il-sung on September 8.[76] A North Korean military delegation led by the Commander of the Navy, Vice Admiral Pang Chol-kap, left Algiers on November 13.[77] Baghdad Radio announced that Iraq's President Bakr received the Indian Chief of Staff, G. C. Bewoor, on March 18. Soviet Defense Minister Grechko visited Iraq March 23-26 for talks with Bakr and others. A large Indian military delegation headed by major generals from the Air Force and Navy visited Egypt in May to survey the latter's defense needs. "Presently Egypt has to send equipment to the Soviet Union for major overhauls of jet fighter engines and tanks. India has what military experts call 'second line maintenance' or overhaul capability . . . Joint training programs are another possibility. The Indian Air Force trained some Egyptian pilots in the late 1950s. The Egyptians have	In January, the Syrian Chief of Staff, General Hikmat al-Shihabi, met his Soviet counterpart, General Viktor Kulikov, in Moscow on his way home from North Korea.[81] On February 11, a North Korean military delegation led by Vice Admiral Pang Chol-kap, Naval Commander of the People's Army, left for a visit to Yugoslavia.[82] On June 6, a Libyan military delegation arrived in Pyongyang for a visit.[83] An Algerian military delegation headed by Major Moussouni Belkacem was received by Kim Il-sung on September 15, 1975. In a banquet honoring the delegation, Lieutenant General O Kuk-yol, Commander of the North Korean Air Force, declared: "Our people and people's army will as ever vigorously fight on shoulder-to-shoulder with the Algerian people in the common struggle against imperialism and for the accomplishment of the cause of socialism."[84] Since early 1975, a delegation of the Palestinian terrorist organizations had been present in Hanoi to follow closely North Vietnam's preparations for the offensive which brought the collapse of the Saigon regime. In May, the delegation went back to Beirut to prepare a report on the lessons stemming from Hanoi's attack.[85]

1974	1975
much more advanced experience in the handling of Russian SAMs and have a dense, diversified defense screen of Russian SAMs on their territory, while the Indians are limited primarily to the high altitude SAM-2 missiles for their defense."[78] Beginning on September 30, Indian Defense Minister J. Ram conducted a four-day official visit to Syria.[79] On November 25, the Indian Air Chief, Marshal O. P. Mehra, arrived in Baghdad for a short visit.[80]	

[56] *Arab Report and Record,* February 16-29, 1972, p. 83; March 16-31, 1972, p. 139; November 16-30, 1972, pp. 554, 567; December 1-15, 1972, pp. 555, 578; June 1-15, 1972, p. 273; *Mid East Report,* October 1, 1972, p. 1; *African Review,* October 1972, p. 2; Rubinstein, *op. cit.,* 1977, pp. 213, 224.

[57] *FBIS* (Eastern Europe), February 28, 1973, p. F1; March 6, 1973, p. G1.

[58] *Arab Report and Record,* March 16-31, 1973, p. 122.

[59] *FBIS* (Eastern Europe), June 13, 1973, p. E2; June 20, 1973, p. E13; June 14, 1973, p. E17.

[60] *Ibid.,* November 27, 1973, p. E1.

[61] *Middle East Intelligence Survey,* cited in *Defense and Foreign Affairs Daily,* February 15, 1974.

[62] *Middle East Intelligence Survey,* December 15, 1974.

[63] *FBIS* (Eastern Europe), March 8, 1974, p. G7; December 10, 1974, p. F3; December 16, 1974, p. F5; *FBIS* (Middle East and North Africa), April 3, 1974, p. H1; April 10, 1974, p. H4; May 15, 1974, p. D1. *Arab Report and Record,* September 1-15, 1974, p. 380; November 1-15, 1974, pp. 492, 495; December 6-31, 1974, p. 589.

[64] Lewis, *op. cit.,* pp. 78-79.

[65] *Krasnaya Zvezda,* July 26, 1975.

[66] *Tass,* October 26, 1975; *Arab Report and Record,* October 16-31, 1975, p. 588.

[67] *Tass,* November 14, 1975.

[68] *Afro-Asian Affairs,* October 23, 1975, p. 2.

[69] *Arab Report and Record,* May 16-31, 1972, p. 254.

[70] *Ibid.,* August 16-31, 1972, p. 398.

[71] *Ibid.,* April 1-15, 1973, p. 173. Note that at the time, deployment of North Korean pilots in Egypt amounted to an operational integration with a Soviet-controlled air defense system.

[72] *New York Times,* June 30, 1973; *Asian Almanac,* August 18, 1973, p. 5967.

[73] *News Review on West Asia* (New Delhi), October 1973, p. 17.

[74] *FBIS* (Middle East and North Africa), June 12, 1974, p. D5; June 26, 1974, p. D9. *Journal of Korean Affairs,* July 1976, p. 36. It is conceivable that the visit dealt with the intended introduction (in November) of North Korean warships into the Mediterranean.

[75] *Ibid.,* June 19, 1974, p. H2.

[76] *Arab Report and Record,* September 1-15, 1976, p. 366.

[77] *Ibid.,* November 1-15, 1976, p. 475.

[78] *Asian Recorder,* July 2-8, 1974, p. 12078. Indian's Defense Minister, J. Ram, visited Moscow in late 1973 and was interested in arranging for India to receive SAM-6s. *New York Times,* November 11, 1973; *Times of India,* November 26, 1974. The recent refusal of India, reportedly under Soviet pressure, to sell spare parts for MIG-21s to Egypt when the latter failed to get them from Russia (*Aviation Week and Space Technology,* March 22, 1976, p. 21), should dispel any illusions about Delhi being a substitute for the Soviet Union in its military relations with Cairo.

[79] *Middle East Journal,* Winter 1975, p. 78.

[80] *Arab Report and Record,* November 16-30, 1974, p. 512.

[81] *Middle East Economic Digest,* February 7, 1975, p. 21; *Journal of Korean Affairs,* April 1975, p. 70.

[82] *Journal of Korean Affairs,* April 1975, p. 71. It is not inconceivable that discussions about the servicing of North Korean warships in Yugoslav ports, whenever such vessels were deployed in the Mediterranean, had taken place; see fn. 74 above.

[83] *Ibid.,* July 1975, p. 42. Note also that on May 26, a military delegation from Uganda led by Major Adrisi Mustafa, Army Chief of Staff, arrived for a visit to North Korea. *Ibid.,* p. 41; for reports on the presence of North Korean military advisors in Uganda, see *Afriscope* (Lagos), May 1975, p. 25.

[84] *FBIS* (Asia and Pacific), September 18, 1975, pp. D9-11.

[85] *Washington Post,* quoted in *Ma'ariv* (Tel Aviv), May 21, 1975.

increased attractiveness of, and consequently attachment to, the West, but because of Sadat's belief that the Soviet alliance had failed him. The distinction is important when one assesses the probable duration of the alleged Egyptian shift. There is ample evidence to suggest that the decisions taken by Sadat regarding his continued membership in the Soviet system were virtually forced upon him. On April 17, 1972, for instance, President Sadat told members of the Central Committee of the Arab Socialist Union that "we have provided the Soviet Union with facilities that serve our interests."[86] In December 1972 (that is, five months *after* the expulsion of Soviet advisors from Egypt), Sadat extended the 1968 agreement on the rights of the Soviet Navy to use Egyptian port facilities, which was to expire in March 1973.[87] In an interview, Sadat said he had drawn a distinction between "advisors" and "strategic presence."[88] In January 1975, when the Western press was full of accounts about the worsening state of relations between Egypt and the USSR, Sadat was asked in an interview with *Le Monde* if he might go so far as to denounce the Soviet-Egyptian friendship treaty of 1971, if Moscow did not change its attitude. He replied: "I can't rule out that possibility, but it is very difficult to make a decision that would go against the *interests of Egypt and the Arab world in a general way.*"[89] Further, in an interview with the Beirut Daily *Al Hawadeth* on March 20, 1975, Sadat said: "They (the Soviets) replied that I want to expel them from the region. But had I really wanted to, I would have cancelled the (friendship) treaty after some of its provisions were violated. But I did not cancel the treaty and did not end the naval facilities extended to them, although these facilities reflect on the independence of my country." On other occasions, he described Egyptian-Soviet relations as of a "principled, strategic character."[90]

A demonstration of this strategic mutual support connection came in an interview given by Sadat on April 12, 1975, to a correspondent

---

[86] *Arab Report and Record,* April 16-30, 1972, p. 203.
[87] Haselkorn, *loc. cit.,* p. 238. As late as September 1975, four Soviet submarines were reportedly tied up at any given time at Alexandria's Al Gabbari shipyards. *Baltimore Sun,* September 23, 1975.
[88] *New York Times,* August 4, 1972; also October 2, 1972.
[89] Cited in *ibid.,* January 23, 1975. Emphasis added.
[90] *Christian Science Monitor,* April 21, 1975. Similarly, the Arab League Secretary General, Mahmoud Riad, said in an interview (GDR Radio, December 23, 1974) that Arab friendship with the USSR and the Socialist countries "is not governed by tactical considerations, but is of strategic importance . . . This friendship we should keep, come what may."

of the leading Kuwait daily, *Al Siyassa,* in which he said that by re-opening the Suez Canal, Egypt was proving at one and the same time its independence of the United States and its friendliness to the Soviet Union, *for this act would permit the latter to move its men of war to the Indian Ocean.*[91] In December, he confirmed that naval facilities for the Soviet Mediterranean fleet had been assured until 1978, adding "an 'even handed policy' does not mean that I will grant similar facilities to the Americans."[92] Sadat also acknowledged that "if I wanted to replace the quantities of Soviet arms I have, I would need at least 20 years, because the war factories in Europe are owned by companies which cannot produce the same quantities as those produced by the Soviet Union, because the Soviet Union allocates an enormous part of its industries to war production. Therefore, it can give quantities which are difficult for others."[93]

Most importantly, our traditional preoccupation with the status of Soviet-Egyptian bilateral relations should not distract our attention from the real dimensions of the Soviet design. This strategy has been seeking to establish *permanent* military relations between *security subsystems,* as opposed to occasional interactions between individual states. Demonstrations of logistic and defensive support performed between the Warsaw Pact and the Middle East subsystems are thus rarely limited to Egypt. Similar widespread activities could be discerned with regard to Syria, Iraq, Libya, PDRY, Somalia, and so forth.

For example, in 1971 there were reports concerning involvement of 80 East Germans with the internal security forces of South Yemen.[94] On October 2, 1972, North Yemen charged that Soviet pilots were taking part in air raids by South Yemen on Northern towns and villages, including night missions.[95] South Yemen Premier Ali Nasser

---

[91] M. Abir, in *Philadelphia Inquirer,* June 30, 1975. Emphasis added. Also J. K. Cooley, "The Shifting Sands of Communism," *Problems of Communism,* March-April 1975, p. 29.

[92] Interview with *Le Monde,* December 12, 1975.

[93] Interview with *Al Hawadeth,* cited in U. Ra'anan, "The Soviet-Egyptian 'Rift,'" *Commentary,* June 1976, p. 30.

[94] *Mid East Report,* January 1, 1972, p. 23; *Frankfurter Allgemeine Zeitung,* May 5, 1972; *Christian Science Monitor,* August 15, 1974. South Yemen's internal security services have been "organized with East German financial support and by East German experts." Abir, *op. cit.,* 1974, p. 93.

[95] *Mid East Report,* October 15, 1972, p. 7. According to the exiled former South Yemen Prime Minister, Abd al-Qawi Makkawi, more than 600 Soviet military advisors went to Aden after their services in Egypt were terminated in July 1972, and they were still there in early 1973. *Al Jaridah* (Beirut), February 2, 1973.

stated in an interview with the Beirut newspaper *L'Orient Le Jour* on October 6 that "the Soviet Union will not stand with folded arms in the event of an invasion of South Yemen." Further, the clandestine Voice of the Free South radio's Aden correspondent reported on November 17 that two Soviet officers had been given command of South Yemen Army brigades. This step was taken, he said, on the recommendation of the Soviet Embassy after the Defense Ministry had "complained of increasing rebel operations against the traitorous lackey regime."[96]

Subsequently, the presence of Polish, East German, Bulgarian, and Cuban military and civilian advisors in South Yemen was reported, some of whom had been spotted with the insurgents in Dhufar (Oman).[97] *Al Nahar* from Beirut said on March 18, 1976, that Fatah Ali Bakhit, a South Yemeni official responsible for security in the border region with Oman, who had arrived in Dhufar to seek political asylum, disclosed that South Yemen's internal security was run by East Germans.

An Iranian police spokesman alleged in 1972 that 120 members of subversive groups facing trial in Iran had received guerrilla training in Iraq and East Germany, and had been supplied with arms by Iraq. The same year, the annual meeting of CENTO in London (June 1-2) discussed a report of Secretary General Nassir Asar of

---

[96] Cited in *Arab Report and Record,* November 16-30, 1972, p. 567.

[97] J. O. Maxwell, "The Arab-Persian Gulf: A Strategic Analysis," *Marine Corps Gazette,* February 1975, p. 26; *Christian Science Monitor,* January 14, 1976. In September 1974, for example, a guerrilla member of the Popular Front for the Liberation of Oman defected to the government side. He revealed how he, with 14 others, had spent several weeks at a training school in Odessa for instruction in weaponry, mainly the RCL rocket launcher and the SAM-7. See D. L. Price, *Oman, Insurgency and Development,* Conflict Studies No. 53, Institute for the Study of Conflict, London, January 1975, pp. 7, 16-17. (Note that PFLO recruits sent to Russia for training passed through Kuwait; and that at Hauf, just across the border in South Yemen, the PFLO set up a "Lenin School" for military training and political education. J. B. Kelly, "Hadramaut, Oman, Dhufar: The Experience of Revolution," *Middle Eastern Studies,* May 1976, p. 225.) In September 1975, press reports indicated the appearance for the first time of the SAM-7 in Dhufar. *Ma'ariv,* September 29, 1975, quoting the Kuwaiti *Al Wattan; Economist,* October 25, 1974, p. 54. Lebanese papers said the missiles came from Libya via South Yemen. In late 1975, Russian advisors were reportedly directing the PDRY artillery barrage of Omani positions in Dhufar. J .E. Peterson, "Guerrilla Warfare and Ideological Confrontation in the Arabian Peninsula: The Rebellion in Dhufar," *World Affairs,* Spring 1977, p. 289. For earlier reports of Soviet involvement in the Dhufar insurgency, see *Al Hayat,* March 11, 14, 1972.

Iran, which told of Soviet arms smuggled from Iraq to revolutionaries in Iran and of Soviet aid to the Iraqi fishing fleet, which was believed to land arms and agents along the Persian Gulf.[98] Further demonstrations of defensive support to Iraq had occurred during 1974. In mid-year, press reports quoting US military sources indicated that Soviet pilots were flying Soviet-built jet fighter-bombers from bases in Iraq against Kurdish rebel forces.[99] In an interview with the *Times,*[100] Masoud Barazani (son of the Kurdish rebel leader Mustafa Barazani), who acted as chief of intelligence, said Tu-22s, Sukhoi-20 fighter-bombers, and MIG-23s were flown by Russians on missions against Kurdish rebels. "The Russians were also involved," he said, "in coordinating infantry advances with artillery action. Sometimes their officers were present at Iraqi divisional headquarters. On August 20, for example,

---

[98] *Facts on File,* June 4-10, 1972, p. 423; *Los Angeles Times,* May 22, November 11, 1975. A joint statement issued on July 2, 1971, by Radio Baghdad on behalf of the Fatah and the Iranian National Front said: "An Iranian fighter, Ali Akhbar Zefani Frehani, has died from torture in prison in Iran. He fought alongside the Fedayeen in Palestine . . . Frehani trained together with a group of young Iranians at Arab Fedayeen bases and participated in Fedayeen actions against the enemy . . . He reached the rank of officer in the resistance forces before transferring to the Iranian front." Further, on the *intrasubsystem* level, it should be noted that the Algerian daily *Al Sha'ab* reported on October 22, 1971, that "the Iranian revolutionary movement has established a 'Palestinian Group' composed of 45 Iranian fighters who fight alongside their Palestinian brethren. Some of them have returned to Iran after obtaining combat experience and advanced training." See also *Al Ahad* (Beirut), December 19, 1971. Note that *Al Hadaf,* the official organ of the Popular Front for the Liberation of Palestine, regularly publishes reports of actions carried out by the Iranian National Front.

[99] *Arab Report and Record,* June 16-30, 1975, p. 250; *Financial Times,* September 11, 1974, reported that one of two Iraqi pilots captured in August after being shot down had admitted direct Soviet involvement. Also *New York Times,* September 27, 1974; *Times,* October 16, 1974, observed that the Russians were working for an outlet to the Gulf and a suitable remote testing ground for Tu-22s; *Los Angeles Times,* October 25, 1974, commented that the Soviets would thus gain operating experience from Iraqi bases. *Washington Post,* December 17, 1974.

[100] November 16, 1974; for names of Soviet pilots involved in bombing missions against the Kurds, see *Soviet Analyst,* January 2, 1975. *Washington Post,* October 20, 1974 reported: "Where there used to be three arms shipments arriving at Basra a month, now there are six, and five or six giant transport planes a week are now arriving at Habbaniyah Air Base instead of two or three. The Iraqi Army has been divided into three main corps; and at the headquarters of each, the Kurds say, there are five Russian experts." At least one Soviet colonel is known to have been killed in combat with the Iraqis against the Kurds. *Washington Post,* February 1, 1975.

when Iraqi tanks made an unexpected breakthrough near the town of Rawanduz, the operation had been supervised personally by Russian Brigadier General Alexander Vasiliev, who had been on top of the mountain with Major General Ismail al-Nouaimi, the Iraqi Assistant Chief of Staff." Barazani put the number of Russian "experts" with the Iraqi Air Force at 1,500, and 4,000 with the Army. Another Barazani aide, Juwammer Ali, said on June 18 that the Kurdish headquarters near Galala had been heavily and continuously bombed by Soviet Tu-22 bombers flown by Soviet pilots.[101]

On November 18, 1974, the Syrian government newspaper *Al Baath* announced that a Soviet naval flotilla, made up of a missile cruiser, a destroyer, and a submarine under the command of Vice Admiral Nikolai I. Khovrin, Commander of the Black Sea Fleet, was due for a five-day visit in Latakia (the port where, Israeli Premier Rabin said several days before, 20 Soviet cargo ships were unloading arms). Of course, Soviet naval ships had visited Latakia and Tartus in the past; but this was the first time that such a visit had been announced publicly. This was regarded as significant in view of the tension after a partial mobilization of Israeli reserves and reinforcement of armored units on the Golan Heights. The visit was seen by officials as a demonstration of a pledge given by Leonid I. Brezhnev, the Soviet leader, to President Hafez al-Assad of Syria in April that Moscow would join in the defense of Syria against any attack.[102] In fact, in February 1975 there was a report of a Bulgarian offer to send combat units to Syria.[103] On the other hand, *Flight International* on June 26, 1976, reported that in addition to Russia, other Communist air forces have been sending military missions to Syria to gain up-to-date combat experience.

With regard to intersubsystem mutual support activity involving Libya, it was reported in 1975 that President Qaddafi agreed to the use of his country's commercial links with Italy for the transfer of funds to the Italian Communist Party and other subversive groups in Western Europe. During Kosygin's visit to Libya in June, a fund of £100 million was established for "special projects" in the Mediterranean area to be decided by the two countries. Some £40 million

---

[101] *Facts on File,* July 6, 1974, p. 541.

[102] *New York Times,* November 19, 1974; also *Observer,* November 17, 1974.

[103] *Middle East Intelligence Survey,* February 1, 1975, p. 168. In a recent speech before the National Assembly, Premier Zhivkov declared that Bulgaria is a "loyal friend and an *ally* of the Arab people confronted by Israeli aggression." *Ha'aretz,* October 16, 1975. Emphasis added.

had reportedly been allocated to the Italian Communist Party in order to enhance its campaign prospects with the aim of joining the coalition government. Under such circumstances, the Soviets (and the Libyans) had expected that the Communist Party would be in a good position to press for the withdrawal of the US Sixth Fleet from its base at Naples.[104] In addition, it is understood that the first of six submarines delivered recently by the Soviet Union to Libya has been manned by a mixed Soviet-Libyan crew, commanded by a Soviet officer.[105] Tripoli Radio on December 12, 1976, while commenting on the completion of Qadaffi's recent visit to Moscow, also described Soviet-Libyan relations as "strategic."

(2) *Between the Middle East and India/Far East Subsystems*

The strategic link between India and Soviet allies in the Middle East, as a segment of the Soviet collective security strategy, directly influences the shape of future military contingencies in these regions. *Daily Telegraph* on June 29, 1970, signalled the existence of this link when it reported that two Soviet-made Egyptian submarines were being extensively refitted at the Indian naval base of Vishakapatnam. The paper added that the vessels were the latest in a series of Egyptian warships to use Indian repair and refitting facilities. On November 26, 1970, Indian Defense Minister Jagjivan Ram announced that Egypt had been given naval facilities suitable for refitting submarines and other vessels in Vishakapatnam. He implied that Egyptian vessels had already called at the base, but declined to say when. Reporting the story, the London *Guardian* said on November 27: "Ram's statement was the first official admission that Egyptian naval vessels were being serviced in Vishakapatnam."

Another indication of this link came on November 19, 1970, when Indian Foreign Minister Swaran Singh attacked Western reports suggesting that Premier Gandhi had persuaded Mauritius to give the Soviet Navy a base on its shores, and also denied a suggestion that the Russians intended to build a naval base at Socotra (South Yemen). Singh declared that these reports were Israeli propaganda.[106] It is interesting to note, however, that allegations about the port of Aden having a Soviet harbormaster were reportedly

---

[104] *Daily Telegraph,* cited in *Ma'ariv,* September 12, 1975; *Ma'ariv,* September 14, 1975.

[105] *Ma'ariv,* January 10, 1977.

[106] On the Indian-Mauritius link, see *Far Eastern Economic Review,* November 19, 1973, p. 28; *Africa Confidential,* July 12, 1974, p. 8; *Baltimore Sun,* October 29, 1975; *Daily Telegraph,* April 9, 1976.

dropped after the Indian harbormaster protested.[107] Further, South
Yemen's Foreign Minister Muhammad Saleh Mouti arrived in India
on March 13, 1974, and told reporters on arrival that both India
and South Yemen were fighting to keep the Indian Ocean as a peace
zone, and that there was great concern over the possibility of a US
base being established on Diego Garcia.[108]

Prior to and during the Indo-Pakistan War of December 1971,
demonstrations of mutual strategic support interactions between the
Middle East and Indian subsystems had occurred again. Thus in
early November, 12 Soviet transport planes carried military supplies,
including advanced versions of SAMs, to New Delhi and Bombay.
Further, during the war 30 An-22 transport aircraft used Cairo's
military airbase (Almaza) as more than just a refueling stop in flying
reinforcements to India; Sadat disclosed that Soviet cargo aircraft
on their way to India picked up Soviet equipment in Egypt. Simultaneously, the Soviets were reportedly transferring some of their jet
warplanes from Egypt directly to India to replace Indian Air Force
losses during the war. About 15 MIG-21 fighters and Tu-16 bombers
were delivered in this way.[109]

This should also be considered background for assessing the hasty
visit (July 22-23, 1972) by Indian Foreign Minister Swaran Singh
to Egypt. A press report from Cairo said, in fact, that it was believed
"the latest developments in Egyptian-Soviet relations in the wake
of withdrawal of the Soviet military mission from Egypt (announced
publicly by Sadat on July 18) . . . were also discussed in the talks."[110]

The other dimension of these strategic mutual support relations
is indicated by growing military links between India and Iraq. As

---

[107] *Third World Reports* (London), vol. 4, no. 12—vol. 5, no. 1, 1974, p. 2.
[108] *Arab Report and Record,* March 1-15, 1974, p. 91.
[109] Haselkorn, *loc. cit.,* p. 241, and references therein. One source claims that a
squadron of MIG-21s and one of Tu-16s were, in fact, involved in this operation. Whetten, *op. cit.,* 1974, p. 208. Still another said that Soviet electronic
equipment was being diverted from Egypt to India. *An Nahar,* December 31,
1971. Note that a Tu-114 Moss AWACS (Airborne Warning and Control
System) aircraft flown by a Russian crew served as the Indian early-warning
and control center. Strike aircraft of the Indian Air Force were guided by the
Moss to targets up to 185 km. behind Pakistani lines. The strike aircraft, which
in addition to Canberras and Su-7s included An-12 Cub transports converted
into bombers, operated from their base in Chandigarh, 230 km. north of Delhi.
See M. Cherikov, "Moss-AWACS with a Red Star," *International Defense
Review,* October 1975, pp. 677-678.
[110] *Asian Almanac,* October 7, 1972, p. 5432.

Table Three indicates, within two months after the signing of the Soviet-Iraqi friendship treaty (April 1972), Indian Admiral E. C. Kuruvila, Commander of the Western Indian Fleet, arrived in Basra, Iraq, for talks with Iraq's Chief of Staff. In 1973, it was reported that India had "30 to 40 and possibly more instructors in Iraq training pilots there to fly Soviet-supplied MIG fighters."[111] Further, it was reported in November 1974 that 150,000 winter military uniforms had been airlifted from India to Iraq to assist the latter in its planned winter offensive against the Kurds.[112]

It should be noted that a press release on July 17, 1973, following talks between Indian Defense Minister Ram and Soviet Premier Kosygin, said that the two had discussed the continuing tension in the Middle East and the reactivation of CENTO, which had found a supporter in China.[113] Subsequently, during Iran Premier Abbas Hoveyda's August visit to Moscow, strong displeasure at the continuous allegiance of Teheran to CENTO was voiced by Kosygin.[114]

Again, the correct analytical perspective regarding Soviet strategy requires a systemic view rather than the one focusing on bilateral relations only. Thus, in addition to India, other countries—members of the India/Far East security subsystem—have been in an increasing measure linked militarily with Soviet allies in the Middle East. Aside from the well-known participation of North Korean personnel in the October 1973 Arab-Israeli War, several other examples should be mentioned. A State Department spokesman, Charles Bray, said on September 21, 1972, that North Korea had provided "direct assistance to at least some organizations in the Middle East which are operating in the field of terrorism. It is an appalling intervention."[115] In fact, following a visit to North Korea by Somali President Barre and Defense Minister Samantar in late May 1972, it was reported that a group of Somalis had been receiving guerrilla warfare

[111] *News Review on West Asia,* March 1974, p. 101; *Aviation Week and Space Technology,* March 20, 1973; *Washington Post,* June 2, 1973. As a result, "all conversion and operational training of Iraqi pilots on the MIG-21 were conducted by Indian personnel." *Air Enthusiast,* September 1973, p. 107.
[112] *Washington Post,* November 15, 1974.
[113] *Asian Almanac,* September 29, 1973, p. 6029. Ram referred to a statement of the Chinese Foreign Minister in Iran virtually endorsing the reactivation of CENTO and Iran's arms build-up.
[114] B. M. Smolansky and O. M. Smolansky, "Soviet and Chinese Influence in the Persian Gulf," in Rubinstein, *op. cit.,* 1975, p. 149.
[115] *Arab Report and Record,* September 16-30, 1972, pp. 466-467.

training in North Korea.[116] A joint communique on June 24, 1973, following a visit by Gustav Husak, Czech Communist Party First Secretary, to North Korea stated: "The two sides are granting active support to the struggle of the Arab nations, including the Palestinian people, against imperialism and the Israeli aggressor."

On the other flank of the mutual support equation, it should be noted that Washington suspended aid to Somalia in May 1970 after ships flying the Somali flag had carried goods to North Vietnam.[117] Further, in a message to Kim Il-sung of North Korea, transmitted through the Ambassador of Somalia to China, President Siad Barre of Somalia "extended militant and full support to the following points: The US imperialists' introduction of weapons of the latest type into South Korea aggravates the tension in this area . . . and that the US imperialist aggression troops should be forced out of South Korea . . . The Somali government expressed militant solidarity with regard to this problem."[118] Recently, it was reported that North Korean advisors were also present in Somalia.[119]

After the Yom Kippur War, North Korean pilots were transferred from Egypt to Syria.[120] In October 1974, Syrian sources reported that 300 North Koreans had arrived in Damascus to help man the capital's air defenses;[121] and in early 1975, it was said that a second squadron of North Korean MIG-21 aircraft might be sent to Syria at the latter's request.[122] Again, the existence of the mutual support

---

[116] *New York Times*, May 23, 1972; *African Review*, October 1972, p. 3.

[117] *Africa Report*, May-June 1975, p. 51; *Washington Post*, July 8, 1975. Thus, Pentagon spokesman Jerry Friedheim disclosed (May 11, 1972) that at the time of the mining of the North Vietnamese port of Haiphong, five Somali ships were trapped in the harbor as well. *Facts on File*, May 7-13, 1972, p. 340.

[118] *FBIS (Asia and Pacific)*, April 2, 1976, p. D1.

[119] *African Development*, March 1976, p. 203.

[120] *Baltimore News-American*, March 12, 1975.

[121] *Observer*, November 17, 1974. Also Israeli Defense Minister Shimon Peres, quoted in *Defense and Foreign Affairs Daily*, February 13, 1975. On May 23, 1975, Israel Radio quoted Peres as saying that "two or three thousand Russian soldiers" as well as troops from "Cuba, North Korea, and other countries" were in Syria. *Washington Post*, quoting "secret Pentagon documents" (February 23, 1976), said the North Korean mission in Syria consisted of 75 men. The paper quoted Pentagon documents as saying they "departed Syria in late 1975." The departure was also confirmed by Israeli Air Force Commander Major General B. Peled on October 26, 1975. *Arab Report and Record*, October 16-31, 1975, p. 573.

[122] *Middle East Intelligence Survey*, February 1, 1975, p. 168.

equation is indicated by a Syrian attack on Israel in the United Nations charging that South Korea was learning from Israel's military experience.[123] Similarly, in a joint communique following the visit of North Korean Prime Minister Pak Sung-chul to Iraq (January 15-23, 1977), which was published in the *Baghdad Observer* (on January 19, 1977), Iraq called for the evacuation of US forces from South Korea and the dissolution of the United Nations Command there. Both countries also called for the withdrawal of US forces from Asia.

Soon after the 1975 flare up in Spanish Sahara, which followed the accord to divide the territory between Mauritania and Morocco, about 200 Cuban and North Vietnamese soldiers arrived to train members of the Polisario Front guerrilla group.[124] North Vietnam's Deputy Premier and Defense Minister, General Vo Nguyen Giap, visited Algeria January 4-10, 1976, and had talks with President Boumedienne and the leader of the Front, Reguibi Louali.[125] It should be noted further that North Korea's Kim Il-sung on March 15,

---

[123] *Ma'ariv*, October 24, 1975.
[124] *Daily Telegraph*, January 26, 1976; *Flight International*, February 7, 1976, p. 268; *Boston Globe*, February 13, 1976; *Middle East Intelligence Survey*, March 15-31, 1976, p. 198. At the same time, *Algerie Presse Service* (January 30, 1976), quoting the French radio station Europe 1, said that Russians "were settling in at Tindouf near the Moroccan border and . . . were going to build a railway line to the Mediterranean." The radio also reported that Soviet tanks were being unloaded from Antonov planes at Dar-al-Beida airstrip. *Ma'ariv* (February 2, 1976) said a Soviet airlift of An-22s overflying Yugoslavia and the Mediterranean brought SAM-7s, heavy mortars, antitank missiles, and SAMs to Algeria "in the last few days." (Also *Boston Globe*, February 13, 1976.) Other Soviet planes were reported to land at Tripoli, Libya, which had sent Soviet arms to Algeria as well. *Washington Post* (January 18, 1976) said the Soviets also increased the number of their advisors in Algeria, which was allowing Soviet material to be transported through Algeria to Angola. Though Algeria's official *El Moujahid* (February 1, 1976) denied the airlifting of Soviet arms to Algeria, *Washington Post* (February 22, 1976) said the Soviets had recently finished erecting new missile defenses in southern Algeria, and that Soviet arms had been arriving almost daily.
[125] *Arab Report and Record*, January 1-15, 1976, p. 15. Note that Giap proceeded from Algeria to Moscow where, on January 14, he participated in a gathering which reportedly included the Soviet Defense Minister, Grechko, the Soviet commander of Warsaw Pact forces, Marshal Yakubousky, Commander-in-Chief of Soviet Armed Forces General Kulikov, Principal Political Commissar of Soviet Armed Forces General Yepishev, Commander-in-Chief of Soviet Air Defense Forces Marshal Batitsky, and Commander-in-Chief of the Soviet Navy Admiral Gorshkov. *Afro-Asian Affairs*, January 21, 1976, p. 5.

1976, "sent a message of congratulations to Mohamad Lamine Ould Ahmed, Prime Minister of the Government of the Saharan Arab Democratic Republic, informing the latter of the decision of the government of the Democratic People's Republic of Korea to recognize it."[126]

(3) *Between the Warsaw Pact and India/Far East Subsystem*

As mentioned above, first indications of strategic mutual support relations between these two Soviet security regions came in the mid-1960s. It has been reported that a Mongolian Army tank regiment was stationed in East Germany with the Soviet Army in 1966, and this practice may have continued.[127] Moreover, *Krasnaya Zvezda* on December 11, 1967, disclosed that Soviet instructors were operating with trainee North Vietnamese antiaircraft missilemen during American attacks. During 1968, Soviet naval units paid eight visits to Indian ports, and Moscow asserted on the occasion of the first of these cruises that its purpose was to "further develop friendly relations and to strengthen ties between armed forces."[128] The mutuality of these strategic relations was once more indicated when India's Foreign Minister at the time, Dinesh Singh, said in the Lok Sabha on April 8, 1969, that India supported the Soviet Union in its border dispute with Communist China. Further, on March 31, 1969, Singh told parliament that India would not permit the USSR to fly military planes to North Vietnam or any other destination over Indian territory. He added, however, that civilian flights between Hanoi and Moscow had been cleared by the government.[129]

It seems that the intensity of military interactions between the Warsaw Pact and the India/Far East subsystems has been increasing in recent years. For instance, beginning in April 1972 Soviet

---

[126] *FBIS (Asia and Pacific)*, March 16, 1976, p. D1.

[127] *Far Eastern Economic Review*, June 3, 1974, p. 28.

[128] Cited in Howe, *op. cit.*, p. 303, fn. 18.

[129] *Facts on File*, April 10-16, 1969, pp. 221-222. The civilian Soviet aircraft were landing in Calcutta on their way to Hanoi. *Military Review*, July 1969, p. 106. Singh was surely aware of Aeroflot's potential, and at times active, military role, and of the fact that many veterans of Soviet military aviation serve with it. Further, top Civil Aviation Ministry officials are active military officers (including the present Minister, Marshal of Aviation Bugaev). At least two or more of his principal deputies are also generals. Another Air Force Major General is the Chief of the Civil Aviation Political Administration, and a third is thought to be Chief of the International Transport Directorate. See also *Neue Zurcher Zeitung*, March 18, 1970.

salvage ships and minesweepers, together with five Indian mine-sweepers, conducted port clearing operations in Chittagong, Bangladesh. In December of that year, the commander of the Soviet flotilla, Admiral Zuyenko, asserted that the Indian minesweeper squadron in Chittagong had been under his operational command.[130] This followed reports that the Indian Navy has switched to Soviet naval procedures.[131] On February 8, 1973, the Indian warship *Andjapid* had begun a four-day visit in the port of Gdansk, as a guest of the Polish Navy.[132]

East Berlin's *Neues Deutschland* announced on January 12, 1973, that Mongolian guests—among them B. Tsog, First Deputy Defense Minister—visited the Group of Soviet Forces in Germany. A GDR military delegation led by Defense Minister General Heinz Hoffman arrived in Mongolia in early May: "The visit is to serve the deepening of fraternal relations betwen the two peoples and their armed forces." Later, during his talks with Y. Tsedenbal, Mongolia's Party First Secretary, Hoffman "reaffirmed the unshakable friendship between the two peoples and armies and the firm unity and indestructible fighting alliance of the two fraternal parties and peoples with the CPSU, the peoples of the USSR, and its glorious Army." Addressing "hundreds of soldiers" of the Ulan Bator garrison, General Hoffman said: "The members of the MPR People's Army, together with the glorious Soviet Army, stand shoulder to shoulder guarding the peace on the eastern frontier of the community of Socialist states."[133] In an article written in *Neues Deutschland* (October 16, 1973), GDR State Secretary Oskar Fischer (member of a high-ranking East German delegation that had returned from a recent visit to Mongolia) stated: "The (GDR) party-government

---

[130] C. C. Petersen, *The Soviet Port-Clearing Operation in Bangladesh, March 1972-December 1973,* Professional Paper 123, Center for Naval Analyses, Arlington, Virginia, June 1974, pp. 28, 34, fn 68. Note that the Commander-in-Chief of the Soviet Navy, Admiral Gorshkov, arrived in New Delhi on April 17, 1972, for a ten-day visit. *Far Eastern Review,* April 15, 1972, p. 4. The first Polish-Indian survey of the Arabian Sea, off India's northwestern coast, has recently begun. The Polish trawler *Murena* was reportedly accompanied by two Indian ships conducting studies on hydrometeorological conditions in the region. *Summary of World Broadcasts* (SWB) (Eastern Europe), January 25, 1977, p. A3/1.
[131] *Middle East,* October 1976, p. 20.
[132] *FBIS* (Eastern Europe), February 13, 1973, p. G13.
[133] *Ibid.,* May 3, 1973, p. E1; May 7, 1973, p. E4; May 9, 1973, p. E6; May 15, 1973, pp. E6-7.

88 *The Evolution of Soviet Security Strategy, 1965-1975*

delegation has returned from the MPR with the firm conviction that the Mongolian people are loyal friends and fellow fighters of the GDR and its people."

A Mongolian military delegation led by Army General Batyn Dorj arrived in East Germany on April 4, 1974. The GDR Deputy Defense Minister, Colonel General Heinz Kessler, described the visit as a sign of the "close class brotherhood-in-arms" which links both peoples and their armies. Dorj said the purpose of the visit was "to study experience in the training and education of army personnel, and to further strengthen the friendship and cooperation between both peoples and their armies." (Among those present in the welcoming ceremony was also the Commander-in-Chief of the Group of Soviet Forces in Germany, Army General Yevgeny Ivanovsky.) The Mongolian delegation visited a motor rifle detachment in the northern part of the GDR, where Dorj said: "In your detachment and everywhere we have been in your country, we have felt we were among faithful comrades and brothers-in-arms." The delegation also visited an East German naval unit and watched naval exercises. General Dorj expressed satisfaction, saying that the Mongolian delegation could see for itself that "the borders of the Socialist community were reliably protected." In a speech on April 4, Erich Honecker, Secretary of the SED Central Committee, told the delegation that because of "counterattacks of the most reactionary and aggressive circles of imperialism, watchfulness remained the order of the day. For this reason, the SED always insured the necessary degree of combat readiness of the GDR's National People's Army, in closest alliance with the Soviet Army, and the armies of the Mongolian People's Republic and other fraternal Socialist countries."[134]

A Hungarian military delegation led by Defense Minister Colonel General Lajos Czinege visited Mongolia between June 3-15, 1974, and a Czech military delegation led by the Defense Minister, Army General Martin Dzur, visited there between September 2-8, 1974.[135] *Krasnaya Zvezda* said that on July 17, 1975, Mongolia's Defense Minister General Batyn Dorj had arrived the day before for an official visit to Hungary.

---

[134] *Ibid.*, April 2, 1974, pp. E2-3; April 4, 1974, p. E6; April 8, 1974, p. E4.
[135] *Ibid.*, June 6, 1974, p. F4; June 14, 1974, p. F1; September 3, 1974, p. D1; September 10, 1974, p. D3.

An official delegation of the Indian Army led by Chief-of-Staff General G. C. Bewoor arrived on June 3, 1974, in Czechoslovakia, while India's Defense Minister J. Ram arrived in Poland on July 2. Among other things, he visited the headquarters of the Silesian Military District in Wroclaw, "where he met soldiers of a communications unit and acquainted himself with their training and equipment." On July 6, Ram arrived in Czechoslovakia, where he also observed a tactical exercise of a motorized infantry unit backed by air force and artillery. In an interview with CTK (July 9), Ram said: "As for the Middle Eastern conflict, India's sympathy has always been with the Arab world." In a Prague radio broadcast to Africa and Asia (July 10), Ram was quoted as saying: "As is known to the world, India does not stand for any defense pact with any country and you don't have any defense pact with any country. Our treaty with Soviet Russia is also a treaty of peace, cooperation, and friendship, and we are prepared to have similar treaties with other countries also."[136]

In September, the Indian Minister of External Affairs, Swaran Singh, arrived in Moscow. In a session with Brezhnev, the two reportedly tried to coordinate the objections of both countries to the development of an American naval base on the island of Diego Garcia in the Indian Ocean.[137] It should be recalled that in February 1974, Indian Prime Minister Gandhi was quoted as saying that in foreign policy there was no difference between her Congress Party and the Communist Party of India (which is affiliated to the Communist Party of the Soviet Union).[138] Further, in November of that year Admiral Gorshkov had again visited India.[139] In February 1975, Soviet Defense Minister Marshal Grechko, accompanied by Air

---

[136] *Ibid.,* June 6, 1974, p. D6; June 14, 1974, p. D10; July 3, 1974, p. G3; July 8, 1974, p. G7; July 9, 1974, p. D3; July 10, 1974, p. D4; July 11, 1974, pp. 3-4. In mid-1975, it was reported that the Indian Air Force would buy 50 Polish Iskra-100 jet trainers, following breakdown of negotiations with Czechoslovakia on price and finance conditions for a similar number of L-39 trainers. *Aviation Week and Space Technology,* May 12, 1975, p. 1; May 19, 1975, p. 25. PAP from Warsaw said September 26, 1975, that Poland had sent a first batch of Iskra planes to India. *FBIS* (Eastern Europe), October 2, 1975, p. G10.
[137] *New York Times,* September 11, 1974. For a general discussion of the Indian position, see S. P. Seth, "The Indian Ocean and Indo-American Relations," *Asian Survey,* August 1975, pp. 645-655.
[138] *Times of India,* February 10, 1974.
[139] *Far Eastern Economic Review,* December 6, 1974, p. 5.

Marshal Pavel S. Kutakhov, Soviet Air Force Commander, and Admiral Gorshkov, Commander-in-Chief of the Soviet Navy, arrived in India. The Western press was quick to observe that "this was the first time such a delegation visited any but a Warsaw Pact country, in other words one of Moscow's formal client-allies."[140]

A recent article in the organ of the Vietnam People's Army hailed the development of East Germany's army: "The growth in strength of the National People's Army has greatly increased the defense potentials of the German Democratic Republic, as well as the armed might of the entire Socialist camp." The editorial went on to wish the militant solidarity and fraternal cooperation between the armed forces of Vietnam and the GDR more fruitful development.[141] On September 14, 1976, a Hungarian military delegation headed by Major General Chevi Karei, Political Secretary of the Defense Ministry, arrived in North Korea at the invitation of the People's Armed Forces Mobilization Department. It had a series of conferences with Korea's Assistant Vice Chief-of-Staff Kim Chol-man, who serves as Vice Minister of the People's Armed Forces Mobilization Department.[142] On October 6, 1976 an East German military delegation arrived in Pyongyang. General Heinz Hoffman, the GDR's Defense Minister and head of the delegation, praised "the just struggle of both peoples for achieving independent reunited states." He added that the SED, as well as workers, peasants, and soldiers of the GDR, "support the fight of the Democratic People's Republic of Korea for reunification by peaceful means."[143]

---

[140] *Christian Science Monitor*, February 24, 1975; *Baltimore Sun*, February 28, 1975.

[141] *FBIS (Asia and Pacific)*, March 3, 1976, p. K1.

[142] *East Asian Review*, Winter 1976, p. 605.

[143] F. W. Scholmann, "Die DDR und die Koreanischen Wiedervereinigungsgespräche," *Deutschland Archiv*, January 1977, p. 42; *Neues Deutschland*, October 6, 7, 1976.

7

The Soviet Collective Security System

We are now in a position to define in general terms the Soviet security strategy. The body of data presented in the preceding chapters indicates that since 1965, at least, the Soviet Union has been working toward the gradual establishment of a collective security system designed to safeguard what Moscow conceives of as its defense perimeter. This security system is based on strategic interactions performed between and within its three subsystems: the Warsaw Pact, the Middle East, and the India/Far East. The "collective" character of the strategy is primarily derived from the fact that the subsystems are designed to, and in reality do, reinforce each other due to their structural strategic intra- and interdependence.

The general failure of the West to grasp these facts may be attributed primarily to a number of common strategic fallacies. The first is a continuous underestimation of the political and strategic consistency of the Soviet effort and its magnitude, particularly when it comes to conventional capabilities. This seems to be a lesser problem with regard to the nuclear strategic field, presumably because this subject has a direct, day-to-day bearing on the security of the United States proper, while conventional capabilities have only indirect bearing on American security. But the US focus on the Soviet strategic effort implies greater attention to the threat of physical annihilation, which is in reality less likely, while at the same time it ignores a process initiated by Moscow which may well bring the destruction of the American political and strategic presence over large parts of the globe—a process which seems, at least to this author, to be more probable. The same applies to the US arms control effort which, as a logical conclusion from the above preoccupation, is directed almost totally toward the strategic balance (for example, the SALT talks).

From the perspective of the present study, it seems that the Soviet strategic build-up is designed to provide the necessary umbrella for the Soviet "push" on its periphery. Presumably, the umbrella is needed to deter the United States from resisting militarily the gradual expansion of the Soviet sphere of domination achieved through the *conventional* collective strategy outlined above and without challenging the United States directly. It should be further emphasized that, as far as the Soviet proxy strategy is concerned, the West is almost completely disarmed no matter how many ICBMs the United States may have.[1] Further, the debate currently in progress in the United States about the Soviet strategic build-up and what kind of strategic arms the United States should acquire in response, is misleading as well as misdirected. The real issue should deal with Soviet *strategy* as opposed to an almost exclusive preoccupation with the Soviet *arsenal*. Consequently, the United States should devote much more attention to questions of developing effective counterstrategies, rather than waste its energies in debating what types of new weapons are needed. Lacking a coherent Western strategy, the most advanced miltary technology would be quite useless. Never before has the American tendency to resort to *technical* solutions for strategic problems been so dangerous. This is so precisely because the adversary seems to be equipped with a set of well-tested, long-range operational strategic guidelines.

A second strategic fallacy is the underestimation of the strategic importance of the various bilateral friendship treaties concluded by Moscow since 1965, particularly when taken in their totality. Even without a detailed analysis of individual bilateral treaties, it should be of interest to us that in contrast to a "neoisolationist" American foreign policy, Moscow has been searching for new commitments all over its periphery. Furthermore, it is the conviction of this author

---

[1] This is not to say that the state of the strategic balance is unimportant, but only that without a viable strategy which can resist and hopefully defeat the Soviet effort, while using a level of forces similar to the one the Soviets are using, the US strategic arsenal may become quite irrelevant.

that Russia is prepared to proceed with this network until the entire periphery of the USSR is (either directly or indirectly) linked in a formal alliance system to Moscow.

Analytically, this implies adopting macro tools of analysis to study Soviet strategy aimed at its periphery. Such a perspective makes the *pattern* of Soviet operations the focus of the strategic debate, and eliminates partial statements (like those made by many during the recent Angolan war) which are usually based on micro analysis. In addition, it avoids the regionalization of American security interests. Viewed from the Soviet collective security system perspective, it seems both unfortunate and anachronistic that US strategic interests along the Soviet periphery have been determined geographically, rather than derived from a general strategic concept.

Further, since the Soviet external deployment is a relatively new phenomenon (for example, the Soviet fleet in the Mediterranean), there is a certain amount of wishful thinking among Western commentators, who tacitly assume this deployment could, somehow or someday, be rolled back to the continental confines of Soviet Russia. Conversely, the prime strategic problem for the West is to address the Soviet *design,* which is a product of Soviet strategic thinking and perceptions, and which views the Middle East, for example, as a part of the Soviet defense perimeter. This is a much more important task than, say, the futile debate over whether Egypt has "defected" or not. There is only a partial link between trying to win away local allies and the real target, which is the apparant existence of a Soviet long-range strategic design.

This design is already hard at work to create other "Egypts," not only in the Middle East but also in Africa and South and East Asia. Furthermore, it should be stressed that the success or failure criteria which the Soviets have consequently adopted may be quite different from the ones we have been ascribing to them for years. Not only are political and strategic costs recognized in advance as an integral part of this operation by Moscow, but the way these costs have been defined is probably different. For example, though many Western observers contend that Soviet involvement in Egypt should be treated as a dramatic failure, there is little doubt that from the Soviet security system perspective it has profited Moscow immensely. Egypt has contributed to the Soviet design as no other single non-Communist country has; it opened the entire Arab

Middle East to Moscow, actively assisting the Soviets in other Middle Eastern and North African countries, and in addition contributed for several years to Russia's own security by allowing its air and naval facilities on its territory, thus improving the Soviet capability to confront the US Sixth Fleet.[2]

In the final analysis, it may be an academic question whether a large Soviet design has been preplanned and blueprinted in advance, or merely may have come together after a process of trial and error, opening up new opportunities and closing others. Nevertheless, from the Soviet security system strategy perspective, the apparent failure of the detente policy, which was supposedly aimed at changing the Soviet *behavior pattern* (that is, the designers' minds), should have been regarded as of greater significance to us than the question of whether Sadat has been moving West or not. The relative permanence of Soviet behavior is highlighted by the fact that the greatest Soviet strides toward its aim of establishing a collective security system were made precisely during the peak years of the detente policy.

Finally, there is a tendency to conceive of Moscow too readily as a low-risk actor. Though this perception might be accurate, the erosion in American political will to resist Soviet expansionism (especially in "grey areas"), *for reasons independent of Soviet behavior,* may well lead to a Soviet forward policy which corresponds to a general low-risk posture.

In contrast, this study leads to the conclusion that in the years to come, one may expect a series of crises along the Soviet periphery, with the prime question being, Which conflict will erupt first? As an unscientific forecast, the author would argue that the part of the Balkans which potentially blocks Soviet access to the other segments of its security system (that is, Yugoslavia, Greece, Turkey), in terms of possible strategic mutual support missions, should become a prime target for Soviet diplomacy and strategy in the future. There

---

[2] A knowledgeable writer confirmed this indirectly in a recent article. "There have been conflicting judgments regarding the US Sixth Fleet's ability to operate in the easternmost Mediterranean in the face of a determined countereffort by the Soviets. The balance must be a very delicate one if informal professional disagreement exists, as it does. This being the case, we should be alert to any factors that would change the balance, such as Soviet access to North African air bases. A move such as this might well tip the delicate balance against the Sixth Fleet, heightening the risk." Admiral Stansfield Turner, Commander-in-Chief, Allied Forces, Southern Europe, "The Naval Balance: Not Just a Numbers Game," *Foreign Affairs,* January 1977, pp. 351-352.

are many signs that this process has already begun, as evidenced in recent Soviet gestures toward Turkey and Yugoslavia.[3] But even if Moscow's success in this respect is by no means complete, we should recall our earlier conclusions regarding Soviet consistency and permanence of objectives. In other words, to content oneself with arguments about alleged Soviet policy failures or successes is far from sufficient. An equally important question has to do with where the Soviets are heading. Or, to use the well-known metaphor, How many doors is the hotel burglar planning to break into, as opposed to where he has already tested the handles?

---

[3] Thus, during the December 1975 visit of Soviet Premier Kosygin to Turkey, the Soviets reportedly renewed their offer of a friendship treaty to Ankara. *Ma'ariv,* December 30, 1975; *Washington Post,* February 5, 1976. Moreover, a breakdown of Soviet economic aid commitments to foreign countries in 1975 shows that fully half of the aid, about $650 million, was promised to Turkey. (US State Department figures, quoted in *New York Times,* August 20, October 6, 1976.) For recent Soviet offers of arms to Turkey, see Radio Bayrak, quoted in *Middle East Economic Digest,* August 8, 1975; *Boston Globe,* December 3, 1975. As for Yugoslavia, it was reported that during Brezhnev's November 1976 visit to Belgrade, he proposed that a Soviet-Yugoslav friendship treaty be concluded. See D. Schlegel, "Yugoslavia's Independence from Moscow," *Aussen Politik,* English Edition, February 1977, pp. 185-186; *Süddeutsche Zeitung,* November 3, 1976. Further, this "southern strategy" was indicated by the fact that the Soviets in 1974 have begun supplying the Bulgarians with sophisticated weaponry previously reserved for the East Germans. Admiral Means Johnston, Jr., in an interview with *U.S. News and World Report,* June 2, 1975, pp. 19-20. In November 1974, a Soviet KGB delegation under KGB Chairman Yuri Andropov visited Sofia to begin better integration of Bulgaria's security and intelligence services with the KGB. According to Western intelligence sources, "this may involve transferring to Moscow's direct supervision of Bulgarian clandestine operations in states like Greece and Turkey." *Christian Science Monitor,* December 24, 1974; January 10, 1975.

Soviet External Deployment, 1966-1975

YEAR: 1966

Infrastructure Development	De Facto Stationing
Middle East Subsystem	

1. On May 10, Soviet Premier Kosygin arrived in Cairo accompanied by Admiral Sergei G. Gorshkov of the Soviet Navy. "Gorshkov's immediate goal was probably to secure a firm agreement from Cairo which would have allowed Soviet warships to make regular calls at Egyptian ports without having to obtain permission for each visit."[1] Three airstrips were turned over to the Soviets in February in a secret pact with the Egyptians. The Soviets agreed to modernize the airstrips, bear all costs, and man the sites "during peacetime." They were Dakhla Oasis, El Kharga, and Qasr Farafra, all in Upper Egypt in the interior of the country, "well away from the Israeli threat. This apparently was preparation for things to come. No known Egyptian Air Force (units) have been stationed at these airfields."[2]

The first official Soviet naval visit to Egypt occurred in August, when a Soviet naval detachment arrived in Alexandria. "The importance to the Soviets of the August port call can be seen in the fact that the detachment was commanded by Vice Admiral G. Chernobay, Chief of Staff of the Black Sea Fleet."[6] At a press conference aboard the guided missile destroyer Boikii, Admiral Chernobay announced that the USSR was going to maintain a permanent naval presence in the Mediterranean. "This was the first official Soviet statement that the USSR's naval presence was to be permanent, and the fact that it was made in Alexandria is highly relevant."[7] Note that the USSR delivered Komar guided missile patrol boats to Algeria and Syria during this period. Soviet naval units paid their first visit to Algeria in April and Admiral Chernobay led a second group of naval units there in November. The Times (London, July 16, 1968) noted amid reports of a growing Soviet presence in Algeria (see the 1968 table): "A few Komar missile launchers under the Algerian flag, with Soviet technicians . . . in attendance, would help to fill a vacuum before any significant Soviet naval presence is established in the western Mediterranean."

YEAR: 1966 (continued)

Infrastructure Development	De Facto Stationing
Indian/Far East Subsystem	

1. In January, a direct railway line between Moscow and Choibalsan was put into operation. Three months later, a daily service between Irkutsk and the Mongolian capital Ulan Bator was inaugurated, which has greatly facilitated troop movements.[3]

2. Since the first session of the Joint Japan-Soviet Economic Committee, in March, there were discussions of Japanese participation in the modernization or construction of Soviet Far Eastern ports. During 1968, attention focused on potential Japanese participation in the construction of a new Soviet port on the Bay of Wrangel.[4]

3. Toward the end of the year, the Soviets completed a road network in Afghanistan (across the Hindukush to Kabul) which links up to Soviet railheads and ports on the Amur Darya.[5]

A month after the signing of the Mongolian-Soviet friendship treaty, top-level talks took place in Ulan Bator to work out plans for military cooperation between the two countries.[8] The *New York Times* (March 16, 1966) said it had received reports of Soviet troop movements in Mongolia on the Sino-Soviet frontier. In 1967, Ulan Bator Radio confirmed the presence in Mongolia of Soviet troops and missiles.[9] The *New York Times* (January 2, 1968) said Soviet troops stationed in Mongolia included tank detachments and antiaircraft units. In August 1968, reports quoting Western intelligence said the Soviets were deploying mobile missiles.[9] The report added that by late 1966, more than 10,000 Soviet troops were in Mongolia.[10]

Footnotes for Year 1966:

[1] Dragnich, *op. cit.*, p. 32.

[2] A. W. Hansen *The Bear in Sheik's Clothing*, Air Command and Staff College, Maxwell Air Force Base, Alabama, May 1972, pp. 28-29.

[3] *Foreign Report* (Economist), January 25, 1968, p. 4.

[4] K. Saeki, "Toward Japanese Cooperation in Siberian Development," *Problems of Communism*, May-June 1972, p. 7. See also the 1970 Table.

[5] *Neue Zurcher Zeitung*, January 18, 1970.

[6] Dragnich, *op. cit.*, p. 37.

[7] *Ibid.*, p. 39.

[8] *Foreign Report*, January 25, 1968, p. 4. Note that on the basis of the text of Article 9 (which exists in the identical text in the friendship treaties with Hungary and Bulgaria), "the existence of a secret military agreement between the Soviet Union and Mongolia is *not* excluded. The appropriate provision says: 'The treaty in question does not touch the commitments of both sides resulting from valid bilateral and multilateral agreements.' '' B. Meissner, "The Political Treaties of China and the Soviet Union in East Asia," in *The Yearbook of World Affairs, 1973*, London Institute of World Affairs, London, 1973, p. 225.

[9] *Current Scene*, July 7, 1971, p. 17.

[10] *Far Eastern Economic Review*, August 8, 1968, pp. 278-279; *Sunday Times* (London), October 6, 1968; *Air Force Magazine*, March 1975, p. 73.

YEAR: 1967

Infrastructure Development	De Facto Stationing
Middle East Subsystem	

1. On January 28, Admiral Gorshkov arrived in Egypt to seek port facilities there. "The timing is relevant. During 1967-68, the Soviet Navy would begin taking delivery of new classes of ships, submarines, and aircraft which would enable their Mediterranean deployment to become operationally significant for the first time."[1] Another observer asserts that "there is some evidence that the Soviet Navy was planning a major winter deployment to the Mediterranean that February, and Gorshkov may have been trying to arrange for some of the ships to call at Egyptian ports or to use anchorages off the Egyptian coast."[2] On October 7, Soviet naval support facilities were established in Alexandria and Port Said, including a submarine tender and other support ships.[3] Toward the end of the year, "Soviet fleet movements to and from Port Said and Alexandria became so frequent as to constitute virtually a permanent naval presence there."[4]

2. A defector from the Republican Army, Lieutenant Abdullah al-Udaini, said at a press conference in Aden on February 7 that the Soviet Union was building a naval base with Egyptian help at Mocha.[5] *Tass* on February 6 said that the Soviet Union was helping Yemen to build its port in Hudeida. Aden reports had said on August 7 that Moscow had offered direct military aid in exchange for facilities at Janad airport about 14 miles from Sana'a. The *Times* (August 7, 1967) said the proposal was made during a visit to Moscow of Republican Deputy Prime Minister Abdullah Guzieilah. The Yemen Embassy in Moscow on August 8 denied the story.[6] Other sources, however, reported later: "Just to the north of Sana'a, an 11,500-foot airstrip was completed under Soviet supervision. The largest airstrip in the Middle East, *its location makes all points in the Mediterranean, Africa, and India accessible to the Soviet Union.*"[7]

3. Between April 18-24, Admiral Gorshkov was heading a naval delegation to Yugoslavia, presumably pressing for port facilities.[8] Note that the visit took place less than a month after five Soviet naval units had paid a four-day "informal" visit

Between 1965 and 1967, Soviet ship operating days in the Mediterranean had doubled (8,500 ship-days in 1967).[11] A naval presence was maintained throughout the Winter for the first time, and the number of naval units on station more than doubled. The normal composition of the Soviet Mediterranean fleet since then has been eight to ten attack/torpedo submarines; two to three guided/cruise missile submarines; two to four cruisers, some or all armed with guided missiles; and often one helicopter missile cruiser of the Moskva class; nine to 12 frigates, destroyers, and escort ships, some armed with guided missiles; one to three minesweepers; one to three amphibious ships; and 15 to 20 auxiliary ships.[12] In an interview with the *New York Times* (October 23, 1967), Admiral Ephraim P. Holmes, Supreme Allied Commander, Atlantic, for NATO, pointed to "the recent appearance of a number of amphibious landing ships, similar to American LSTs, in the Mediterranean," as an example of the extension of Soviet naval capability beyond the periphery of the Soviet Union. "In the past," he added, "the Soviets had a few small landing craft that looked like they were built to operate in rivers and lakes. Now they have built a number of oceangoing landing ships and deployed them well beyond their shores. This signified an awareness of what it takes to project force forward."[13] Soviet anchorages have been identified off the Greek island of Kithera, in the Gulf of Hammet off Tunisia, in the Gulf of Sirte off Libya, and off Alboran Island east of the Strait of Gibraltar.[14] A Soviet submarine tender and a missile support ship spent five months in the general area of the Cape Verde Islands in company with a number of submarines.[15]

YEAR: 1967 (continued)

Infrastructure Development	De Facto Stationing
Middle East Subsystem	

to the Yugoslav port of Split.
4. Beginning in June, soon after the Six
Day War, Soviet naval units made almost
regular monthly calls at Algeria.[9] A leading Soviet commentator on Asian affairs, V. Matveyev, stated in *Izvestiia*
(August 31, 1967): "Only a policy can
have a future in Asia . . . which takes into account forces of national independence and freedom. To think in terms of
'bases' and 'spheres of influence' is not
only vain but even dangerous." Thus in
1967, for example, in the name of facili-
tating future delivery of heavy equipment,
"'but to provide bunkering for Soviet
ships as well,'" the USSR undertook to
rebuild and modernize the Somali port
of Berbera.[10]

Footnotes for Year 1967:

[1] M. MccGwire, "The Mediterranean and Soviet Naval Interests," in MccGwire, *op. cit.,*
1973, p. 354.

[2] Dragnich, *op. cit.,* pp. 46-47.

[3] M. MccGwire, "The Evolution of Soviet Naval Policy: 1960-1974," in MccGwire, *et al.,*
op. cit., 1975, p. 524. Soviet President Nikolai Podgorny visited Egypt in June 1967. In a
meeting with Nasser, he "asked for a command post and a repair shop in Alexandria, and
then proposed that both these should be guarded by Russian marines. Next, he suggested that
the whole area—command post, repair shop, and quarters for the guards—should be handed
over to them . . . (Further,) Podgorny asked for permission to raise the Red Flag over the
area allocated to them. At this, Nasser lost his temper. 'This is just imperialism,' he said.
'It means we should be giving you a base.' Podgorny backed down, but the damage had been
done." M. Heikal, *The Road to Ramadan,* Quadrangle, New York, 1975, p. 48.

[4] *Middle East Record, 1967,* pp. 11-12, 26; *New York Times,* March 23, 1968. One source
claims further that Mersa Matruh, west of Alexandria, became a Soviet air base in 1967. G.
Lenczowski, *Soviet Advances in the Middle East,* American Enterprise Institute, Washington,
D.C., 1972, p. 157.

[5] *Arab Report and Record,* February 1-14, 1967, p. 46; *Asian Recorder,* March 12-18, 1967,
p. 7591.

[6] *Arab Report and Record,* August 16-31, 1967, p. 284; and see below.

[7] W. D. Toole, "Soviet Interest in Arabia," *Military Review,* May 1968, p. 96. Emphasis
added. *Africa Confidential,* August 7, 1970, p. 8.

[8] MccGwire, *op. cit.,* 1973.

[9] Joshua and Gibert, *op. cit.,* p. 26; Lenczowski, *op. cit.; New York Times,* January 23, 1968.

[10] E. R. Zumwalt, *On Watch,* Quadrangle, New York, 1976, p. 361.

[11] Blechman, *op. cit.,* p. 13, Table 4.

[12] *Understanding Soviet Naval Developments,* Office of the Chief of Naval Operations,
Department of the Navy, Washington, D.C., April 1975, p. 11.

[13] Admiral Holmes was probably referring to the Soviet Alligator-type LST, described
earlier.

[14] *New York Times,* June 2, 1967. See also the 1969 and 1975 tables.

[15] M. MccGwire, "Parallel Naval Developments," in MccGwire, *op. cit.,* 1973, p. 170.

YEAR: 1968

Infrastructure Development	De Facto Stationing
Warsaw Pact Subsystem	

During the night of August 20-21, 14 Soviet divisions supported by half a dozen East German, Polish, Hungarian, and Bulgarian divisions, in all some 200,000 men, invaded Czechoslovakia.[19] On October 16, Soviet Premier Kosygin and Czech Premier Cernik signed a treaty legalizing the presence of Soviet troops in Czechoslovakia.[20] By early December, following the first announced withdrawal of some occupation units several weeks earlier, it became known that the number of Soviet divisions in Eastern Europe had risen to 31 (16 armored and 15 motorized infantry), compared with 26 divisions (13 armored and 13 motorized infantry supported by about 1,200 tactical aircraft) stationed there before the invasion. (Note, however, that there was no increase in the standing size of Soviet theater forces, and the number of ground force divisions was kept at about 140.[21]) One European observer[22] contended that since the "October Storm" maneuvers in 1965, the Soviet General Staff had suspected that the Czechoslovak Army would be incapable of holding its sector of the line with conventional arms against a US attack. Moscow had, therefore, raised the question of stationing Soviet troops on the Czechoslovak-West German border to stiffen resistance there and insure that the Warsaw Pact forces would not be the first to escalate to the tactical nuclear level. Note also that during the invasion of Czechoslovakia, the Soviets had airlifted an entire airborne division overnight, using a fleet of some 200 An-12 Cubs.

YEAR: 1968 (continued)

Infrastructure Development	De Facto Stationing
Middle East Subsystem	

1. Soviet Defense Minister Andrei Grechko arrived in Cairo on April 1, following visits to Iraq and Syria. "The granting of port facilities (in Egypt), which entailed jurisdictional control by Soviet personnel over the repair shops and warehouses needed for the maintenance, repair, and provisioning of the Soviet fleet, was extended *de facto* in January 1968 and formalized in a secret five-year agreement in April 1968, at which time Soviet Tu-16s were also deployed in Egypt for surveillance of the US Sixth Fleet and Israeli positions." It was learned later that the Soviets were also negotiating for naval access to facilities at the Iraqi port of Umm Qasr.[1]

2. South Yemen Defense Minister Ali Salim al-Beedh led a military delegation to Moscow in February; and on March 30, South Yemen President al-Shaabi conferred with a six-man Soviet delegation headed by General Alexander Pozharsky (on a visit to South Yemen since March 21).[2] The Soviet press agency *Novosti* was reported to have announced early in the year that South Yemen had agreed to allow the USSR to acquire naval and air facilities in Aden.[3] The Soviets had also signed an agreement to improve the harbor and docks at the port of Aden.[4] It is also reported that at "the moment of extreme crisis in Sana'a (North Yemen) 1968, when the Yemeni republican regime seemed about to fall to the royalists, Moscow attempted to send further aid to it, contingent on a site for a communication base in the heights above the capital."[5]

3. NATO diplomats, June 24, warned Borg Oliver, Prime Minister of Malta, against allowing the use of Malta's port facilities to Soviet naval ships. The Soviets reportedly had proposed sending a naval squadron to visit Malta.[6]

4. On January 31, France completed the withdrawal of its forces from the Mers-el-Kebir naval base. US Senator Peter A. Dominick (R.-Colo.) told the Senate June 28 that "the Russians are now negotiating for the huge NATO-built (naval) base (at Mers-el-Kebir) . . . which was turned back to Algeria by France."[7] On July 15, Soviet Defense Minister Grechko arrived in Al-

Since 1968, Western carriers have been marked "without fail" when in the eastern basin, and are nearly always shadowed elsewhere in the Mediterranean. Intelligence units were stationed off the Polaris base at Rota in Spain and in the Sicilian channel.[23] The Italian monthly *Aviazione Marine* reported in May 1968 that the USSR had set up an electronic espionage network covering the Middle East through the anchorage of four of their "spy ships" in Arab ports. These Soviet vessels had been reportedly stationed at Basra, Iraq (since November 1968), Tartus, Syria (since December 1968), Port Said in Egypt, and Hudeida in the Yemen Arab Republic.[24] The Commander of the Soviet Mediterranean Fleet "normally keeps his flag and staff aboard a submarine tender that frequently visits Tartus, Syria."[25] Note that a new NATO air arm—Maritime Air Forces Mediterranean (MARAIRMED) was commissioned on November 21. It was formed to keep watch on the "USSR's growing naval strength in the area." Attention would be concentrated, it was reported, on the nature of the Soviet naval presence in Syrian and Egyptian ports and on the possible takeover by the USSR of the former French naval base at Mers-el-Kebir, in Algeria.[26] In an interview with *Der Spiegel* (May), Admiral Horacio Rivero, Commander-in-Chief, South, disclosed the Soviets were maintaining one to four Alligator LSTs in the Mediterranean at all times, as well as some smaller Polnocny amphibious vessels. He added the Soviets may have as much as a battalion of Marines on these ships.[27] The *New York Times* (March 29, 1968) reported that "Soviet bomber squadrons fly (in Egypt) for maneuvers." On October 27, the paper reported that Soviet pilots in Egypt had been "flying separate all-Soviet missions, including bombing, strafing, and air defense exercises. From time to time, flights of Tu-16 bombers fly to Egypt from bases in the Soviet Union, move from air base to air base conducting bombing practice, and then fly home." Some analysts say the Soviets were focusing in these exercises on "stand-off" bombing.[28] In August, US Assistant Secretary

YEAR: 1968 (continued)

Infrastructure Development	De Facto Stationing
Middle East Subsystem	

giers for a one-week visit. Among military installations visited by him was the former French naval base at Mers-el-Kebir.[8] In September, reports emanating from "the highest level of the Moroccan government and confirmed by US officials," said Moscow had arranged to post its technicians in Mers-el-Kebir, 260 miles from the Strait of Gibraltar. Algerian diplomats, when asked about it, had avoided an answer, confining themselves to the statement that the Russians had not been granted rights to a permanent base at Mers-el-Kebir.[9] *Observer* (November 9, 1968) said 40 Russian technicians were maintaining the Mers-el-Kebir installations. French Foreign Minister Michel Debre, commenting November 13 on reports of increased Soviet control over military installations in Algeria, said Algeria had not handed over any bases to foreign control. He said he would visit Algeria soon to discuss outstanding problems. A report in the *Sunday Telegraph* (November 10, 1968) said Debre had asked for an immediate report on Soviet penetration into Algeria. The *Financial Times* (November 12, 1968) said that there had been "considerable anxiety" in French government circles over the Soviet build-up in Algeria. Privately, it said, French officials had admitted that they were more concerned by the possibility of the takeover of air bases than of naval stations. It is also reported that toward the end of the year, the French government had asked President Boumedienne for formal assurances that Mers-el-Kebir would be neither ceded nor leased to the Soviets before 1977, until which year the French-Algerian independence accords of 1962 gave France the right to use it.[10] 5. *Daily Telegraph* (October 19, 1968) reported the arrival of considerable numbers of Soviet naval officers and technicians in civilian clothes in Damascus following a secret agreement Syria had made with Moscow to grant the latter "extensive facilities . . . in Latakia and Tartus." The Soviets were "supervising building by Syrian workers of docks, stores, and maintenance facilities." Further, Soviet specialists were reportedly "working on modernization of Syrian air-

of State William Macomber told a Congressman that Tu-16 bombers supplied by the USSR to Egypt were making surveillance flights over the Sixth Fleet.[29] One observer maintains that starting in May, the land-based air arm of the Soviet Navy was allowed to use the Cairo West airport for regular Tu-16 reconnaissance flights over the Sixth Fleet in the Mediterranean as far west as the boot of Italy. "Instructively, the Badgers used Egyptian markings."[30] Admiral Rivero also commented that at least some of the crews of these bombers had Soviet technicians.[31] On September 20, the Soviet helicopter carrier *Moskva* entered the Mediterranean; "most Soviet exercises (were) held in the eastern Mediterranean, the main emphasis being on ASW, with aircraft from Egyptian airfields working with the helicopter carriers."[32] Soviet ship operating days in the Mediterranean for the year totaled 12,000.[33]

YEAR: 1968 (continued)

Infrastructure Development	De Facto *Stationing*

Middle East Subsystem

fields to enable them to take Soviet-made aircraft supplied to Syria. These airfields were visited from time to time, openly or secretly, by Soviet long-range bombers."[11]

6. *Daily Telegraph* (December 18, 1968) said the USSR was preparing large-scale development plans for the Al Gabbari shipyard in Alexandria to meet the needs of its Mediterranean fleet. The paper added that 130 Soviet engineers and technicians were due to arrive shortly in Alexandria to plan and supervise big extensions to the shipyard to provide it with a capacity to build tankers up to 40,000 tons. The report also said that an agreement had been reached on the procedure for the repair and maintenance of Soviet warships under the direction of Soviet technicians.

India/Far East Subsystem

1. On February 9 (that is, within a month after British Prime Minister Wilson's "East of Suez" withdrawal announcement), Soviet Admiral S. G. Gorshkov, accompanied by Rear Admiral L. Meezin, Chief of Staff of the Russian Black Sea Fleet, arrived in India for a ten-day visit, "presumably to explore the possibility of securing refueling and repairing facilities for Russian warships in Indian ports and docks."[12] On April 1, Indian Defense Minister Swaran Singh announced (in the Lok Sabha) the purchase of Soviet-made submarines.[13] On July 6, India's first Soviet-built F-class large attack-type submarine sailed into the naval base of Vishakapatnam to take Soviet-type submarines are yet to come . . . and at least one more . . . crew is now being trained in the USSR."[14] In December, it was announced that a second Soviet submarine intended for India was being commissioned at the Russian naval base of Riga in the Baltic Sea.[15] At the same time, reports indicated that Soviet advisors were assisting in construction and adaptation of the Indian east coast naval base of Vishakaptnam to take Soviet-type submarines, and that India had been offered in return the use of the base facilities by Moscow.[16] Some six months later, there

In March, a squadron of the Soviet Navy made up of a Sverdlov-class cruiser, two guided missile destroyers, and a submarine conducted the first publicized tour by a group of Russian naval ships in the Indian Ocean in recent years. Since then, excluding ten days in 1969, the Soviet Union has maintained a steady presence of combatant and support forces in the Indian Ocean tailored to satisfy multiple missions. The "spotlight has been on the northwest quadrant adjacent to the Middle East."[34] Soviet ship operating days in the Indian Ocean (surface combatants and auxiliaries) totaled 1,760 for the year[35] (529 days for combatants only).[36]

By the Summer, the Russians were ready for their first series of large-scale maneuvers in the Mongolian area. Rail lines had been built between Chita, a major Soviet military base, and Choibalsan, Mongolia's second largest city, where a new Soviet base was said to have been established. (Non-Communist Chinese sources in Hong Kong reported that after the Soviet-Mongolian maneuvers, several Chinese divisions were redeployed to the Soviet-Mongolian border, and that significant numbers of artillery pieces were withdrawn from the

YEAR: 1968 (continued)

Infrastructure Development	De Facto Stationing
India / Far East Subsystem	

were reports of "a considerable increase in Soviet submarine activities (in the Indian Ocean), illustrated a few weeks ago when a Soviet submarine surfaced in Malaysian territorial waters for repairs."[17] A knowledgeable observer writes: "The Royal Navy's withdrawal from East of Suez did not prompt the decision to deploy Soviet units to the Indian Ocean. More significant, I believe, was Britain's inability to meet India's request for modern diesel submarines. Russia's unprecedented action in supplying India with submarines of the up-to-date F-class gained Russia access to naval bases on the east coast of India."[18]	Fukien region, ostensibly for shipment to the Soviet border region.)[37]

Footnotes for Year 1968:

[1] Rubinstein, *op. cit.*, 1977, p. 46. On Umm Qasr, see T. B. Millar, *Soviet Policies in the Indian Ocean Area*, Canberra Papers on Strategy and Defense No. 7, Australian National University Press, Canberra, 1970, p. 15.

[2] *Times,* February 3, 1968; *New York Times,* March 31, 1968.

[3] *Middle East Record,* 1968, p. 50. On January 2, 1969, four Soviet warships arrived in Aden for a five-day visit. See also the 1970 table.

[4] Millar, *op. cit.,* 1970, p. 13.

[5] J. B. Bell, "Strategic Implications of the Soviet Presence in Somalia," *Orbis,* Summer 1975, p. 406.

[6] *Facts on File,* June 27-July 3, 1968, p. 265.

[7] *Ibid.* Considering the magnitude of Soviet economic and military aid to Algeria, "it may have been a significant factor in persuading Algerian leaders that they could afford to press the French to evacuate bases before the date (1972) provided by the Evian accords." J. D. Esseks, "Soviet Economic Aid to Africa, 1959-72, An Overview," in W. Weinstein, ed., *Chinese and Soviet Aid to Africa,* Praeger, New York, 1975, p. 109.

[8] *Arab Report and Record,* July 16-31, 1968, p. 201.

[9] *Asian Recorder,* September 16-22, 1968, p. 8533.

[10] *Middle East Record,* 1968, p. 16.

[11] A. Yodfat, "The USSR, Jordan and Syria," *Mizan,* March-April, 1968, p. 84.

[12] Vivekanandan, *loc. cit.,* p. 61. *Christian Science Monitor,* March 23, 1968, said Gorshkov's visit to India was a "part of his effort to line up a worldwide system for ports of call and bases for his navy."

[13] Note that the shift toward acquiring Soviet naval equipment "had met with considerable opposition at (the Indian) naval headquarters." Thomas, *loc. cit.,* 1975-76, p. 502.

[14] *Baltimore Sun,* July 7, 1968; *Warship International,* Winter 1969, p. 7.

[15] R. G. C. Thomas, "The Politics of Indian Naval Re-armament, 1962-1974," *Pacific Community,* April 1975, p. 464. In 1968, two commands were set in operation: a Western Fleet with headquarters in Bombay, and an Eastern Fleet with headquarters in Vishakapatnam.

[16] T. B. Millar, *The Indian and Pacific Oceans, Some Strategic Considerations,* Adelphi Paper No. 57, International Institute for Strategic Studies, London, May 1969, p. 5; *Time Magazine,* October 3, 1970, p. 33; *New York Times,* March 21, 1972; *Far Eastern Economic Review,* June 4, 1973, p. 15. One source which reported this story added that India has given Russian vessels a kind of de facto base in the Andaman and Nicobar Islands. *Asian Letter,* Tokyo, September 30, 1969, p. 3. See also the 1970 table.

[17] *Far Eastern Economic Review,* January 29, 1970, p. 25. J. M. van der Kroef, "Soviet Security Strategy in Asia," *Aussen Politik,* English edition, March 1970, pp. 297-298.

[18] M. MccGwire, in *Guardian,* August 26, 1970.

[19] R. R. Gill, "Europe's Military Balance after Czechoslovakia," *Military Rivew,* January 1969, p. 47.

[20] *Financial Times,* October 18, 1968.

[21] Wolfe, *op. cit.,* 1970, pp. 466-471.

[22] J. Erickson, in Gill, *loc. cit.,* p. 52.

YEAR: 1968 (continued)

23 MccGwire, *loc. cit., 1973*, p. 347.

24 Cited in *Arab Report and Record*, June 1-15, 1969, p. 251. See also the 1970 table.

25 J. W. Lewis, *op. cit.*, p. 59; *Aviation Week and Space Technology*, January 17, 1977, p. 48.

26 *Arab Report and Record*, November 16-30, 1968, p. 387.

27 See also *Middle East Record*, 1968, p. 15.

28 Hansen, *op. cit.*, p. 46.

29 *Middle East Record, 1968*, p. 16; *Ha'aretz*, August 18, 1968; *Daily Telegraph*, August 19, 1968.

30 J. C. Hurewitz, "Weapons Acquisition: Israel and Egypt." Paper presnted to the Interuniversity Seminar on Armed Forces and Society, Chicago, October 1973, p. 11. Thus, for example, two Soviet-piloted Tu-16 reconnaissance aircraft with Egyptian markings kept track of NATO vessels participating in the April 1969 *Dawn Patrol* exercises. *Jerusalem Post*, April 25, 1969; *Times*, June 3, 1969. *Daily Telegraph*, on April 11, 1969, while noting the deployment of Soviet Tu-16s in Cairo West, added that Soviet bombers also had facilities at sections of the civil airports of Cairo, Luxor, and Aswan reserved for military use.

31 Interview with *Los Angeles Times*, March 24, 1969. See also *Times*, October 1, 1968; *Washington Post*, October 26, 1968. One source indicated that 100 Soviet pilots were assigned to the Egyptian Air Force, taking part in operational training exercises. A. Yodfat, "Arms and Influence in Egypt—the Record of Soviet Military Assistance Since 1967," *New Middle East*, July 1969, p. 30.

32 MccGwire, *loc. cit., 1973*, p. 347; Polmar, *op. cit., 1974*, p. 73.

33 Blechman, *op. cit.*, p. 13, Table 4.

34 *Means of Measuring Naval Power with Special Reference to U.S. and Soviet Activities in the Indian Ocean*, prepared by the Foreign Affairs Division, Congressional Research Service, Library of Congress, May 12, 1974, p. 5.

35 *Ibid.*, p. 4, Table 1.

36 "Indian Ocean Security," *Bulletin of the Africa Institute of South Africa*, November 2, 1975, p. 45.

37 Robinson, *op. cit., 1971*, pp. 30-31.

YEAR: 1969

Infrastructure Development	De Facto *Stationing*

Warsaw Pact Subsystem

	It was announced in April that Marshal P. F. Batitsky, Commander-in-Chief of the Soviet National Aerospace Defense Forces, was also Commander of the Troops of Aerospace Defense of the Warsaw Pact countries. "This signified a marked improvement in the Soviet early warning antiaircraft capability."[8] The Czech Air Force has reportedly provided seven of its air bases for use by the Soviet Union. The Soviets stationed MIG-21s, Yak-28s, and Su-7s at the bases, which were also being used as terminals for air operations to and from the Balkan and Mediterranean areas.[9]

Middle East Subsystem

1. Moscow had reportedly sounded the Madrid government about the possibility of establishing a base on the tiny Mediterranean island of Alboran about 150 miles from Gibraltar and 250 miles from the American base at Rota. Earlier in the year, a shipping agreement was concluded between Spain and Russia which secured Spanish port facilities for Soviet ships in the port of Barcelona. The Russians originally requested Cadiz—just across the bay from the American Polaris submarine base at Rota. A fishing agreement concluded between the two countries permits use of the port of Santa Cruz de Tenerife in the Canary Islands as a refueling and supply base for the 200 Soviet trawlers operating off the coast of West Africa.[1] (In 1976, a high Spanish official complained that Soviet fishing trawlers based at Spain's Canary Islands were ranging as far south as Angola for electronic monitoring of US-backed forces fighting in the former Portuguese colony. The source said that Spanish intelligence had intercepted coded messages from trawlers off Morocco and the Spanish Sahara on the fighting there. The source made it clear that US intelligence was aware of the activities of trawlers in both areas of conflict.)[2] Note also that in mid-1969, Russia came out strongly in support of the Spanish claim to Gibraltar, even though this meant backing the Franco regime and quarreling with the under-

In January, the MIG-25 Foxbat was reported to be in Egypt.[10] "Since operations were short-lived, this was more than likely a desert operational test in anticipation of future full-squadron deployment."[11] The *Daily Telegraph* (July 24, 25, 1969) reported that Russia had recently deployed "several batteries" of SAMs in order to protect medium-range bombers bearing the insignia of the USSR and Egypt, which had been deployed in Algeria since March. The bombers had been originally based in Egypt, but had been sent to Algeria "after the Israeli forces demonstrated their ability to penetrate as far as the Nile." Algeria's official daily *El Moudjahid* denied the story, July 29, 1969. But the *Christian Science Monitor* (August 7, 1969) identified Batna and Laghouat, in Algeria, as the airfields the Soviet bombers were deployed in. (Note that an Algerian military delegation led by Major Abd-al-Kader Shabu, Secretary General of the Ministry of National Defense, flew to Moscow on April 28 and returned to Algiers on May 9. The delegation included the Commander of the Air Force, Captain A. Latreche, and the Commander-in-Chief of the Navy, Captain Ben Moussa. No results from the visit were announced either in Moscow or Algiers.)[12] Another source said that the Soviet Union "has, in several military airbases in the (Algerian) Sahara—Laghouat, Ouargla and Amguel—carried out

YEAR: 1969 (continued)

Infrastructure Development	De Facto *Stationing*
Middle East Subsystem	

ground Spanish Communist Party.[3] 2. Additional work on the existing Soviet-built port of Berbera in Somalia began in 1969, and the harbor was completed the same year.[4]

a lengthening of runways which the nature of Algeria's present air fleet hardly justifies. The Soviet Union would seem to have already taken possession of one of these bases."[13]

The *Jerusalem Post* (March 3, 1969), quoting NATO officials, said the average figure of 40 Soviet warships and at least ten submarines in the Mediterranean was to be compared with an average of 20 surface ships and three to four submarines before the Six-Day War. The build-up was both quantitative and qualitative, as some "very interesting and sophisticated" naval craft had been sent to the area since the beginning of 1969. The *Sunday Telegraph*, on March 9, 1969, reported that the first known visit of a Russian nuclear submarine to a non-Soviet port took place early in 1969 when an N-class submarine entered Alexandria harbor. The *New York Times*, on March 17, said that the visit was made in January for servicing. Soviet ship operating days in the Mediterranean totaled 14,000 for the year.[14] The *Daily Telegraph* (March 17, 1969) reported that an armored Soviet supply depot ship was based in Port Said, with five to eight other warships. The newspaper added that the Soviet fleet was making extensive use of the Bay of Salum, a sheltered deep-water anchorage near the Egyptian-Libyan border. In June, the Soviets had deployed a floating barracks machine shop in Alexandria, Egypt.[15]

Indian/Far East Subsystem	

1. Indian reports said in June that Soviet assistance had been promised to improve the port of Gwadar in West Pakistan, on the northern shore of the Gulf of Oman. These reports indicated that "India had challenged Russia to deny that Pakistan was to be supplied with Soviet submarines, and that Gwadar was to be developed as a base able to accommodate and service submarines of the Soviet fleet. The Soviet government denied any such intentions, but India recalled that Moscow had also previously denied any plans of arms to Pakistan and yet was now doing so."[5] According to some Pakistani diplomatic sources,

Soviet yearly ship operating days in the Indian Ocean totaled 3,688 (for surface combatants and auxiliaries),[16] and 1,138 for combatants only.[17] Australian Minister for External Affairs Mr. Freeth said in August that the Soviet flotilla in the Indian Ocean at no time consisted of more than 12 ships in all, including seven fighting vessels.[18]

YEAR: 1969 *(continued)*

Infrastructure Development	De Facto *Stationing*
India/Far East Subsystem	

Moscow would also like to establish a road link with the port of Gwadar by building a road through Baluchistan.[6]

2. There have been reports that Moscow sought permission to develop an island near Singapore for bunkering and supplying Soviet vessels, but this was refused; and that they were seeking to lease part of the naval base when the British finally left.[7]

Footnotes for Year 1969:

[1] *Foreign Report* (Economist), September 18, 1969, p. 5; November 20, 1969, p. 2.

[2] *Washington Post,* January 31, 1976.

[3] *Foreign Report* (Economist), July 17, 1969, p. 5.

[4] *African Review,* October 1972, p. 2; W. H. Lewis, "How a Defense Planner Looks at Africa," in H. Kitchen, ed., *Africa, From Mystery to Maze,* Lexington Books, Heath, Lexington, Massachusetts, 1976, p. 308.

[5] Millar, *op. cit.,* 1970, p. 16, fn. 30; van der Kroef, *loc. cit.,* p. 300; *Baltimore Sun,* July 12, 1969. Note the similarity between the Indian charges and reported Soviet activities in Vishakapatnam (see the 1968 table).

[6] A. H. Syed, *China and Pakistan, Diplomacy of an Entente Cordiale,* University of Massachusetts Press, Amherst, 1974, p. 48. See also the 1970 table.

[7] Millar, *op. cit.,* 1970, p. 2.

[8] W. F. Scott, "Soviet Aerospace Forces: Continuity and Contrast," *Air Force Magazine,* March 1976, p. 45.

[9] *Military Review,* September 1969, p. 106.

[10] US Department of State, "United Arab Republic," *Background Notes,* Publication No. 8152, US Government Printing Office. Washington, D.C., April 1971, p. 8.

[11] Hansen, *op. cit.,* pp. 31-32.

[12] *Arab Report and Record,* April 16-30, 1969, p. 158; May 1-15, 1969, p. 178.

[13] G. De Carmoy, "France, Algeria and the Soviet Penetration," *Military Review,* March 1970, p. 87.

[14] Blechman, *op. cit.,* p. 13, Table 4. In April, 65 Russian vessels assembled to monitor NATO's exercise *Dawn Patrol.* In August, 63 ships participated in large-scale Soviet exercises led by the helicopter carrier *Moskva.* With her in the Mediterranean were three cruisers, ten destroyers, eight escorts, eight landing ships, about 15 submarines, and the usual assortment of tenders, supply ships, and oilers. Fairhall, *op. cit.,* p. 218.

[15] Bell, *loc. cit.,* 1975, p. 404; A. Hottinger, "The Arab States on the Eastern Mediterranean," in *Military Forces and Political Conflicts in the Mediterranean,* Atlantic Paper No. 1, Atlantic Institute, Paris, January 1970, p. 37.

[16] *Means of Measuring Naval Power,* p. 4, Figure 1.

[17] "Indian Ocean Security," *loc. cit.,* p. 45.

[18] Millar, *op. cit.,* 1970, p. 2, fn. 2.

YEAR: 1970

Infrastructure Development	De Facto Stationing

Middle East Subsystem

1. Admiral of the Soviet Fleet Sergei G. Gorshkov visited Algiers between March 24-April 1, reportedly to seek facilities at Mers-el-Kebir. Algeria failed to grant any of the naval installations, but did authorize landing rights for naval reconnaissance aircraft[1]
2. In June, press reports indicated the Soviets were building a naval base or a port near Port Sudan (in Sudan), claiming that the new harbor was protected by SAM-2 missiles, a radar system, and a military airfield. Over 500 Russian experts were believed to be working on the base.[2]
3. In October, the Soviet Union and Turkey signed a road pact that allowed Soviet trucks to cross eastern Turkey on a 500-mile land route into Syria and Iraq. Some two months earlier, the Turkish press carried pictures of a Bulgarian truck loaded with Soviet military equipment (jeeps) on the way to Iraq.[3]
4. Construction of a Soviet base at Ras Banas on the Egyptian coast just north of the Sudanese border was also reported.[4] In November, reports indicated the Soviet Union was developing a deepwater naval base at Mersa Matruh, Egypt (150 miles from the Libyan border), intended for naval craft up to destroyer size.[5]

By the end of June, the Soviet Air Force had control over six airfields in Egypt: Aswan, Beni Suef (south of Cairo), Cairo West, Inshas (northeast of Cairo), Mansura, and Gianaklis (south of Alexandria). Some 20 Tu-16s (armed with Kelt air-to-surface missiles) and Il-38 maritime reconnaissance/ASW planes were operating from Egypt and performed missions over the US Sixth Fleet in the Mediterranean. Operating from Cairo West, these aircraft ranged as far as Malta. Recovering in Algeria, they could extend surveillance to the entire western Mediterranean.[8] By mid-year, the Soviets had three intelligence ships in the Mediterranean,[9] and the number of medium-size Polnocny-class amphibious craft was doubled to 12.[10] Soviet ship operating days in the Mediterranean for the year totaled 17,500.[11]

India/Far East Subsystem

1. On January 24, Japan and the Soviet Union concluded an agreement for the construction and modernization of a seaport on Wrangel Bay, near the town of Nakhodka (60 miles from Vladivostok).
2. After persistent pressure on Pakistan to close the US communication center at Bedaber near Peshawar (which accomplished its aim by 1968), the Russians by mid-year proposed to set up a radio relay communications center near the same area where the former American center was located.[6]
3. In July, Soviet engineers completed a strategic four-lane highway which runs through the mountains of northern Afghanistan. It could link Russia with the Indian Ocean provided Pakistan granted transit facilities.[7] On October 22, Sultan Mohammed Ghazi (President of Afghanistan's Civil Aviation Authority) stated (on his return from an official visit to the

By midyear, a regular deployment cycle was established in the Indian Ocean, with ships deploying from Vladivostok and spending about five months on station.[12] Soviet ship-days in the Indian Ocean (surface combatants and auxiliaries) numbered 3,579.[13] The redeployment of two Alligator LSTs from the west might have been associated with the provision of naval support facilities in the area. "It seems possible that the transfer of (these LSTs) . . . was exploited to deliver specialized equipment to the Indian Ocean, either because it was less suited for shipment by merchant ship or because of problems with unloading it away from the necessary port facilities . . . Both of these Alligators called at Somalia on arrival in the area. The first visited two ports (Kismayu and Mogadishu) and also called at Port Sudan and Vishakapatnam; the second visited Ber-

YEAR: 1970 (continued)

Infrastructure Development	De Facto Stationing

| *India/Far East Subsystem* ||

| USSR) that the Soviet Union had expressed its readiness to assist in building six airports in the Pamir region (northeast Afghanistan bordering on the USSR, China, and Pakistan). | bera and Aden. A 'freighting' task would provide a reason for the anomalous single Soviet naval visit to the Indian naval base at Vishakapatnam by an unimpressive pair of warships."[14] |

Footnotes for Year 1970:

[1] Whetten, *loc. cit.*, 1971, p. 16. Admiral Thomas H. Moorer, Chairman of the Joint Chiefs of Staff, said on February 24, 1970, at a Congressional hearing that the Soviets were "gradually edging their way westward" looking toward Malta and Algeria for ports of access. *Jerusalem Post,* April 23, 1970.

[2] Abir, *loc. cit.*, 1972, p. 28; *Time Magazine,* October 5, 1970, p. 33; *Times,* June 24, 1971; *Mid East Report,* New York, July 1, 1971, p. 15. According to one source, the Soviets had established air bases north and east of Khartoum, the Sudanese capital. *Neue Zurcher Zeitung,* December 6, 1970. As early as November 1968, there was speculation in the British press that Sudan had offered the Russian Navy the use of harbor and supply facilities at Suakin and Port Sudan. Van der Kroef, *loc. cit.*, p. 248. It was later reported, however, that the Soviet activity near Port Sudan had been terminated. See *Al Hawadeth,* June 3, 4, 1972.

[3] On the Soviet-Turkish road pact, see *New York Times,* October 21, 1970; *Sunday Times,* November 1, 1970. On overland transit of Soviet military aid to Iraq via Turkey, see *New York Times,* October 6, 1970; and *Middle East Intelligence Survey,* November 15, 1974, p. 126. Also *Middle East Record, 1969-70,* vols. 1-4, Shiloah Center for Middle Eastern and African Studies, Tel Aviv, 1977, p. 457.

[4] Wegener, *op. cit.*, p. 90, fn. 26.

[5] *Washington Post,* November 15, 1970; *Arab Report and Record,* April 16-30, 1971, p. 230; R. F. Pajak, "Soviet Arms and Egypt," *Survival,* July-August, 1975, p. 168; J. W. Lewis, *op. cit.*, p. 67. It was reported that the construction of the port had begun a year previously. Nominally, the port was to be under Egyptian control, but in fact the Soviets would operate it. US experts listed the following advantages to the Soviet Navy on having use of this port: avoidance of surveillance by foreign espionage services; inaccessability to air attack or reconnaissance by Israel; ability to repair in dry dock Soviet vessels capable of traversing the Suez Canal en route to the Indian Ocean; and proximity to Libya, which would be useful should the Soviets supply arms to that country. A disadvantage was that the port was within the range of the US Sixth Fleet air arm. *Le Monde,* November 17, 1970. *Al Akhbar* from Cairo denied the reports November 15, 1970.

[6] Choudhury, *loc. cit.*, 1974, pp. 110, 112-113, 114. Also *Foreign Report* (Economist), June 13, 1968, pp. 5-6.

[7] Z. Mustafa, "The 1971 Crisis in Pakistan: India, the Soviet Union and China," *Pacific Community,* April 1972, p. 513. V. Yeh, "Reopening of the Suez Canal and the New Situation in the Indian Ocean," *Asian Outlook,* March 1974, p. 10. Note that on January 28, 1971, Afghanistan and the Soviet Union signed an agreement under which Pakistan and the Soviet Union would be allowed road transit facilities through Afghanistan for their bilateral trade. It provided for the first time that goods could be transported through Afghanistan from the Soviet Union to Pakistan and vice versa. *Asian Almanac,* April 10, 1971, p. 4505. But, "since the highway's present traffic consists of goats, the assumption is that the Russians must have a military purpose in mind," *New York Times,* January 22, 1975. See also information contained in the 1968 table.

[8] *Washington Post,* February 6, 1970; April 29, 1970. *New York Times,* May 11, 1971; August 4, 1972. *Ha'aretz,* August 17, 1971. One source, quoting American intelligence circles, said that the Soviets also had a secret radar base west of Alexandria and made preparations to build missile sites capable of being used against vessels of the Sixth Fleet. *Ma'ariv,* June 9, 1975.

[9] *Ha'aretz,* August 21, 1971. One of these ships has been exclusively covering Israel. The former Commander of the Israel Navy, Rear Admiral Benyamin Telem, revealed during the 1975 Navy Day that the Soviet intelligence ship was still in position, usually 30 to 50 miles off the Israeli coast. He said it was capable of picking up all broadcasts made in the country. *Jerusalem Post Weekly,* June 17, 1975, p. 9. Further, *Ma'ariv* on April 26, 1976, said the Soviet spyship Krim, which usually cruised some 45 km. off the Israeli coast, had been sighted opposite the Lebanese coast by an Israeli naval patrol, its mission probably related to Syria's military intervention in the Lebanese civil war.

[10] Whetten, *op. cit.*, 1974, p. 393. The Polnocny-class landing ship has a capacity for a marine company and from eight to ten vehicles. Pritchard, *loc. cit.*, p. 21.

YEAR: 1970 (continued)

[11] Blechman, *op. cit.,* p. 13, Table 4.

[12] Mccgwire, *loc. cit.,* 1975, p. 528.

[13] *Means of Measuring Naval Power,* p. 4, figure 1. Considering combatant ships only and excluding auxiliaries, support ships, and mine clearing operations in Bangladesh, Russian ship-days in 1970 totaled 1,670. "Indian Ocean Security," *loc. cit.,* p. 45. Lord Balniel, Minister of State for Defense, told the House of Commons in November 1970 that at the time the Soviets had 21 ships in the Indian Ocean: seven surface ships, four submarines, and nine or ten auxiliaries. The UK Defense White Paper, issued on February 17, 1971, presented similar numbers for 1970. K. Subrahmanyam and J. P. Anand, "Indian Ocean as an Area of Peace," *Indian Quarterly, October-December* 1971, p. 294.

[14] M. Mccgwire, "The Pattern of Soviet Naval Deployment in the Indian Ocean, 1968-71," in Mccgwire, *op. cit.,* 1973, pp. 434-435.

YEAR: 1971

Infrastructure Development	De Facto Stationing
Middle East Subsystem	

1. A SEATO report issued on April 23 pointed out that the Russians were digging massive tunnels on the island of Socotra (PDRY). The report linked this activity with the probable construction of a Soviet radio station and ammunition depot.[1]

2. It was reported (and has never been denied by South Yemen) that the Soviet Union has the right to the use of Khormaskar and other airfields; and that Aden, "which has a Soviet harbormaster," marine engineers, and technicians, was an important servicing port for Soviet warships.[2] The *Los Angeles Times* (May 12, 1976) said the Soviets "have a naval base and an airfield in South Yemen . . . The Russians have between 2,000-5,000 men there, working in the Soviet military facilities and providing training and maintenance for the Yemeni forces. Sources said ships from the Soviet Indian Ocean fleet visit the South Yemen facility frequently, and Russian reconnaissance planes fly on patrol about twice a week from the city of Aden." Former South Yemeni Premier Muhammad Ali Hartan stated in an interview with *Al Gomhouria* (Cairo, August 12, 1976) that the Soviet Union has naval and air bases in South Yemen, including a major airfield in the Lahej region for long-range reconnaissance flights over the Indian Ocean and the Red Sea. Another source indicates that "Soviet military advisors are active down to the lowest level of command both in the (South Yemeni) Army and the Air Force."[3]

3. Soviet Defense Minister Marshal Grechko reportedly visited Russian military installations in Egypt during his June 10-13 tour of Soviet Mediterranean fleet units. "He particularly visited missile sites at Huwargatah, on the Red Sea, where a military base is under construction on Egyptian territory."[4]

4. Premier Kosygin discussed the extension of Soviet facilities in Algeria during his visit there early in October.[5] "Colonel Boumedienne rejected Russia's renewed requests for the use of Mers-el-Kebir . . . The Soviet Navy has bunkering, revictualling, and repair facilities at Annaba, Oran, and Algiers, but must

In April, it was disclosed that MIG-25 Foxbats with Soviet pilots had been stationed in Egypt.[11] Subsequent reports indicated that two of the Soviet-controlled air bases were being operated exclusively by the Soviet Naval Air Force. These were Aswan in the south and Mersa Matruh in the west (where 12 MIG-25s had reportedly been stationed).[12] Late in the year, Israel revealed that Soviet Yak-28 Brewer light bombers had been deployed in Egypt as well.[13] Further, electronically configured An-12 Cub-C transports and several Be-12 Mail amphibious patrol craft, all manned by Soviet crews, were located at bases in Egypt.[14] *Aviation Week and Space Technology* reported in April that the Soviets had moved approximately 15 MIG-25 fighters and a squadron of 9-18 Su-7 ground attack aircraft into Algeria under terms of a "new and hitherto secret military pact" between the two countries. "Soviet pilots flying the aircraft have free access to Algerian airfields under the agreement, which basically covers the use of the former French naval base at Mers-el-Kebir. Two Soviet submarines are based there. The agreement runs through 1988."[15] Other sources confirming the presence of Soviet MIG-25s in Algeria said the Soviet Air Force's bomber and transport aircraft reserve had been shifted from Algeria to Libya —possibly to the former US base at Wheelus.[16] A reliable source confirmed recently the use in the past of Libyan airfields, including the former US Air Force base at Wheelus, by Soviet strike aircraft.[17] Three Samlet naval surface-to-surface missile sites had been constructed around Alexandria (Egypt), where vessels of the Soviet Mediterranean fleet were constantly deployed.[18] Soviet ship-days in the Mediterranean totaled 19,000 for the year.[19]

YEAR: *1971 (continued)*

Infrastructure Development	De Facto *Stationing*
Middle East Subsystem	

make a specific request each time. The Soviet Air Force will continue to be able to fly submarine reconnaissance flights from the same airfields in Algeria where it is training the Algerian Air Force. . . . Civil aircraft flying from Algiers to Rabat or Casablanca must fly abeam the coast to the border to avoid fly-spying over these fields."[6]

5. After establishing a small naval base at Mersa Matruh on the Mediterranean 270 miles northwest of Cairo, the Soviets began dredging the harbor at Salum still farther west, near the Libyan border.[7] Refit and replenishment facilities were available in Alexandria and Port Said, and the Soviet fleet possessed its own fuel and supply depots. Soviet access to these two ports had been unrestricted.[8]

6. Soviet pressure on Yugoslavia for naval facilities was also reported.[9]

India/Far East Subsystem	

1. It was reported that civilian trawlers operating out of Port Louis (Mauritius) were serving fleet logistic purposes along with a Soviet LST. Currently, there is an understanding permitting Soviet technicians to use Mauritian yards for ship repair.[10]

In April, the US Department of Defense published a picture giving first confirmation of Soviet missile-submarine deployments in the Pacific Ocean.[20] An average of 283 Soviet warships, not including submarines, sailed through the Soya, Tsugaru, and Tsushima Straits each year since 1971. "Actually, the total number of Soviet warships passing through the Straits was far bigger if more than 100 submarines in the Soviet Pacific fleet are added to the above."[21] Soviet ship-days in the Indian Ocean totaled 3,804 (surface combatants and auxiliaries),[22] and 1,480 days for combatants only.[23] A typical deployment (until later in the year) comprised a destroyer, a landing ship, a submarine, and submarine escort, plus some six to seven auxiliaries. In December, however, in connection with the Indo-Pakistan War, this concentration had grown to include two cruisers, four destroyers, two minesweepers, four submarines, and a tank landing ship. Altogether, this force had 24 SSM launchers, and 12 SAM launchers[24]

Footnotes for Year 1971:
1 Subrahmanyam and Anand, *loc. cit.,* p. 206. Also A. Hottinger, "Ferment in the Persian Gulf," *Swiss Review of World Affairs,* February 1971, p. 15; Y. Wu, *Strategic Significance of Singapore,*

YEAR: 1971 (continued)

A Study in Balance of Power, American Enterprise Institute, Washington, D.C., 1972, p. 13. Note that while reporting the landing of Soviet marines on Socotra, the *Sunday Telegraph* on August 30, 1970, said they were to protect a radio station set up by the Soviets there.

[2] Abir, *loc. cit.*, 1972, p. 27; *Times*, December 16, 1970; *New York Times*, May 5, 1971; February 7, 1975. On Soviet assistance in managing the port of Aden, see also W. H. Lewis, *loc. cit.*, 1976, p. 308.

[3] Singh, *op. cit.*, p. 92.

[4] *Mid East Report*, July 1, 1971, p. 15. See also relevant information in 1972 table.

[5] Whetten, *loc. cit.*, 1971, p. 16.

[6] *Africa Confidential*, November 19, 1971, p. 5; and see below.

[7] *New York Times*, May 11, 1971. Salum was used as a port by the British Navy in World War II. See also item concerning Mersa Matruh in the 1972 table.

[8] *Strategic Survey, 1971*, International Institute for Strategic Studies, London, 1972, p. 32. Also *Economist*, July 22, 1972, p. 16. *Corriere della Serra's* special correspondent, who had observed the activities of Soviet vessels docked at Alexandria, said Soviet vessels have four berths "at their exclusive disposal which the Egyptians and others know they may not go near." Cited in *Ma'ariv*, May 20, 1969.

[9] *Ibid.*

[10] *Means of Measuring Naval Power*, p. 10; M. W. J. M. Broekmeijer, "The Future of Communism in South Asia," *Asia Quarterly*, no. 1, 1974, p. 62; *International Herald Tribune*, May 7, 1971.

[11] *New York Times*, April 11, 1971; *Times*, April 12, 1971; *Aviation Week and Space Technology*, April 19, 1971, p. 14; October 4, 1971, p. 11. One source claims the Foxbats began operating from Egypt on March 26, 1971. Hansen, *op. cit.*, p. 44.

[12] *Strategic Survey, 1971, op. cit.*, p. 32; Whetten, *loc. cit.*, 1971, p. 17; *New York Times*, May 11, 1971; *Daily Telegraph*, January 5, 1972. The Aswan base was used by the USSR for reconnaissance flights as far as the Indian Ocean. *Ha'aretz*, January 27, 29, 1972. The total number of MIG-25s stationed in Egypt at the time was put at 24. *Flight International*, April 20, 1972, p. 562. The remaining 12 operating from Cairo West airfield. Hansen, *op. cit.*

[13] Whetten, *loc. cit.*, 1971, p. 16. One source had put the number of the Yaks at ten. *Mid East Report*, March 1, 1972, p. 8.

[14] Pajak, *loc. cit.*, p. 168; N. Polmar, "Soviet Naval Aviation," *Air Force Magazine*, March 1976, pp. 71, 72; also p. 99.

[15] April 19, 1971, p. 14. According to the report, the MIG-25s were being airlifted to Egypt by An-22s, where they were assembled and flown by Soviet pilots to Algiers. See also relevant item in the 1970 table, and *Baltimore News-American*, October 22, 1975.

[16] *Africa Confidential*, November 19, 1971, p. 5.

[17] *Understanding Soviet Naval Developments*, pp. 7, 11; also Polmar, *op. cit.*, 1974, pp. 66-67. For analysis of the strategic significance involved in Soviet access to a network of airfields in Egypt, Algeria, and Libya; see comments of the Italian Air Force Chief of Staff, General Duilio S. Fanali, *Flight International*, January 14, 1971, pp. 69-70. For similar estimates, see Admiral Horacio Rivero, Commander-in-Chief of NATO forces in Southern Europe, in *Le Monde*, June 4, 1970; General Lyman L. Lemnitzer, Supreme Allied Commander, Europe, in *Ha'aretz*, May 15, 1969.

[18] Whetten, *op, cit.*, 1974, p. 163.

[19] Blechman, *op. cit.*, p. 13, Table 4.

[20] *Strategic Survey, 1971*, p. 86.

[21] *FBIS* (PRC), April 1, 1976, p. A3.

[22] *Maens of Measuring Naval Power*, p. 4, Figure 1.

[23] "Indian Ocean Security," *loc. cit.*, p. 45.

[24] See J. M. McConnell and A. M. Kelly, *Superpower Naval Diplomacy in the Indo-Pakistani Crisis*, Center for Naval Analyses, Arlington, Va., Professional Paper No. 108, February 1973.

YEAR: 1972

Infrastructure Development	De Facto *Stationing*

Warsaw Pact Subsystem

The Committee of Defense Ministers of the Warsaw Pact agreed in February to the formation of new military air-transport regiments in Poland, the GDR, Czechoslovakia, and Hungary. These regiments were to come directly under the Joint Command of the Pact.[1]

Middle East Subsystem

1. In February, Soviet Defense Minister Marshal Grechko visited Somalia for the signing of a Soviet-Somali agreement. Grechko agreed to improve the airstrip and the port at Berbera in return for future access to the new facilities. In addition, modernization projects began at the airfields at Hargeisa and Gallacio, and a new airfield was begun at Uanle Uen. Construction in Berbera began in October with work on three sections of a floating pier, a new POL storage tank farm, and a pipeline between the port and the site of the new military airfield.[2]

2. In March, the London *Times* reported Egypt had refused a request by the Soviet Union for a naval base on its Red Sea coast. In May, the same source said that Grechko was understood to have pressed the Egyptians for additional facilities for the Soviet Indian Ocean fleet along Egypt's Red Sea coast. *Al Akhbar* (Cairo, May 16, 1972) said that during the May Grechko visit, an agreement was reached concerning continued Soviet presence in Egyptian ports. It should be noted that in March, Egyptian sources announced that a new port was being built at Bernis (sheltered by Ras Banas), to be connected by a new road to Aswan. Reliable sources said the Russians were pressing also for permanent port facilities in general, and had announced their willingness to set up a sophisticated arms manufacturing plant in Egypt in exchange.[3]

3. On May 14, Soviet Defense Minister Grechko, on a visit to Syria, signed a military agreement. The Soviets were permitted to build naval facilities in two Syrian ports, Latakia and Tartus.[4] The Beirut daily *Al Nahar* reported[5] that Syria had agreed to let the Soviet Union use the Latakia port as "a main Mediterranean base." Cairo's *Middle East News*

Soviet ship-days in the Mediterranean totaled 18,000 for the year.[8] After their expulsion from Egypt, Soviet Tu-16s for reconnaissance operations against the US Sixth Fleet were transferred from Egypt to Syria.[9]

YEAR: 1972 (continued)

Infrastructure Development	De Facto Stationing

Middle East Subsystem

Agency reported on October 20 that shipping reaching Syria from the USSR had been diverted to the port of Tartus, instead of being accepted at Latakia according to normal practice for the past 16 years. The step was taken, the agency said, after recent press reports that Syria had agreed to let the USSR use Latakia as a "main Mediterranean base." A team of Soviet experts arrived in Latakia on June 29 to participate in an expansion plan of the Syrian harbor.[6]

India/Far East Subsystem

The Soviets are understood to have approached Taiwan for permission to use the Pescadores for refueling and repair purposes.[7]

From 1972, a larger number of Soviet ships were deployed in the Indian Ocean. The typical force consisted of five to six warships and eight to nine auxiliaries. Total number of ship-days (surface combatants and auxiliaries) reached 8,000.[10] Ship-days for combatants only totaled 2,387.[11] Australia's Foreign Minister Nigel Bowen stated in parliament on May 9: "The significance for us of the Russian presence in the Indian Ocean lies not so much in the actual number and power of Russian naval vessels there at any one time, as in the rapidly increasing capacity of the Soviet Union to place and sustain large naval forces of considerable power in the area very quickly. This capacity would, of course, be considerably augmented by the opening of the Suez Canal."[12]

Footnotes for Year 1972:

[1] D. Holloway, "The Warsaw Pact in the Era of Negotiations," *Military Review,* July 1973, p. 54.

[2] Bell, *loc. cit.,* 1975, p. 404; *Times,* May 18, 1972. Admiral Gorshkov, who accompanied Marshal Grechko during the May visit, "had revived the idea of our giving the Soviet Navy 'facilities' at Mersa Matruh and Bernis in the Red Sea. The Army and Navy were strongly opposed to the idea, but Admiral Gorshkov was very insistent, claiming that only with these facilities would the Soviet Navy be able to operate properly, and that it would enable them to give Egypt much better reconnaissance information, and so on." Heikal, *op. cit.,* p. 164.

[3] Hansen, *op. cit.,* pp. 48-49.

[4] Haselkorn, *loc. cit.,* p. 238, and references therein.

[5] August 27, 1972. Also *Arab Report and Record,* August 16-31, 1972, p. 419.

[6] *Mid East Report,* July 15, 1972, p. 12.

[7] On August 28, 1972, Chou En-lai held a four-hour talk with a group of Taiwanese scholars. In the talk, Chou praised Chiang's refusal to let the Russians use the Pescadores as a Soviet naval facility. He said this proves Chiang still possesses the basic independent nationalist spirit. C. L. Chiou, "Super Powers in the Taiwan Straits," *World Review,* October 1974, pp. 37-38; also *Far Eastern Economic Review,* June 11, 1973, p. 17.

[8] Blechman, *op. cit.,* p. 13, Table 4.

[9] J. D. Glassman, *Arms for the Arabs, The Soviet Union and War in the Middle East,* Johns Hopkins University Press, Baltimore, Maryland, 1975, p. 97.

[10] *Means of Measuring Naval Power,* p. 4.

[11] "Indian Ocean Security," *loc. cit.,* p. 45.

[12] *SEATO Record,* Bangkok, June 1972, p. 5.

YEAR: 1973

Infrastructure Development	De Facto *Stationing*

Warsaw Pact Subsystem

Since 1970, the number of tanks deployed in Warsaw Pact divisions has increased by 9,000. Almost 3,000 of them went to 15 Soviet motor rifle and 16 tank divisions stationed in East Europe, among them some 1,200 new T62s (to Soviet forces in East Germany, Czechoslovakia, and Poland). *Frankfurter Rundschau* said (February 17, 1973) that the Soviet Union has in fact moved 2,000 new tanks into East Germany in "recent months." The paper said the action had been detected by "Western intelligence services" and confirmed by the Defense Ministry in Bonn. Note that "the replaced equipment (T-54/T-55s) has not been withdrawn, but stored up."[7] The crews for these older armored fighting vehicles were retained. Western analysts concluded that the Soviets have been moving toward a dual basing system by which tanks are kept both in depots and in field storage. More than 4,000 new armored personnel carriers have been moved into Eastern Europe also, averaging 1,000 per year since late 1969. Conventional artillery has been substantially increased (the number of guns in divisions almost doubling), and more than 1,000 guns have been brought in since the beginning of 1973. Soviet forces in Germany were given further weapons and equipment sufficient for an extra company in each regiment. There has also been an expansion of the number of tactical aircraft obtaining in each air regiment, which follows the pattern of the ground forces in fitting out existing units with additional weapons or equipment. (See the 1974, 1975 tables.) Two squadrons of MIG-23s Flogger strike fighters were believed to be operational with Soviet forces in Germany.[8]

Middle East Subsystem

1. In January, Libyan President Qaddafi refused to permit the Soviet fleet to use the facilities that had been used by the US Sixth Fleet prior to the Libyan closing of US bases there. Qaddafi reportedly stated that such permission would merely have meant replacing the US fleet with the Soviet fleet.[1]
2. A July report originating in Beirut said the Russians were exerting pressure on

In February, a report quoting Western intelligence sources said the Soviets were keeping a large cache of MIGs and Sukhois in varying degrees of operational readiness in storage In Egypt, Syria, and Iraq.[9] On September 26, US Deputy Defense Secretary William Clements said that the Soviet Union had "put supersonic bombers in Iraq that were never there before."[10] Within a week, it be-

YEAR: 1973 (continued)

Infrastructure Development	De Facto Stationing

Middle East Subsystem

South Yemen to grant them naval facilities on the Mukalla coastline. Russian experts reportedly also examined the air strip at Ras Karma, near the former RAF barracks at Muri.[2]

3. Reports quoting NATO sources indicated Moscow was negotiating with Somalia about the accelerated expansion of Birikao harbor, approximately 137 miles east of Berbera. The sources added that the Soviets want to build submarine maintenance yards there.[3] Late in the year, construction of what has subsequently been identified as a missile storage and handling facility in Berbera had begun.[4]

4. In addition to the Umm Qasr facility, an ostensibly Iraqi base in the same port was being built under the supervision of Soviet technicians; and the nearby deepwater port of Basra has been used by a large Soviet Navy repair ship to support warships on patrol in the Persian Gulf and the Strait of Hormuz.[5]

came known that the Russians deployed about a Dozen Tu-22 Blinder medium bombers in Iraq. "This is the first time the bomber . . . has been deployed outside the Soviet Union or Eastern Europe."[11] Since the Yom Kippur War, Soviet-piloted MIG-25 Foxbats have been redeployed in Cairo West Airport.[12] Some sources had put the number of MIG-25s deployed there as high as two squadrons,[13] others at four, operating from Cairo West and Aswan.[14] By October 31, the Soviets had also boosted their Mediterranean fleet to 98 ships, including 29 combatants, 46 auxiliary support ships, and 23 submarines (compared to 43 surface ships plus 14 submarines they had on October 5). On November 1, the Russians reportedly requested that control of the Syrian naval bases of Latakia and Tartus should rest with the commander of the Soviet Mediterranean Fleet, and that the Jezirah airfield should also be under total Soviet authority.[15] In April, a press report quoting American military sources indicated that Somalia had agreed to allow Soviet use of staging, maintenance, and refueling facilities for "medium range jets" scheduled to operate from the Berbera airfield in return for Soviet agreement to expand and modernize that airport. Some 2,500 Soviet advisors and technicians were reportedly stationed in Somalia as well.[16]

India/Far East Subsystem

During Brezhnev's visit to India in November, the Indian press confirmed that the USSR had made a formal request for port facilities in that country.[6]

During the Yom Kippur War, the Kremlin (simultaneously with the concentration in the Mediterranean) had massed 30 ships in the Indian Ocean. "The concentration east of Suez has remained fairly constant ever since."[17]

Footnotes for Year 1973:

[1] Radio Moscow, January 17, 1973, cited in R. E. Kanet, "The Soviet Role in the Middle East," in B. W. Eissenstat, ed., *The Soviet Union, The Seventies and Beyond*, Heath, Lexington, Mass., 1975, p. 309; *Arab Report and Record*, January 1-15, 1973, p. 12.

[2] *News Review on South Asia*, August 1973, p. 97. Since 1971, there has been a growing Soviet presence and activity in the port of Mukalla, South Yemen. Abir, *op. cit.*, 1974, p. 125.

[3] *Military Review*, August 1973, p. 93. Another source said some Komar-type missile boats were transferred from the USSR to Somalia in 1973-74 in exchange for use of port facilities at Birikao. *Warship International*, no. 2, 1974, p. 160. Soviet development of port facilities at Birikao was already reported in late 1972. *African Review*, October 1972, p. 2.

[4] Statement by US Secretary of Defense James R. Schlesinger, *Disapprove Construction Projects on the Island of Diego Garcia*, p. 7.

[5] Zumwalt, *op. cit.*, p. 362.

[6] Haselkorn, *loc. cit.*, p. 251, and references therein. *New York Times*, November 29;

YEAR: 1973 (continued)

December 7, 12, 1973. *Christian Science Monitor,* November 28, 1973. Note also the coincidence of Brezhnev's visit to Delhi (November 26-30, 1973) with the visit of a Russian delegation headed by Secretary of the General Committee Ponamarev to Iraq during the period November 27-30.

⁷ Admiral Armin Zimmerman, Inspector General of the Bundeswehr, quoted in *Intelligence Digest,* March 1, 1975, p. 2; *The Military Balance, 1973-1974,* International Institute for Strategic Studies, London, 1973, p. 6; *Frankfurter Allgemeine Zeitung,* April 21, 1973.

⁸ Data derived from J. Erickson, "Soviet Combat Force on Continent Grows," *NATO Review,* June 1974, pp. 18-21; J. Erickson, "MBFR: Force Levels and Security Requirements," *Strategic Review,* Summer 1973, pp. 32-36; which claim that, in fact, *additional* T55s were moved up to storage areas in Eastern Europe. C. G. Jacobsen, "The Emergence of a Soviet Doctrine of Flexible Response?" *Atlantic Community Quarterly,* Summer 1974, pp. 235-236. *Aviation Week and Space Technology,* March 26, 1973, p. 11; November 12, 1973, pp. 12-13; *New York Times,* April 6, 1973; *Intelligence Digest,* April 1, 1975, pp. 4-5. Note the *multioptional* character of the Warsaw Pact's dual basing system (and other "oversupplies" which result from equipment augmentations not accompanied by corresponding personnel increases). Such stocks would be essential in contingencies of logistic support for other parts of the Soviet collective security system as well—for example, the Middle East. Indeed, on October 12 (during the Yom Kippur War), US intelligence authorities detected a huge movement of Soviet rail traffic in Eastern Europe moving to the *east*—away from Soviet bases in Central Europe. At the time of the movement, it was not clear to US officials whether Moscow was moving material from stockpiles in Central Europe to resupply Arab forces, or moving it to airports to support an airborne intervention. *New York Times,* October 30, 1973. Within one month, Russia had replaced 2,500 tanks the Arabs lost during the war with 2,600 new ones. Moscow also brought in replacements for 400 airplanes. (Former Israeli Defense Minister Moshe Dayan in *Los Angeles Times.* April 17, 1975.) It is difficult to estimate what portion of these tanks had come from Soviet production, estimated by Dayan and Secretary of Defense Schlesingr at 3,000 per year (*Ma'ariv,* December 27, 1974; *Christian Science Monitor,* August 4, 1975;) and which from Warsaw Pact stocks. But there is little doubt that the latter played a significant part in it.

⁹ *Aviation Week and Space Technology,* February 5, 1973, p. 28; November 19, 1973, p. 15.

¹⁰ *Daily Telegraph,* October 3, 1973.

¹¹ *New York Times,* October 3, 1973; January 25, 1974; *Aviation Week and Space Technology,* October 8, 1973, p. 11. The bombers have remained under Soviet control and are piloted by Soviet pilots. Glassman, *op. cit.,* p. 116. For an analysis of this deployment's multioptional character, see Haselkorn, *loc. cit.,* pp. 241-242.

¹² *Aviation Week and Space Technology,* November 5, 1973, p. 12.

¹³ G. Golan, "Soviet Aims and the Middle East War," *Survival,* May-June, 1974, p. 112.

¹⁴ *Washington Post,* February 9, 1975. Some sources reported that at least three MIG-25s which were being operated in Syria, "and a number of MIG-25s stationed in Egypt, all flown by Soviet pilots, alternated between airfields in both Syria and Egypt." *Intelligence Digest,* December 1974, p. 5; also *Christian Science Monitor,* June 26, 1975; F. W. Voss, "Moglichkeiten der Arabischen Staaten un einem Neuer Nahostkrieg," *Wehrkunde,* September 1975, p. 456. Israeli sources were reported to have identified an airfield 175 miles northeast of Damascus as the one from which the Foxbats were operating. *Air Enthusiast,* Kent, England, March 1972, p. 107. Recent reports have indicated, however, that the MIG-25s were withdrawn from Egypt after a Russian refusal to share control over their missions with Cairo (*Economist,* July 26, 1975, p. 46; *Sunday Times* quoted in *Ma'ariv,* July 27, 1975; *Middle East Economic Digest,* August 1, 1975, p. 7). *Christian Science Monitor,* August 7, 1975, reported, however, that the Russian-piloted MIGs had resumed their flights over the Sinai and the eastern Mediterranean on intelligence-gathering missions. On September 15, President Sadat in a speech before the membership of the Arab Socialist Union, claimed four MIG-25s stationed in Egypt had refused to fly anywhere near the Sinai. Therefore, he had come to the conclusion, he said, that the planes which were being flown by Russian pilots were in Egypt for reasons which had nothing to do with Egyptian security. For this reason, he had grounded the planes and they were withdrawn "three days ago," he added. *New York Times,* September 16, 1975. According to the paper, Communist bloc sources were responsible for the reports circulating two months earlier saying the planes were withdrawn at that time. *Baltimore Sun,* September 23, 1975, reported that three An-22 transports had been engaged in moving the MIG-25s and their support equipment and crews since September 13. The removal of the planes from Egypt was also confirmed by the Chief of the Israeli Air Force, Major General Peled. *Ma'ariv,* October 26, 1975.

¹⁵ *Afro-Asian Affairs* (London), August 27, 1975, p. 1.

¹⁶ *New York Times,* April 9, 1974.

¹⁷ *Means of Measuring Naval Power,* p. 9. *Los Angeles Times,* July 13, 1975. The extra ships included a cruiser (with SSMs and SAMs), one destroyer (SSMs and SAMs), two destroyers, three submarines (one nuclear), two supply ships, and one oiler. *SIPRI Yearbook, 1975,* p. 69.

YEAR: 1974

Infrastructure Development	De Facto Stationing

Warsaw Pact Subsystem

	The Soviet Army, which has been stationed in Hungary since 1956, has had reinforcements added to its two armored divisions, two motorized infantry divisions, and its Air Force division of 70,000 men. During the Yom Kippur War, Soviet Army units were reportedly transferred from their usual stations near Odessa to the Bratislava district. When orders to enter the war did not materialize, they were stationed along a possible invasion route towards Yugoslavia. At least eight armored and motorized divisions took up positions in South Hungary at Nagykanisza and Baja.[23] In July, during the Cyprus crisis, 2,000 Soviet military personnel in civilian clothes crossed Rumania into Bulgaria, and about 500 Soviet aircraft landed at staging bases in South Hungary, according to senior Greek defense sources.[24] Note that the US Defense Department reported July 19 that the Soviet Union had placed seven airborne divisions on alert.[25] (An *AFP* dispatch from Athens said July 21 that Bulgarian troops were massing along the northern border of Greece.) In mid-September, the Austrian press reported the movement of the equivalent of five Soviet divisions (60,000 men) into Hungary from East Germany and Czechoslovakia at a time of internal tension in Yugoslavia.[26]

Middle East Subsystem

1. Three new Syrian airfields were being constructed with Soviet assistance at Abu a-Dubor, Sueda, and Sarat. The perimeters of existing airbases have been hardened by building concrete shelters for combat aircraft.[1] On June 18, Syria and the Soviet Union signed an agreement to expand the Syrian port of Latakia. It was reported that Moscow would start work before the end of the year, and that the project included the extension of the existing breakwater by about 700 meters and the construction of another harbor with berths totaling 1,700 meters in length. In 1975, it was reported that Russian personnel were also employed in the expansion of port facilities at Tartus, Syria.[2] Subsequently, the Russians were reported to be pressing Syria

In addition to four brigades of Scud-B SRBMs which have been stationed in Egypt under Soviet control since the Yom Kippur War, it was revealed in January that Scud missiles were stationed in Syria under similar arrangements.[27] Western intelligence sources in the Emirate of Oman reported late in the year that Soviet Tu-20 Bear aircraft based in Iraq were flying reconnaissance missions over the Strait of Hormuz and Oman.[28] The Cyprus crisis of July found the Soviet Union at a numerical disadvantage in the Mediterranean. Moscow had only 12 major combatants—guided missile cruisers, destroyers, and a helicopter carrier. There were also 38 minor war vessels and support ships in the squadron. Reports from London indi-

YEAR: 1974 (continued)

Infrastructure Development	De Facto *Stationing*
Middle East Subsystem	

for greater use of its ports of Latakia and Tartus. "The Soviet request to expand its use of Syrian ports . . . was believed to have been broached . . . during a May 1976 visit of a delegation headed by (S.) Skachkov, Chairman of the Soviet State Committee for Foreign Economic Relations. Although a civilian, he was met and later seen off at the airport by General Mustafa Tlass, Syrian Defense Minister. It had been learned the Soviet delegation visited Tartus and Latakia."[3]
2. In September, General Viktor Kulikov, Chief of the General Staff of the Soviet armed forces, visited Yugoslavia. It is understood the visit was connected with possible Russian naval facilities in Yugoslavia (possibly in the harbor at Kotor). The Belgrade government "is seeking a formula whereby some facilities can be given to the USSR in the Adriatic without jeopardizing Yugoslav nonalignment."[4] Russian submarines were observed entering and leaving the Yugoslav submarine base at Split from September 1973 to March 1974, "but whether Split may be regarded as a Russian base remains an open question."[5] In 1975, it was revealed that a Soviet submarine tender and submarine of the F-class underwent repairs in Tivat, Yugoslavia, "an event made possible by the 1974 Yugoslav port rights law permitting foreign naval vessels to be repaired in its ports."[6] Late in 1975, a large Soviet floating drydock was delivered to that port, "enhancing the capabilities for support of the Mediterranean Eskadra."[7] On November 16, 1976, in private talks with President Tito, Brezhnev had asked for an increase in servicing of Soviet warships at Adriatic ports. The request, however, was rejected. Further, Tito was said to have rejected a Brezhnev request to permit Soviet airplanes to enter Yugoslav airspace unless a third country friendly to Belgrade asked for it.[8]
3. In September, President Ford revealed the Soviets had three bases in the Indian Ocean: Aden in South Yemen, Umm Qasr in Iraq, and Berbera in Somalia.[9] In earlier testimony, Admiral Zumwalt revealed the Soviets were engaged in building a new military airfield near

cated, however, that reinforcements were on their way from the fleet base at Sevastopol, in the Crimea. A Soviet flotilla of cruisers and destroyers had been detected, apparently by patrol aircraft, in Cypriot waters.[29] Pentagon spokesman W. Beecher noted the movement of several Soviet cruisers and destroyers toward Cyprus July 15.

YEAR: 1974 (continued)

Infrastructure Development	De Facto Stationing
Middle East Subsystem	

Mogadishu, Somalia.[10] In November, *Aviation Week and Space Technology*[11] gave the following details on Soviet-used facilities in the Indian Ocean: Hudeida—"A base that will take submarines and guided missile destroyers. The Russians have constructed two berths and two more are being built. The approach channel is being dredged to 28 ft. depth." In Aden, the Soviets were believed about to supply a medium-sized floating dock. Umm Qasr in Iraq will take cruisers of 6,000 tons. The Soviets have use of facilities at Vishakapatnam (also *Indonesian Times,* December 7, 1974) and Vizianagaram, both in India. Logistic facilities were in use at Port Louis, Mauritius, and tank farms at Berbera, "the center of Soviet activity in the Indian Ocean," Kismayu, and Mogadishu in Somalia.

4. Reports asserted a Soviet intention to acquire anchorage facilities at Larnaca (Cyprus) following a visit there in November of a squadron belonging to the Soviet Black Sea Fleet.[12]

5. It is understood that Russia's mine-sweeping fleet in the Red Sea (clearing the southern approaches to the Suez Canal) had been laying detection devices on the seabed to monitor ship movements.[13]

6. In December, Beirut's *Al Nahar* reported that Moscow had offered Egypt MIG-25s and advanced versions of SAMs, but had tied the offer to a return of Soviet military experts.[14] Indeed, a Soviet contingent which arrived in Egypt during the winter to assemble MIG-25s had reportedly tried to set up a Soviet enclave again at the Mersa Matruh air base.[15] Israeli sources said that Soviet Foreign Minister Gromyko told Egyptian President Sadat in their talks of February 1975 that aircraft and other advanced weapons systems would be provided only if Soviet military personnel were readmitted. According to the sources, the Soviet offer remains open.[16]

7. Political observers in contact with the PAIGC—the African Party for the Independence of Guinea-Bissau and the Cape Verde Islands—have constantly maintained that the party has a secret

YEAR: 1974 (continued)

Infrastructure Development	De Facto *Stationing*

Middle East Subsystem

agreement with the Soviet Union to grant it a base in Bissau and in the Cape Verde Islands in return for Moscow's support of the guerrilla movement.[17]

(The *London Daily Mail* reported in January 1976 that the Soviet Union was bargaining with Guinea's President Sekou Touré to set up a naval base off the West Africa coast, presumably on Tamara.[18] *New York Times,* January 19, 1976, reported a Russian offer to build a naval base on Tamara Island in Guinea, "where the Soviets already operated an airfield. Long-range bombers and reconnaissance aircraft regularly fly out of Guinea to patrol the South Atlantic." According to the paper, President Touré of Guinea was informed by the Soviet Union that it would build the naval base for his government, provided Soviet naval units could retain part of it for their exclusive use.)

India/Far East Subsystem

1. On January 20, a Chinese attack drove South Vietnamese forces off the Paracel Islands in the South China Sea. "Peking may have wanted to reassert its own claim (to the islands) partly out of fear that in the event of Hanoi acquiring control over South Vietnam, it might allow the Soviet Union a base on the islands in accordance with Moscow's slogan of Asian 'collective security.' "[19]

2. In mid-March, Brezhnev, in a speech at Alma Ata, revived plans for a second Siberian rail connection: The Baikal-Amur Magistral (BAM) started from Tayshet by forced labor before World War II. The BAM should extend about 2,000 miles from Ust'Kut to Komsomol'skna-Amure, where there are connections to Khabarovsk and Vladivostok. It would provide an east-west transport route deeper in the Siberian interior, and thus a safe back-up to the exposed and over-loaded Trans-Siberian Railroad close to the Chinese border.[20] Note that early in the Japanese-Soviet negotiations over Japan's participation in the Tyumen oil project, "the Soviet Union at first insisted that Japan should finance a pipeline along the Sino-Soviet frontier as part of the project and then shifted its position

In January, the Soviet garrison in Mongolia was reportedly increased from two to five divisions and reinforced with up-to-date armor-like T62 tanks and added SAM batteries.[30] Between 30,000 and 50,000 Soviet troops were thus estimated to have been stationed in Mongolia.[31] Further, in mid-1976, the Soviet Union reportedly moved part of a third tank division into the area around Bulgan, in Mongolia, about 50 miles from the Chinese border.[32] Between April and mid-June, the Japanese Maritime Self-Defense Force reportedly sighted 30 Soviet destroyers, submarines, and cruisers in the Tsugaru and Tsushima Straits. Soviet naval order-of-battle in the Pacific was estimated at more than 100 submarines, of which 18 to 20 were nuclear-powered and 62 diesel-powered attack submarines. There were one Kresta-I, two Kresta-II, and two Kynda-class guided missile cruisers. In addition, the Soviet Pacific Fleet had five Kashin, one Kanin, and two Kotlin destroyers, all equipped with guided missiles. Other Soviet destroyers and destroyer escorts numbered about 40—in all, over 52 major Soviet combat ships in the Pacific Fleet.[33] In February, reports said the Soviet Kresta-II-class cruiser

YEAR: 1974 (continued)

Infrastructure Development	De Facto Stationing
India/Far East Subsystem	

and insisted on double tracking of the Trans-Siberian Railway. China reacted strongly to the construction of either a pipeline or a double tracking of the railway along the frontier with its major enemy, and the Japanese felt that a project which would increase Soviet military and naval capabilities in the Far East would be bad for Japan as well as for China."[21]

3. In June, a South African newspaper reported Mauritius was to provide a naval base to Russia in the terms of a secret agreement between the two parties.[22]

Marshal Voroshilov, a destroyer, and a supply ship, were en route to the Indian Ocean and may become attached to the Aden base.[34] In July, the Russians introduced for the first time into the Indian Ocean the 18,000-ton helicopter carrier *Leningrad*.[35] On November 12, Australian Defense Minister Barnard gave the following information about the Soviet naval presence in the Indian Ocean between August 1973 and November 1974: four cruisers (including the helicopter cruiser *Leningrad*), eight destroyers, four diesel-powered submarines, two landing ships, 29 auxiliaries, and 29 miscellaneous vessels employed in minesweeping operations in Bangladesh and the Red Sea. Among the auxiliaries, there was one intelligence-gathering vessel stationed in the Persian Gulf. The average length of stay has now risen from five to six months to one year.[36] Soviet ship-days in the Indian Ocean totaled 7,662 for the year.[37]

Footnotes for Year 1974:

[1] *Air Enthusiast International*, April 1974, p. 155.

[2] *FBIS* (Middle East and North Africa), June 19, 1974, p. H2; *Middle East Economic Digest*, February 28, 1975, p. 19; Admiral Means Johnston, Jr., Commander-in-Chief, Allied Forces Southern Europe, "The Southern Flank of NATO: Problems of the Southern Region in the Post-Yom Kippur Period," *Journal of the Royal United Services Institute for Defence Studies*, June 1975, p. 20; *Tass*, December 14, 1975.

[3] *Boston Globe*, May 24, 1976.

[4] *Intelligence Digest*, November 1974, pp. 4-5.

[5] L. Griswold, "Base Necessities: The World Lineup," *Sea Power*, August 1974, p. 19.

[6] Johnston, *loc. cit.*, p. 23. J. W. Lewis, *op. cit.*, p. 67; *Christian Science Monitor*, April 7, 1976. See also S. Clissold, *Yugoslavia and the Soviet Union*, Conflict Studies No. 57, Institute for the Study of Conflict, London, April 1975, p. 12. Note that with facilities in Italy and (at least until recently) in Greece, US Sixth Fleet need for Yugoslav facilities is minimal, a fact Belgrade is obviously well aware of. The former US Chief of Naval Operations, Admiral Zumwalt, repeatedly implied that the Soviets were also using Yugoslav airfields. *Wall Street Journal*, July 1, 1975; interview with *San Diego Union*, September 21, 1975.

[7] Manthorpe, *loc. cit.*, p. 208. The Soviet Mediterranean flagship *Zhdanov* made port calls in Split during March.

[8] S. S. Stanovic, "Yugoslav-Soviet Relations Following Brezhnev's Visit," *Radio Free Europe Research*, Background Paper No. 43, February 28, 1977, p. 3; *Sueddeutsche Zeitung*, December 14, 1976; *New York Times*, December 19, 1976. Yugoslavia permitted Soviet aircraft to fly over its territory to deliver weapons to Angola in 1975. Note *Al Ahram*, May 19, 1972, reported that Yugoslav President Tito told President Sadat "in a recent message" that in the event of a new war in the Middle East, Yugoslavia "will open its door wide to Soviet military supplies going to Egypt." A Yugoslav government spokesman on June 1 denied the *Al Ahram* story (*Arab Report and Record*, June 1-15, 1975, p. 276). But Yugoslavia's conduct during the October 1973 war indicated the *Al Ahram* report might have been accurate: a land link was established from Hungary to the Yugoslav port of Rijeka in order to sealift heavy equipment, including tanks, to the Middle East. Also, a Soviet air transport unit of approximately 30 aircraft was reportedly moved from Prague to Belgrade to support a possible Soviet airborne intervention in the late phases of the war. Haselkorn, *loc. cit.*, pp. 234-235.

YEAR: 1974 (continued)

⁹ Haselkorn, *loc cit.*, p. 250; *New York Times*, September 1, 1974. It is estimated that the port of Berbera, which is defended by SAM sites, allows for the accommodation of ships up to 12,000 tons. R. M. Burrell, "The USSR and the Indian Ocean," *Soviet Analyst*, January 31, 1974, p. 5. *Middle East Intelligence Survey* reported that seven Soviet military missions have secretly visited South Yemen and Somalia since November 1973. One of them included top-level naval engineers, who looked into the possibilities of expanding the two countries' port facilities. Cited in *Defense and Foreign Affairs Daily*, June 11, 1974.

¹⁰ Statement in *Proposed Expansion of US Military Facilities in the Indian Ocean*, Hearings before the Subcommittee on the Near East and South Asia, House Committee on Foreign Affairs, 93rd Congress, 2nd Session, March 20, 1974, p. 139; *Christian Science Monitor*, March 5, 1974.

¹¹ November 25, 1974, p. 22.

¹² A. O. Ghebhardt, "Soviet and US Interests in the Indian Ocean," *Asian Survey*, August 1975, p. 682. Greek Cypriot Interior and Defense Minister Veniamin went to Moscow at the invitation of the Soviet Defense Minister, Marshal Grechko. *Impact International*, May 23-June 12, 1975, p. 7.

¹³ *Army Quarterly and Defence Journal*, October 1974, p. 625. For a general discussion, see C. C. Peterson, *The Soviet Union and the Reopening of the Suez Canal, Mineclearing Operations in the Gulf of Suez*, Professional Paper No. 137, Center for Naval Analyses, Arlington, Va., June 1975.

¹⁴ Quoted in *Washington Post*, December 28, 1975, p. 7.

¹⁵ *Aviation Week and Space Technology*, July 7, 1975, p. 7.

¹⁶ *New York Times*, February 8, 20, 1975.

¹⁷ *To the Point International* September 7, 1974, p. 23; also *Daily Telegraph*, January 24, 1972; *Christian Science Monitor*, March 5, 1975. During Soviet naval exercise *Okean-75*, a group of Krivak destroyers exercised north of the Cape Verde Islands with the apparent mission of interdicting northbound surface shipping into the Mediterranean and European waters with its SSN-10 cruise missiles, and conducting ASW operations against NATO defensive activities. L. L. Whetten, "Recent Developments in the Soviet Navy," in L. L. Whetten, ed., *The Future of Soviet Military Power*, Crane, Russak, New York, 1976, p. 107.

¹⁸ Cited in *Christian Science Monitor*, January 13, 1976. Note that in 1971, US intelligence services reported that Soviet naval warships were seen off the coast of Guinea, and appeared to be stationed there permanently. *Le Monde*, October 14, 1971; *Africa Research Bulletin*, October 1-21, 1971, p. 2268. For subsequent reports, see *New York Times*, December 16, 1973; *Daily Telegraph*, March 25, 1974. For Soviet denials, see *Tass*, January 31, 1974.

¹⁹ Hinton, "The United States and the Sino-Soviet Confrontation," *Orbis*, Spring 1975, p. 27. For Soviet reaction to the attack see *New York Times*, February 10, 1974; *Christian Science Monitor*, February 19, 1974. On recent polemics between North Vietnam and Communist China regarding the offshore islands, see *Los Angeles Times*, December 7, 1975; *Baltimore Sun*, December 23, 1975.

²⁰ E. Kux, "Strategic Railway in Siberia," *Swiss Review of World Affairs*, June 1974, pp. 17-18; V. Conolly, "The Second Trans-Siberian Railway," *Asian Affairs*, London, February 1975, pp. 23-29; *Times*, October 4, 1974; *New York Times*, November 17, 1974. For some estimates of the load on the existing Trans-Siberian line in case of a Sino-Soviet war, see D. C. MacCaskill, "The Soviet Union's Second Front: Manchuria," *Marine Corps Gazette*, January 1975, p. 24; J. A. G. Kielmansegg, "War or Peace in the Far East?" *Aussen Politik*, English edition, April 1974, p. 443.

²¹ W. J. Barnds, "Japan and Its Mainland Neighbors: An End to Equidistance?" *International Affairs*, January 1976, p. 33. The proposals concerning Japanese participation in the development of the Tyumen oil fields and construction of a 6,660 km. pipeline from Anzhero Sudzhensk to the port of Nakhodka were tabled by the USSR as early as at the first session of the Joint Japan-Soviet Economic Committee in March 1966. Saeki, *loc. cit.*, pp. 7-8. Recent reports say the Soviets have been putting great efforts in developing the naval base at Korsakov in Sakhalin Island, and the submarine base at Sovetskaia on the mainland, to enable the Soviet Pacific Fleet to disperse. In addition, a new "Summer" base is reportedly being built in the north at Petropavlovsk Kamchatsky. *Daily Telegraph*, May 17, 1976. The Japanese *Sekai Shuho* (World Weekly) noted in an article on March 23, 1976, that the Soviet Union has set up a series of naval and air force bases in the Far East with Vladivostok as the center and fanning out to Alexandrovsk, Sakhlinsk, and Korsakov as well as Kunashiri and Etorofu Islands, "which are Japan's inherent territory." *FBIS* (PRC), April 1, 1976, p. 43.

²² *Sunday Times*, Johannesburg, June 23, 1974. Albania's ATA quoted an AFP dispatch as saying Moscow had reached an agreement with Mauritius to establish a Soviet naval base there in an exchange for economic and military aid to the island. "This effort of the Soviet Union," ATA added, "is done after its continuous demands to ensure from India the right of the stay of Soviet ships in the ports of that country . . ." *FBIS* (Eastern Europe), June 17,

YEAR: 1974 (continued)

1974, p. B1. There were reports of overtures made by Moscow for a base on the uninhabited Mauritian dependency of St. Brandon. According to these, the Russians also wanted landing rights for military aircraft and a tracking station. *To the Point International,* February 8, 1975, p. 35; also *African Review,* June 1970, p. 10; *Foreign Report* (Economist), June 11, 1970, pp. 7-8. Other sources characterized the Mauritian stance as an "open port" policy in which the island plays host to the warships of one or another great power. *Washington Post,* September 12, 1975; interview with Mauritian Premier Ramgoolam, *To the Point International,* June 28, 1975, p. 30. Thus, on December 5, 1972, Premier Ramgoolam declared that Mauritius would offer naval facilities to Iran. (S. Chubin, "Naval Competition and Security in South-West Asia," in *Power at Sea, III: Competition and Conflict,* Adelphi Paper No. 124, International Institute for Strategic Studies, London, Spring 1976, p. 25; Singh, *op. cit.,* p. 144; Adie, *op. cit.,* 1975, pp. 24-25; *Far Eastern Economic Review,* June 4, 1973, p. 15; May 27, 1974, p. 30.) One source said recently France has asked for naval facilities in the island and might sign a defense treaty with Mauritius. *Army Quarterly and Defence Journal,* July 1975, p. 362.

[23] *To the Point International,* July 27, 1974, p. 20.

[24] *Christian Science Monitor,* December 27, 1974.

[25] *Facts on File,* July 27, 1974, p. 591. *Tass* denied the story on July 21.

[26] Erickson, *loc. cit.,* 1975, p. 69, fn. 8.

[27] Admiral Thomas H. Moorer, Chairman, Joint Chiefs of Staff, on NBC's "Today" show, cited in *Christian Science Monitor,* January 11, 1974; UPI dispatch from London, January 8, 1974. On Soviet control over Egyptian Scuds, see Haselkorn, *loc. cit.,* p. 237; *New York Times,* October 19, 1973. Another source claims that "though partially serviced and operated by Soviet personnel, the Scuds had been placed under Egyptian operational control." Glassman, *op. cit.,* p. 113. But he, too, is of the opinion that the actual firing of the missiles could not have been done without Soviet authorization. *Ibid.,* p. 138, 159-160.

[28] *Washington Post,* December 17, 1974. The Soviet military designation for this aircraft is Tu-20. US publications generally identify the Bear as the Tu-95, which is the Tupolev design bureau designation.

[29] *New York Times,* July 18, 1974.

[30] Chaplin, "The Sino-Soviet Conflict: How Soon?" *Journal of the Royal United Services Institute for Defence Studies,* September 1974, p. 55. Neville Maxwell (*Washington Post,* November 25, 1974), citing Chinese sources, claims that three times during 1974 the United States had warned Peking that an attack by the Soviet Union appeared imminent. Such warnings, he claims, were received in April, June, and mid-August, and drew on satellite intelligence. (For earlier claims that the United States was supplying China with intelligence about Soviet dispositions and movements along the border, including photographs from American satellites, see H. Gelber, *Nuclear Weapons and Chinese Policy,* Adelphi Paper No. 99, International Institute for Strategic Services, London, 1973, p 35.)

[31] W. R. Heaton, "Mongolia at Fifty," *Pacific Affairs,* Winter 1974-75, p. 494.

[32] *Aviation Week and Space Technology,* June 14, 1976, p. 13.

[33] R. A. Kilmarx, *Soviet-United States Naval Balance,* Center for Strategic and International Studies Report, Georgetown University, Washington, D.C., April 1, 1975, pp. 130, 149-150; *FBIS* (Asia and Pacific), April 12, 1976, p. C3.

[34] *Defense and Foreign Affairs Daily,* February 15, 1974.

[35] *Intelligence Digest,* November 1974, p. 5.

[36] *SIPRI Yearbook, 1975,* p. 70; J. Meister, "Spotlight on the Indian Ocean," *Swiss Review of World Affairs,* March 1975, p. 18. Former CIA Director William Colby confirmed the establishment of a Soviet AGI patrol in the Strait of Hormuz in 1974. See his testimony before the Senate Subcommittee on Military Construction, Committee on Armed Services, August 1, 1974. Normally, 75 percent of the Soviet ships in the Indian Ocean belong to the Kremlin's Pacific Fleet, with the remaining 25 percent coming from Soviet European ports. It should be stressed, however, that air support is provided from the Black Sea Fleet (Polmar, *loc. cit.,* 1976, p. 75); this, in turn, makes Soviet access to Middle Eastern airfields a necessity (at least in the short run), and proves that strategic mutual support performed between the Warsaw Pact, Middle East, and India/Far East subsystems is basic to Moscow's collective security system.

[37] R. F. Ellsworth, Assistant Secretary of Defense for International Affairs, in *Washington Post,* July 31, 1975. A Russian naval task force was photographed off Durban by a South African Air Force Maritime Command reconnaissance aircraft. The group of three vessels included the *Leningrad,* a new missile cruiser, and a destroyer. *To the Point International,* November 16, p. 7.

YEAR: 1975

Infrastructure Development	De Facto Stationing

Warsaw Pact Subsystem	

It was estimated that though the number of divisions has remained constant, the combat strength of the Soviet troops stationed in the "frontal zones" has increased by about 40 percent. General Alexander M. Haig, Commander of Allied Forces in Europe, said Soviet military manpower in East Germany has risen from 250,000 to 350,000 men in the last five years. Other European analysts estimated that the Russians had added 120,-000 men, and that the strength of Soviet forces in Germany was approximately 370,000 men, including artillery, engineers, transport, and other supporting forces.[30] In the case of the Soviet Army, there were at least 4,000 T-62 tanks stationed in the forward Warsaw Pact zone, in addition to the older T-54/T-55s, which have not been withdrawn. Similarly, the number of aircraft per regiment in the tactical air forces (the Frontal Aviation Army) has been continuously increasing. New aircraft types, some with all-weather capability such as the MIG-23 Flogger and the SU-20 Fitter, were entering service without, however, the older types being withdrawn.[31]

Middle East Subsystem	

1. A reliable source confirmed recently that the Soviets were assisting Iraq in the construction or rebuilding of a number of major airfields which "will be able to handle the largest Soviet aircraft. The possibility of staging a Soviet military force from these facilities has surely not escaped their attention."[1]

2. In early February, it was reported that the Soviet Union had asked Portugal (a NATO member) for port facilities for its Atlantic fishing fleet. Quoting official Portuguese sources, the report added that the site for the fishing base had not yet been determined. One possibility was the port of Figuiera da Foz, 150 miles north of Lisbon. (Just outside Lisbon in Oeiras are the headquarters of the Iberian Atlantic Command of NATO). Western observers predicted that if the Russians obtained this base, they would ask permission to build an air base at Coimbra, inland from the fishing port.[2]

3. In March, a press report said the air-

In January, it was reported that the Soviet Union had delivered Scud-B SRBMs to Iraq. "New groups of Soviet military technicians have also been seen in Iraq and are assumed by Western sources to be the crews that will man the Scud missiles, which are likely to remain under Russian control."[32] Reports of increased Soviet activity on the island of Socotra also came in early 1975. "Twice in recent months, marines have landed from amphibious warfare vessels for exercises."[33] Soviet mine sweepers were based in Basra, reportedly equipped also for intelligence gathering duties.[34] Also, electronically configured An-12 Cub-C transports were identified over the western Indian Ocean,[35] and were probably based in Somalia. At a parliamentary hearing in mid-January 1976, Greek Minister of National Defense Averov officially confirmed for the first time the existence of anchorages for the Soviet fleet on both the eastern and western

YEAR: 1975 (continued)

Infrastructure Development	De Facto *Stationing*
Middle East Subsystems	

field at Uanle Uen, 50 miles from Mogadishu, Somalia, had been expanded "in recent months" by 90 percent under Soviet instruction and with Soviet equipment.[3] In April, press reports (quoting a Pentagon spokesman) said the Soviet Union was believed to be building a cruise missile support base at Berbera, Somalia.[4] On June 10, Secretary of Defense James Schlesinger revealed the Soviet Union had begun storing antiship missiles at the Berbera facility. In addition, aerial photographs of Berbera revealed a naval communication site, barracks capable of housing 1,500 men, petroleum storage facilities, and a three-mile-long airstrip under construction.[5] An on-site inspection conducted by Senator Dewey F. Bartlett, accompanied by four American military experts, in Berbera resulted in "absolute confirmation" of Schlesinger's revelations.[6] A subsequent intelligence report[7] said that about 3,000 Soviet specialists were present in Somalia, and at least one Soviet admiral had been seen on shore and was believed to be in command there. One of the newest reported developments was construction of an underground complex reinforced with thousands of tons of concrete and steel about eight miles southwest of Berbera. "US analysts do not yet know its purpose." The report added that the airfield near Berbera may be ready by the end of 1975. Other sources indicated that additional Soviet airfields exist at Hargeisa in the north, and at Galacio and Belet Uen, and that Berbera had a Soviet harbormaster.[8] Late in the year, a large Soviet floating drydock was transferred to Somalia.[9] American military sources disclosed further in November that the Soviet Union was building three combination navy and missile bases in Somalia. "One base at Berbera is virtually finished, and high Navy sources said the other two are in the early stages of construction. The bases would handle missiles and missile ships of the Soviet's Indian Ocean Fleet."[10]

4. The Egyptian semiofficial newspaper *Al Ahram* said[11] that Moscow had agreed to supply some $4,000 million worth of tanks, missiles, and other weapons to Libya in return for permission to build air, naval, and land bases in that coun-

flanks of Crete.[36] By the end of the year, American and Israeli sources indicated that 20 MIG-25 Foxbats—with Soviet pilots—were to be deployed in Syria. Later reports said a squadron of MIG-25s, apparently to be flown by Soviet pilots, had already been sent to Syria.[37]

YEAR: 1975 (continued)

Infrastructure Development	De Facto *Stationing*
Middle East Subsystems	

try. This followed earlier reports[12] that the number of Soviet advisors and equipment experts in Libya have more than doubled since 1974. It was estimated that 480 Russians were working with Libyan military units (compared to 200 in early 1974), and that they had established a base of their own "near the large air base near Tripoli" (which was operated by the US Air Force until 1970 under the name of Wheelus Air Force Base). The arms/bases agreement was signed during an official visit to Libya by Soviet Prime Minister Kosygin (beginning May 12). According to the pro-Libyan Beirut daily *Al Safir,* the groundwork for Kosygin's visit was prepared during a visit by Libyan Prime Minister Abdel-Salam Jalloud to East Germany in April.[13] Quoting intelligence sources in Washington, the *Los Angeles Times* said in connection with the deal that Moscow had gained Libyan agreement for limited use of naval base facilities at Tobruk.[14] The *Boston Globe* (May 24, 1976) said: "The Russians are known to be modernizing the Libyan naval base at Tobruk, probably with the hope of being able to establish a naval base there . . . work there will take another 18 months to complete." In July, *Al Ahram* reported that a team of Soviet experts visited the Libyan port of Bardia to conduct a survey on establishing a naval base there.[15] In an interview with the weekly *Beirut al Masa* (August 26, 1975), President Qaddafi said Libya was trying to build a "strategic, not just passing, relationship" with the Soviet Union. 5. Press reports quoting "reliable sources" in London said that the Soviet Union was seeking to acquire Perim and two other islands in the Bab-el-Mandeb Strait and to establish Soviet bases on them. According to these sources, the South Yemen government, under Soviet pressure, was asking the renunciation of its contract with Egypt which leased those islands to Cairo for 50 years. The South Yemeni Premier, Ali Nassir Mohammed, met the Egyptian Foreign Minister and War Minister in Cairo on May 25 to discuss the transfer of Perim and the other two islands back to South Yemeni control. "The reason for this was a Soviet request for the use of the islands . . . by the Soviet Navy."[16]

YEAR: 1975 (continued)

Infrastructure Development	De Facto Stationing
India/Far East Subsystem	

1. In January, an official of India's space research organization confirmed that the Soviets had asked for port facilities for their tracking and recovery ships in the Indian Ocean. The source commented that the Indian government had not yet reached a decision on the request, first made about 18 months earlier.[17] Recent reports[18] indicated that with the political crisis in India (which led to the proclamation of a state of emergency by Mrs. Gandhi), Soviet pressure on New Delhi to grant it naval base rights had intensified. *U.S. News and World Report* (September 15, 1975) said one of its manifestations apparently was a Soviet rejection of an Indian request for Kresta-class missile cruisers.[19] Former US Ambassador to India William B. Saxbe confirmed recently the Soviet pressure on New Delhi for a naval base. "This has not been granted, but we know that Russia continually puts pressure on to get the base," he added.[20]

2. "Recent reports have confirmed a longstanding suspicion that the Soviet Union is engaged in secret diplomatic talks with the government of the Maldive Islands for facilities for its fleet operating in the Indian Ocean."[21]

3. Under an agreement between Afghanistan and the Soviet Union initialed in January and signed at the end of February (covering a wide range of economic projects), the USSR agreed to construct six airfields in the north of Afghanistan.[22]

4. In May, the *New York Times* quoted "qualified military sources" as saying that the Soviet Union has asked North Vietnam and the Revolutionary Government in South Vietnam for the use of Cam Ranh Bay as a naval and air base.[23] Japan's *Kyodo* news service said that Peking had indicated that Moscow asked the new Communist government in Saigon for the use of former US military bases "in compensation for the huge amount of aid" extended by Moscow during the Vietnam War. According to the report, the statement was made to a visiting Japanese delegation by Chinese experts on international problems during talks with Peking about the Indochina situation.[24]

On June 27, the sentry post of the Japanese Ground Self-Defense Force at Wakkanai, Hokkaido, noted that 13 Soviet landing craft and escort vessels transited the Soya Strait and assembled at Aniwa Bay off Sakhalin Island. "Then the Soviet ships brought 2,000 Soviet soldiers in two batches westward through the Soya Strait . . . the Vladivostok-based Soviet warships were conducting a landing exercise at the Soviet coastal areas with a 'certain region of a certain country' as the hypothetical target."[38] In early July, Soviet Defense Minister Marshal Grechko, Navy Commander-in-Chief Gorshkov, and a Deputy Defense Minister, inspected the Pacific Fleet at Vladivostok.[39] The Director General of Japan's National Defense Agency, Michita Sakata, disclosed in August that Chinese planes had been observing Soviet naval maneuvers in the Yellow Sea.[40] Vice Admiral Thomas B. Hayward, Commander of the US Seventh Fleet, said (in an interview with the *San Diego Union*, December 26, 1975) that "there has been a significant Soviet build-up in the Pacific. The Soviets now have more than 100 submarines and a large number of modern surface combatants, including Kresta-II cruisers and Krivak-class destroyers . . . in the Pacific." On March 31, 1976, Japan's Defense Agency disclosed that the Soviet Union had deployed MIG-23 aircraft at the Vladivostok base.[41] Subsequently, the Agency said that a Maritime Self-Defense Force P2J antisubmarine patrol plane sighted a Soviet Krivak destroyer on April 7, 1976, cruising some 180 km. west of Okinawa, southern Japan. Another destroyer of the same class was seen near Japan toward the end of November 1975, and Agency officials surmised that the Soviet Pacific Fleet now had two destroyers of this class.[42] "During 1975, the Soviet Indian Ocean contingent was built up significantly. It now usually includes at least one major combatant armed with guided missiles. In addition, the force was augmented by three landing ships, at least one of which had military vehicles embarked, during the year."[43] A Soviet task force which entered the Indian Ocean in

YEAR: 1975 (continued)

Infrastructure Development	De Facto *Stationing*
India/Far East Subsystem	

5. Press reports quoting US intelligence sources also indicated that Russia was moving quietly to establish close military ties with Mozambique. It was learned that in advance of Mozambique's scheduled independence (June 25), a high-level Soviet delegation visited there for ten days in May to discuss development of the country's main port at Lourenco Marques (which, according to the *Washington Post*, March 30, 1977, may well have Soviet harbor pilots by now). The sources said it was also learned that the Russians may train the new Mozambique Navy, and suggested the Russians may be trying to lay the groundwork for possible use of the Mozambique port by Soviet naval units.[25] Indeed, in December it was reported that a first bid by the Soviet Union to gain use of Mozambique ports for its warships had been rejected by the New Front for the Liberation of Mozambique (Frelimo).[26] The *Daily Telegraph* on August 12, 1977, reported that Russia was establishing substantial naval and air force facilities at the port of Nacala, in northern Mozambique. "Five miles inland (from Nacala), the Russians are believed to be developing air base facilities at a two-miles-long reinforced airstrip once used by the Portuguese Air Force. Soviet specialists are reported to be installing the latest radar equipment at the air base, which is defended by SAMs and antiaircraft batteries."
6. Burmese Deputy Premier U Lwin, on a recent visit to Moscow, sounded out the Soviet stance on the possible supply of arms. The Soviet Union was reported to have countered by renewing a suggestion that Burma grant it naval facilities at the Coco Islands in the Andaman Sea.[27]
7. According to the Vientiane correspondent of the *Bangkok Post,* the Soviet Union has sent 1,500 advisors in various fields to assist Laos. The paper said the figure was disclosed by Deputy Premier and Foreign Minister Phoune Sipraseuth. The report followed statements by Thai officials that Laos has recently acquired 70 Soviet patrol boats.[28] Vientiane's KPL in English (March 29, 1976) said that on

December included, for example, two destroyers, two mine sweepers, a tanker, an ocean-going tug, and a landing ship.[44]

YEAR: 1975 (continued)

Infrastructure Development	De Facto Stationing
India/Far East Subsystem	

March 29, 1976, Laos and the Soviet Union signed an agreement on postal and telecommunications cooperation. "Present on the occasion was Khatmai Siphandon, Vice Premier and Minister of National Defense and Commander-in-Chief of the Lao People's Liberation Army . . . In their speeches afterwards, Laotian Minister of Ports and Telecommunications and the Soviet Ambassador to Laos both praised the militant solidarity and close cooperation between the two countries." On April 4, 1976, *AFP* from Bangkok reported that "the Soviet Union is about to ship a vast quantity of electronic communications equipment into Laos, where it is already at work improving and building airfields, according to diplomatic sources here. The sources said the material would come in under an agreement signed on March 29 in Vientiane in the presence of Laotian Defense Minister and Armed Forces Chief General Khatmai Siphandon. Several hundred more Soviet technicians would arrive in the next few days to boost the total there to more than 1,500, they said. Under the new pact, the Soviet Union will train Laotians to maintain the new equipment, which would, in the meantime, be looked after by the Russians, the sources added. The equipment is expected to comprise the establishment of a major satellite radio-communications network, radar surveillance, electronic signalling and radar for air navigation, and telex. The main work on airfields is going on at Phonsavan, in the western part of the Plain of Jars. The air strip there, which is being improved to take modern jets, will become an important strategic junction in the heart of the Indochinese Peninsula, less than two hours flying time from southern China, Bangkok, and Hanoi."[29] The *Nation* (Bangkok, May 3, 1976) reported that Russia had established an electronic listening post in Laos for the purpose of monitoring communications in southern China.

Footnotes for Year 1975:
   [1] Johnston, *loc. cit.,* p. 20. Another source reported recently that Iraqi bases were being regularly used by the Russian Air Force. *Flight International,* June 26, 1976, p. 1744.

YEAR: 1975 (continued)

² *New York Times,* February 1, 1975; *Washington Post,* February 1, 1975. For Soviet denial of the story, see *Christian Science Monitor,* February 5, 1975. For Portugal's denial, see *Washington Post,* February 2, 1975. On the roles of the Soviet fishing fleet, see R. T. Ackley, "The Fishing Fleet and Soviet Strategy," *U.S. Naval Institute Proceedings,* July 1975, pp. 31-38. Fairhall, *op. cit.,* pp. 149-178. In March, radical elements in the Armed Forces Movement (MFA) confirmed through the Information Ministry in Lisbon that the Portuguese government was considering giving the Russians fishing facilities for their merchant fleet in the Portuguese-owned Atlantic island of Madeira. *Christian Science Monitor,* March 17, 1975; *Daily Telegraph,* March 18, 1975.

³ *New York Times,* March 10, 1975.

⁴ *Ibid.,* April 7, 1975; *Washington Post,* April 8, 1975; *Philadelphia Inquirer,* April 8, 1975.

⁵ *New York Times,* June 11, 1975; *Los Angeles Times,* June 11, 1975; *Christian Science Monitor,* June 11, 1975; *Baltimore Sun.,* June 11, 1975. For pictures, see *Aviation Week and Space Technology,* June 16, 1975, p. 19; *Air Force Magazine,* August 1975, pp. 28-29. For Somalia's denial of the story, see *Christian Science Monitor,* June 10, 19, 1975; *Los Angeles Times,* June 12, 27, 1975; *Washington Post,* July 4, 1975. For Soviet denials, see *Krasnaya Zvezda,* June 20, 1957; *Pravda,* June 29, 1975. Air-to-surface missiles were also reportedly stored in the Berbera facility. *Aviation Week and Space Technology,* June 16, 1975. In January 1976, the US information office in Nairobi issued a press release to the effect that the Soviet Union was constructing an "antishipping missile installation" at Kismayu. The release added that if construction of the airfield at Berbera should continue at its present rate, "it will be completed this year and be capable of accommodating any known aircraft in the Soviet inventory, including the new socalled 'Backfire' bomber." *The Weekly Review,* Nairobi, January 19, 1976, p. 6. Somali Defense Minister Samantar formally "opened" the Berbera airfield on January 9, 1977. *SWB* (Middle East and Africa), January 13, 1977, p. B1.

⁶ *New York Times,* July 7, 8, 1975; *Washington Post,* July 7, 8, 13, 1975. The Somalis repeated their denial even after Bartlett's visit. See interviews with Somalia's President Barre and Defense Minister Mohamed Ali Samantar, *Afrique-Asie,* July 14, 1975, pp. 11-13; *New York Times,* July 20, 1975. A second American delegation, composed of eight House Armed Services Committee members, reached similar conclusions. See report of Samuel S. Stratton, the chairman of the delegation, in *Armed Forces Journal International,* September 1975, p. 20. For an earlier visit by foreign correspondents which was blocked by the Somalis, see *New York Times,* June 30, July 6, 1975; *Washington Post,* June 30, 1975.

⁷ *Los Angeles Times,* July 9, 1975; *Washington Post,* July 9, 1975.

⁸ *African Development,* September 1975, p. 38. Bell, *loc. cit.,* 1975, p. 405. It was also reported that the "reopening of the (Suez) Canal had led to a new Soviet military build-up in Aden . . . the Russians were quietly helping South Yemen expand facilities (there)." *African Development,* October 1975, p. E14; *Afro-Asian Affairs,* May 19, 1975, p. 2; May 31, 1975, p. 1.

⁹ Manthorpe, *loc. cit.,* p. 208.

¹⁰ *Chicago Tribune,* November 13, 1975; *New York Times,* November 28, 1975. Nine years earlier, Kenya's Vice President Joseph Narumbi told a Commonwealth Prime Minister's Conference in London that the real danger involved in large Soviet arms supplies to Somalia was that the USSR would establish itself in East Africa and win control of the Aden Strait and the Suez Canal. *Sunday Nation,* Nairobi, September 18, 1966; also *Ethiopian Herald,* Addis Ababa, May 11, September 22, 1966. *East African Standard,* Nairobi, September 22, 1966. For the Soviet response, see *Krasnaya Zvezda,* October 10, 1966.

¹¹ May 23, 1975. For different estimates of the deal's value, see *Washington Post,* September 5, 1975, quoting *The Military Balance,* 1975-1976, International Institute for Strategic Studies, London, *Middle East Economic Digest,* May 30, 1975, p. 18. *Ash-Shaab* (Amman, March 6, 1976), quoting diplomatic sources, said Libya had concluded a $1 billion contract with the Soviet Union for the supply of 25 MIG-23s, a squadron of Tu-22 bombers, and the construction of a naval base. For Soviet denial that it plans bases in Libya, see *New York Times,* May 28, 1975. For Libya's Qaddafi denial, see *Washington Post,* July 16, 1975.

¹² *New York Times,* February 21, 1975; see also statement by the Israeli Chief of Staff, General Mordekhai Gur, in *Christian Science Monitor,* February 20, 1975; *Air International,* March 1975, p. 107.

¹³ Quoted in *Middle East Economic Digest,* May 9, 1975, p. 20. It was reported that a week before Kosygin's visit, a Soviet ship delivered 13 MIG-23s to Benghazi Harbor. *Baltimore Sun,* May 9, 1975; *Air International,* July 1975, p. 3.

¹⁴ May 29, 1975. Also *New York Times,* May 29, 1975. *To the Point International,* May 31, 1975, p. 11; *Baltimore Sun,* March 17, 1976; *The Weekly Review,* April 26, 1976, p. 13. A short time after Kosygin's visit, a flotilla of nine Soviet ships belonging to the Soviet Mediterranean fleet paid a visit to Tripoli. *To the Point International,* June 28, 1975, p. 24.

¹⁵ Quoted in *Times,* July 14, 1975. Note that Cairo newspapers associated the June presence of "a high-level Soviet military mission in Libya" with the aim of "using Soviet presence in

YEAR: 1975 (continued)

Libya to confront the US Sixth Fleet and the American influence in the area." Cited in *Christian Science Monitor*, June 17, 1975. *Daily Telegraph*, September 21, 1975, reported that the port of Tobruk was being extended to provide facilities for the Soviet Navy. The paper said also a naval base was being built at El Bardia, 12 miles from the Egyptian frontier, which was likely to offer facilities for Soviet submarines in the Mediterranean. Other sources reported that Libya was building a submarine base in Ras Hillal, near Benghazi, where six Soviet-supplied submarines will be based.

[16] *Afro-Asian Affairs*, June 16, 1975, p. 2; *Ma'ariv*, June 22, 1975; *Los Angeles Times*, May 12, 1976. The Soviets have reportedly built a sophisticated radio monitoring station at Tarshyne (South Yemen), to which even the South Yemenis have no access. Another station, at Socotra, has also been opened for operations recently. *Daily Telegraph*, February 18, 1975; *Weekly Review* (Intelligence Digest), March 12, 1975, p. 4.

[17] *Washington Post*, January 1, 1975; *Christian Science Monitor*, January 3, 1975. Note that the initial request had been made close to Brezhnev's November 1973 visit to India. At that time, press reports that confirmed the Soviet move failed to mention it was limited to space tracking and recovery vessels only. Even if only space tracking recovery vessels are in question, the granting by India of port facilities for these, should it come, will demonstrate strategic mutual support between Delhi and Moscow. This is because Soviet space-associated ships appear in two distinct contexts: "usually four or so missile observation ships are stationed in the expected descent areas of Soviet missiles launched from the Baykonur test range in Central Asia to splash down in the Pacific. They also tend to appear when American missiles or French nuclear weapons are being tested, obviously in order to record telemetry or operators' radio conversation for processing in the Soviet Union. In that sense, they perform a spying function similar to that of ELINT (electronic intelligence) trawlers . . . Soviet space-program ships in the Indian Ocean frequently perform a different function. Both the United States and the Soviet Union make extensive use of reconnaissance satellites to safeguard themselves against surprise attack . . . US-launched satellite capsules are usually recovered in or over the Pacific or western Atlantic, Soviet ones in the Indian Ocean." Jukes, *op. cit.*, 1973, pp. 83-84.

[18] *Christian Science Monitor*, August 15, 1975; *New York Times*, August 26, 1975.

[19] Also *Marine Rundschau*, October 1975, p. 625.

[20] Interview with *U.S. News and World Report*, January 24, 1977, p. 41. Nevertheless, one observer believes that the Indo-Soviet friendship treaty of 1971 contains a secret clause giving the Soviet Union a naval base at Vishakapatnam. Zumwalt, *op. cit.*, p. 364. A. B. Vajpayee, the new Indian Foreign Minister, publicly denied that the Gandhi regime had entered into any secret agreements regarding Soviet naval rights in Indian ports. *India News*, June 20, 1977. Note that on December 9, 1976, Admiral Gorshkov arrived in New Delhi, leaving on December 14 for a three-day official visit to Sri Lanka (Ceylon). Reporting his departure from India, New Delhi radio quoted him as saying that his visit there would further strengthen co-operation between the navies of the USSR and India. The radio added that Gorshkov would be returning to Delhi on December 17 for further talks with Bansai Lal, the Indian Defense Minister. *SWB* (Far East), December 15, 1976, p. 1.

[21] *Christian Science Monitor*, March 4, 1975. The Soviet Union is understood to offer in return substantial doses of economic aid under favorable terms to develop the island's fishing and tourist potential.

[22] *Middle East Economic Digest*, March 19, 1975, p. 12; *Christian Science Monitor*, February 14, 1975.

[23] Also *Japan Times*, May 19, 1975. For the Soviet denial of the story, see *Tass*, May 28, 1975; for Vietnam's, see *Frankfurter Allgemeine Zeitung*, August 18, 1976. It was reported subsequently that Japan would like to increase its antisubmarine surface and air forces to counter Soviet movement into the South China Sea based on the use of Cam Ranh Bay in Vietnam. *New York Times*, August 23, 1975.

[24] *Christian Science Monitor*, May 29, 30, 1975. *New York Times*, August 15, 1975. Early in September, General Chen Hsi-lien, China's leading military man, warned the Vietnamese against allowing the Soviets the use of naval and air bases on Vietnamese soil. *Los Angeles Times*, October 8, 1975. See also J. Kun, "Vietnam: Soviet Economic Penetration," *Radio Liberty Research*, February 25, 1976, p. 6.

[25] *Washington Star*, June 12, 1975; *Philadelphia Inquirer*, June 13, 1975; *Christian Science Monitor*, June 13, 1975. Earlier there were reports that Soviet weapons, including SAM-7s, have been supplied to Frelimo and to Rhodesian guerrillas in base camps in Mozambique. In January and again in March, arms shipments were unloaded from the 17,000-ton Soviet freighter *Akademik Shimansky* at the Mozambican port of Beira. *To the Point International*, January 25, 1975, p. 5; *Johannesburg Star* quoted in *Washington Post*, March 18, 1975; *Christian Science Monitor*, March 18, 1975. A Bulgarian delegation visited Mozambique in February 1975. Mr. Videnov, head of the African Department in the Ministry of Foreign Affairs, said Bulgaria would continue to give material assistance to Frelimo to continue the liberation struggle until

YEAR: 1975 (continued)

"full independence is achieved." *Sunday News* (Dar-es-Salaam), February 6, 1975. In March, Zambia received its second shipment of Russian arms, including armored cars, through the port of Beira by the East German vessel *Volga*. The vessel also unloaded arms and ammunition in the Northern Mozambique port of Nacala. *To the Point International*, March 22, 1975, p. 33. On Soviet participation in the development of the port of Nacala, see *Marine Rundschau*, April 1977, p. 205. For a general discussion, see P. Vanneman, "Mozambique: A New Soviet Opportunity," *Strategic Review*, Fall 1975, pp. 45-53.

26 *Washington Post*, December 3, 12, 1975; *African Development*, February 1976, p. 117; *New York Times*, March 25, 1977. Also *Africa Report*, January-February 1975, p. 52. The Soviet Navy's Kashin-class guided missile destroyer *Odarennyy* arrived in Maputo (Lourenco Marques) on January 18, 1977. Radio Maputo said that "the visit comes under the (February 1976) agreement governing relations of friendship, solidarity, cooperation, and mutual aid between the governments of the People's Republic of Mozambique and the USSR." *SWB* (Middle East and Africa), January 20, 1977, p. B1. In the same vein on April 23, 1976, Soviet Defense Minister Marshal Grechko received the head of a Mozambican military delegation, Defense Minister Alberto Chipande. *Krasnaya Zvezda*, April 24, 1976. Recent reports say: "Algerians who have been helping Frelimo with training have now been joined by some East Germans and Bulgarians, but there are no Cubans, and the Chinese are confining their help to nonmilitary work, mainly training village doctors." Mozambique's President Samora Machel is reported to have replaced Africans with Portuguese and East Germans "in his 80-strong personal bodyguard." *Africa Confidential*, April 16, 1976, p. 2.

27 *New York Times*, August 7, 1975.

28 *Christian Science Monitor*, September 2, 1975; *New York Times*, October 9 ,1975.

29 *FBIS* (Asia and Pacific), April 5, 1976, p. 14. On May 27, the Laotian government daily *Sieng Pasason* denied reports that Soviet radar stations had been set up in Laos. The Pathet Lao newspaper also denied that Laos had taken delivery of MIG-17 and MIG-21 aircraft. Cited in *Washington Post*, May 28, 1976.

30 *New York Times*, March 3, 1976. J. Erickson, "Soviet Military Posture and Policy in Europe," in R. Pipes, ed. *Soviet Strategy in Europe*, Strategic Studies Center, Stanford Research Institute, Washington, 1976, Table 1, pp. 178-179.

31 *International Defense Review*, April 1975, p. 175. See also *Air Force Magazine*, March 1975, p. 67. Note the multioptional (that is, not necessarily European-oriented) character of this "oversupply." Some sources estimate that about half of the 15,500 Warsaw Pact tanks in Poland, East Germany, and Czechoslovakia are T-62s. *New York Times*, September 29, 1975. For latest reports on the introduction of T-72 tanks into East Germany, see *Boston Globe*, January 14, 1977. Deputy Defense Secretary William P. Clements disclosed recently that the Soviet Union has also begun replacing its MIG-17 Fresco fighters with the SU-19 Fencer. "Evidence of this is already visible in Eastern Europe." *New York Times*, September 25, November 19, 1975; *Aerospace Daily*, September 19, 1975, p. 158; *Defense and Foreign Affairs Daily*, February 19, 1975. For a general discussion, see J. Erickson, "Some Developments in Soviet Tactical Aviation," *Journal of the Royal United Services Institute for Defence Studies*, September 1975, pp. 70-74; P. Borgart, "The Air Attack Potential of the Warsaw Pact," *International Defense Review*, April 1976, pp. 193-197, who also pointed out that "older aircraft (which were) replaced are not withdrawn but are kept in service as an operational reserve."

32 *Washington Post*, February 1, 1975.

33 *New York Times*, March 10, 1975.

34 *Ibid.*, February 21, 1975; July 17, 1975.

35 Polmar, *loc. cit.*, 1976, p. 71.

36 *Ma'ariv*, January 20, 1976; *FBIS* (PRC), February 11, 1976, pp. A3-5. Emphasis added.

37 *New York Times*, November 18, 1975; December 11, 1975; March 7, 1976; *Ma'ariv*, November 18, 1975; *Defense Space Business Daily*, November 19, 1975; *Christian Science Monitor*, November 19, 1975; December 12, 1975; also remarks by Israeli Defense Minister Peres in *International Herald Tribune*, December 13, 1975. Subsequent reports said MIG-25s were conducting daily surveillance missions over the Mediterranean and the Middle East. *Aviation Week and Space Technology*, March 22, 1976, p. 19. Reinforcement of the Soviet military advisors' group in Syria—estimated at the time at 3,500 men—was also expected. *New York Times*, October 26, 1975.

38 *FBIS* (PRC), December 19, 1975, p. A4.

39 *Ibid.*, April 5, 1976, p. A12.

40 *New York Times*, August 1, 1975. For some general data, see J. R. Dewenter, "The East China and Yellow Seas," *U.S. Naval Institute Proceedings*, Naval Review 1975, pp. 204-210.

41 *FBIS* (PRC), April 5, 1976, p. A12.

42 *Ibid.* (Asia and Pacific), April 12, 1976, p. C3.

43 Manthorpe, *loc. cit.*, p. 207.

44 *Los Angeles Times*, December 16, 1975.

National Strategy Information Center, Inc.

STRATEGY PAPERS
Edited by Frank N. Trager and William Henderson
With the assistance of Dorothy E. Nicolosi

The Evolution of Soviet Security Strategy, 1965-1975 by Avigdor Haselkorn, November 1977

The Geopolitics of the Nuclear Era, by Colin S. Gray, September 1977

The Sino-Soviet Confrontation: Implications for the Future by Harold C. Hinton, September 1976

Food, Foreign Policy, and Raw Materials Cartels by William Schneider, February 1976

Strategic Weapons: An Introduction by Norman Polmar, October 1975

Soviet Sources of Military Doctrine and Strategy by William F. Scott, July 1975

Detente: Promises and Pitfalls by Gerald L. Steibel, March 1975

Oil, Politics, and Sea Power: The Indian Ocean Vortex by Ian W.A.C. Adie, December 1974

The Soviet Presence in Latin America by James D. Theberge, June 1974

The Horn of Africa by J. Bowyer Bell, Jr., December 1973

Research and Development and the Prospects for International Security by Frederick Seitz and Rodney W. Nichols, December 1973

Raw Material Supply in a Multipolar World by Yuan-li Wu, October 1973

The People's Liberation Army: Communist China's Armed Forces by Angus M. Fraser, August 1973 (Out of print)

Nuclear Weapons and the Atlantic Alliance by Wynfred Joshua, May 1973

How to Think About Arms Control and Disarmament by James E. Dougherty, May 1973

The Military Indoctrination of Soviet Youth by Leon Goure, January 1973 (Out of print)

The Asian Alliance: Japan and United States Policy by Franz Michael and Gaston J. Sigur, October 1972

Iran, the Arabian Peninsula, and the Indian Ocean by R. M. Burrell and Alvin J. Cottrell, September 1972 (Out of print)

137

Soviet Naval Power: Challenge for the 1970s by Norman Polmar, April 1972. Revised edition, September 1974

How Can We Negotiate with the Communists? by Gerald L. Steibel, March 1972 (Out of print)

Soviet Political Warfare Techniques, Espionage and Propaganda in the 1970s by Lyman B. Kirkpatrick, Jr., and Howland H. Sargeant, January 1972

The Soviet Presence in the Eastern Mediterranean by Lawrence L. Whetten, September 1971

The Military Unbalance
   Is the U.S. Becoming a Second Class Power? June 1971 (Out of print)

The Future of South Vietnam by Brigadier F. P. Serong, February 1971 (Out of print)

Strategy and National Interests: Reflections for the Future by Bernard Brodie, January 1971 (Out of print)

The Mekong River: A Challenge in Peaceful Development for Southeast Asia by Eugene R. Black, December 1970 (Out of print)

Problems of Strategy in the Pacific and Indian Oceans by George G. Thomson, October 1970

Soviet Penetration into the Middle East by Wynfred Joshua, July 1970. Revised edition, October 1971 (Out of print)

Australian Security Policies and Problems by Justus M. van der Kroef, May 1970 (Out of print)

Detente: Dilemma or Disaster? by Gerald L. Steibel, July 1969 (Out of print)

The Prudent Case for Safeguard by William R. Kintner, June 1969 (Out of print)

AGENDA PAPERS
Edited by Frank N. Trager and William Henderson
With the assistance of Dorothy E. Nicolosi

Understanding the Soviet Military Threat, How CIA Estimates Went Astray by William T. Lee, February 1977

Toward a New Defense for NATO, The Case for Tactical Nuclear Weapons, July 1976

Seven Tracks to Peace in the Middle East by Frank R. Barnett, April 1975

Arms Treaties with Moscow: Unequal Terms Unevenly Applied? by Donald G. Brennan, April 1975

Toward a US Energy Policy by Klaus Knorr, March 1975

Can We Avert Economic Warfare in Raw Materials? US Agriculture as a Blue Chip by William Schneider, July 1974

OTHER PUBLICATIONS

Arms, Men, and Military Budgets, Issues for Fiscal Year 1978 edited by Francis P. Hoeber and William Schneider, Jr., May 1977

Oil, Divestiture and National Security edited by Frank N. Trager, December 1976

Alternatives to Detente by Frank R. Barnett, July 1976

Arms, Men, and Military Budgets, Issues for Fiscal Year 1977 edited by William Schneider, Jr., and Francis P. Hoeber, May 1976

Indian Ocean Naval Limitations, Regional Issues and Global Implications by Alvin J. Cottrell and Walter F. Hahn, April 1976